WHAT'S LEFT

TED RALL

To read my cartoons and columns and watch my podcasts and broadcast material, please check out Ted Rall Online at Rall.com. You can also contact me with feedback and invitations to speak and/or attend a book signing at Rall.com.

All cartoons published in *What's Left* are © 2025 Ted Rall, All Rights Reserved. To request permission to display or publish, please contact Ted Rall via Rall.com.

Page 13: Woodcut of Martin Luther defending himself under questioning by papal legate Cardinal Thomas Catejan in 1518: Public Domain, https://commons.wikimedia.org/w/index.php?curid=552755

Page 17: Sculpted head of a Parthian soldier, from the Parthian royal residence and necropolis of Nisa by Zereshk at English Wikipedia, CC BY 2.5: Public Domain, https://commons.wikimedia.org/w/index.php?curid=18210634

Copyright © 2025 Ted Rall
All rights reserved.
ISBN: 979-8-9986622-0-1
Adjy Publishing

What's Left?
A Manifesto

Introduction — 7

A Mini-Manifesto About Manifestos — 13

1. What Is "The Left"? — 17

The Left is the political orientation that prioritizes the duty of the state to the individual by fighting for rights to which every human being is entitled because they are alive. Though marginalized and ridiculed by the current system, Leftists account for four out of ten American adults. Despite the Left's numerical strength, organization is elusive due to marginalization by the establishment. Organization will only become possible after the Left defines itself. The way to do that is by articulating a coherent set of ambitious demands.

2. Identity Politics Must Die — 29

The Democratic Party, formerly a party that claimed to represent the interests of the average working person, has metastasized into a corporatist entity that captures and holds prisoner its progressive voter base inside its tent by emphasizing symbolic identity politics. Identitarianism distracts from the class analysis we need and the party's military aggressiveness. It is the inherent enemy of Leftist Americans.

3. Where to Start? Defund the Pentagon — 41

Propped up by a cult of militarism reinforced by the education system, news media propaganda and politicians purchased by campaign donations, the military-industrial complex is wasteful, counterproductive and fails at its stated mission of keeping us safe. We could slash over 90% of defense spending and still be able to protect our borders from all threats.

4. We Waste $3.8 Trillion a Year. Let's Spend It on People — 51

Under the present U.S. federal budget and tax structure, it is possible to find close to $4 trillion a year to spend on long-neglected wants and needs like national healthcare, free college and ending homelessness. This means slashing wasteful military spending, raising taxes to appropriate levels on the wealthy individuals and corporations who can afford to bear the burden and taking a second look at expenses like the interest on the national debt.

5. Octuple the Minimum Wage — 59

The federal minimum wage, stuck at $7.25 since 2009, is an affront to basic human decency because it is impossible to live on. A low minimum wage depresses wages for workers higher up on the pay scale as well. It must be increased to a real living wage that takes inflation and increases in worker productivity into account. Make the minimum wage universal, including for tip workers.

6. Pay Everyone — 65

There are two classes of people in the workforce: the employed and the unemployed. Employed people deserve the right to negotiate on an even playing field with their employer. At-will employment, in which employers can get rid of you for no reason whatsoever, should be abolished. Most people want to join a union; they should be able to. As artificial intelligence and other new technologies disrupt the workplace and replace jobs, we need to decouple income from employment.

7. House the Homeless — 73

Homelessness is the result of systemic economic violence against the extremely poor. It serves as a deterrent to people who might otherwise try to negotiate more aggressively for their economic rights. It destroys communities, wrecks infrastructure and serves as the ultimate indictment of the existing system, because it denies the fundamental right to shelter to citizens.

8. Free Healthcare for All — 81

For-profit healthcare is an atrocity. Healthcare is a basic human right, not a privilege or an optional commodity that consumers can shop for in a free and open marketplace. We are all sick or going to be sick. The goal of the American healthcare system should be to keep us as healthy as possible for as long as possible.

9. Make Higher Education Free — 91

As long as employers continue to insist upon college degrees before they consider applicants for a job, a college education will remain an essential requirement for millions of young people to enter the workforce. Therefore, we must make college as financially accessible as possible for as many people as possible.

10. Create a Foreign Policy for Peace, Not War   99

American exceptionalism is a toxic lie. No country is exceptional, nor should claim to be. The United States spends an inordinately high percentage of its resources on a massive military that bullies other countries to little end other than to create new enemies. We should take our place as an equal among the nations of the world. We should seek friendship and full diplomatic ties with every other country that wants them with us.

11. Police Can Do Something New: They Can Help People   107

Policing is necessary. The Left accepts that. But the system is completely toxic and should therefore be reinvented from scratch. Cops' jobs ought to be to protect us, not themselves. Militarization of local police must cease. Municipalities' current practice of relying on the police for generating revenue should be stopped, along with the legalized highway robbery of civil asset forfeiture.

12. Redefine Crime; Rethink Punishment   115

We send too many people to prison. Prison sentences are too long. Prison conditions are inhumane. The prison-industrial complex is a profit center rather than a vehicle for rehabilitation. We should view every person as more than the worst crime they have committed and strive to integrate them into society to redeem them and make us safer. Follow the Scandinavian model of liberal imprisonment and low recidivism. Close America's overseas gulag at Guantánamo Bay.

13. Make Legal Immigration Easy   123

Under our current economic system, we require constant population growth. Until we replace that system, we require more immigration because of our declining population. Unchecked illegal immigration is a security risk and destabilizing political force, so we need to make it easier for people from other countries to migrate to the United States while controlling our borders, as would any other nation-state.

14. Punish Corporations Like Humans   131

Fifteen years after the Supreme Court declared that "corporate personhood" extends to many privileges previously accorded to individual Americans, we still haven't begun to hold corporations accountable under the law the same way that we hold individual persons accountable when they violate a statute or regulation. It's time to remedy that oversight.

15. Make Income Taxes Fully Progressive   135

    The progressive tax system is one of the most efficient and fair methods of wealth redistribution available under the system as it currently stands. We should not roll it back. Instead, we should expand upon it.

16. Protect Political Expression   139

    A society cannot be free if people do not feel free to express themselves, especially when the subject is politics. Currently, employers may fire or retaliate against an employee due to their political opinions, with no redress whatsoever. It's time for the United States to make political expression a protected class under civil rights laws.

17. Guarantee the Right to Bodily Autonomy   143

    Even more important than many abstract rights that individuals enjoy or ought to enjoy is the right to remain physically unmolested. The Left must protect everyone's right not to be infected, injected or otherwise physically invaded or encumbered upon.

18. Prioritize Human Survival by Prioritizing the Earth's Environment   147

    If the Earth isn't healthy enough to sustain human life, nothing else matters. The environment must always be our top priority.

19. A People's Government Is Transparent   153

    A government by and for the people works only if it's out in the open.

20. What Is To Be Done Now?   155

INTRODUCTION

"Be reasonable. Demand the impossible."
—*slogan of the Situationist movement, Paris 1968*

Democrats are not "the Left."

The Democratic Party is not a Left party.

Many if not most Leftists can and do vote Democratic, but that does not make them Democrats. Nor does garnering votes from Leftists make the Democratic Party a Left or Left-leaning party. Nor does being more liberal than the Republicans make the Democrats a Left party.

There are Leftists and there are Democrats. They are not the same.

You've been told the opposite zillions of times. Right-wing media loves to conflate the Democrats with the Left. Right-wing politicians constantly call Democratic politicians "socialists" or even "communists."

Republican politicians and media outlets don't really believe that Democrats are "far-left extremists." They say that stuff because they still have a Cold War mentality. They also assume most voters are centrists and moderates who will shy away from Democrats if they think they're lefties. The Democrats are a capitalist party. They don't want to change the basic economic or social systems. They want the class structure to remain as is. At their most radical, Democrats want modest reforms. If Democrats were 100% in charge of everything, the people who are rich today would remain rich tomorrow, the people who are poor today would remain poor tomorrow, and corporations would continue to accumulate more wealth and power at the expense of individuals. They agree with the Republicans about these things.

The Left is entirely different. Leftists are anti-capitalist.

There are many strains of Leftists: communists, socialists, left libertarians, left anarchists, progressives and others. Their goals differ in some respects. But the primary defining characteristics of these variations are identical. If the Left were 100% in charge of everything, there would be no rich or poor; everyone would have equal access to everything. Giant corporations would not exist. No one would want for the basic necessities of life, like housing, food and medical care. Everyone would be unconditionally entitled to those by virtue of existing as a living, breathing human being.

As noted above, Leftists can and often do vote Democratic. This is due to the two-party system. Most U.S. Leftists do not vote for a Left party—a party that they agree with—for numerous reasons. Left parties are not on the ballot. They are censored by the media, so their message doesn't get out. Laws, including the constitution, are written to make it almost impossible for them to win. People don't want to waste their votes on a marginal also-ran with no chance of success.

As things stand, these Leftists are steeped in the relentless political culture and propaganda of the Democratic-Republican duopoly. As a result, many of them do not—and cannot—distinguish their own politics outside this hegemonic paradigm. This is tragic, primarily because Democratic Party nonsense diverts attention and energy that true Leftists, non-Democrat Leftists at heart, could otherwise dedicate to the Left politics they genuinely believe in and support.

Defining the real Left, the ideological space to the left of the Democrats, must be our first task.

One of Mao Zedong's famous quotes is: "There is great disorder under heaven. The situation is excellent." In other words, crisis and instability create opportunities for ideas and political movements that might not be able to gain traction at other times.

The defeat of Kamala Harris by Donald Trump in the 2024 presidential election has created a moment that Leftists may be able to exploit. A rightward lurch has left Democrats so dispirited that many liberal voters have vowed to disengage for the next four years. They're canceling subscriptions to newspapers and political magazines and switching off cable news. Though their margin of loss was just one percentage point, Democrats sense this defeat isn't just another election result—*better luck next time.* Something fundamental is wrong. They feel it so much, but what is it? Poor messaging? A failure to connect with the working class? They wonder: Are most voters stupid?

As Democrats survey their losses in the election, they are absorbing a key fact. The biggest data point of the results is that they haven't really won a presidential election since

2012. 2020 was a fluke. Had Trump capitalized on the success of his Covid vaccine initiative, Operation Warp Speed, and urged his supporters to vote early or by mail—any vote, any time, is a good vote—he almost certainly would have beaten Joe Biden. Democrats haven't had a strong enough candidate to beat a sane Republican running normally in a conventional presidential campaign since Barack Obama defeated Mitt Romney. Trump didn't win so much as Biden lost.

Democrats have now effectively lost three consecutive presidential elections. This points less to a divided country wobbling back and forth between two parties than to a systemic realignment in favor of the Republicans.

Trump and the Republicans have claimed a sweeping mandate for a sharp shift to the Right. Whether or not this claim holds true, Democrats appear either unable or unwilling to counter Trump's flurry of executive orders and radical policy changes, such as dismantling environmental regulations, expanding deportation efforts, or slashing federal funding for progressive programs.

Approval for the Democratic Party is plummeting, with surveys showing favorability ratings sinking to historic lows, such as 27% in an NBC News poll from March 2025, reflecting widespread voter frustration. Disillusionment among the party's own base is intensifying the decline, as only 40% of Democrats approve of congressional leaders' performance in a Quinnipiac poll, a sharp drop from 75% a year earlier, reflecting an implosion of confidence in the party's direction and leadership.

The crisis inside the Democratic Party leaves the American Left, long marginalized and excluded from electoral politics and "mainstream" political dialogue, at a crossroads.

The communists, socialists, left libertarians, left anarchists, progressives and other Americans who oppose capitalism can coast. They can continue to do what Leftists in America usually do: boycott elections, support a third party, or hold their noses and support the Democrats.

Alternatively, Leftists could attempt a hostile takeover of the Democratic Party, much like Trump's MAGA movement seized control of the GOP—a strategy Bernie Sanders and Alexandria Ocasio-Cortez are arguably pursuing through their "Fighting Oligarchy" tour, which rallies massive crowds to push the party toward economic populism and aggressive opposition to Trump.

Or Leftists can try to build an organization of their own.

I am agnostic on whether it's better to capture an existing apparatus than to create a new one from the ground up. Both have their advantages and disadvantages. Many Leftists, having tolerated Democrats' anti-Leftist stance, see little value in persisting with this flawed electoral game, especially given their losing streak. The corporatists and conservatives who control the Democratic Party have held sway for decades. They have repeatedly led us to disaster yet they refuse to step aside. Why stick around, hoping against hope for things to get better?

Is it the Left's time? It ought to be. But it won't be our time unless we take it by force.

When I was younger, I concluded that only a popular revolution could succeed. Now, I believe this more fervently than ever. This would mean the violent overthrow of the corporate-capitalist state and its political structure by the Left, effecting drastic and dramatic changes in social, political and economic organization necessary in order to address and nourish our human instinct to survive and our ambition to thrive.

Revolution is necessary and overdue. However, as Che Guevara wrote in his book *On Guerrilla Warfare*, not only is revolution exceedingly challenging to achieve and to maintain, a situation can become pre-revolutionary only after citizens become convinced that their situation is dire and highly unlikely to improve under the existing order, and that nothing can improve unless and until it is overthrown: "Where a government has come into power through some form of popular vote, fraudulent or not, and maintains at least an appearance of constitutional legality, the guerrilla outbreak cannot be promoted, since the possibilities of peaceful struggle have not yet been exhausted."

Clearly, as in other developed countries, "possibilities of peaceful struggle have not yet been exhausted" in the United States. Two-thirds of eligible U.S. voters turned out to cast ballots in the 2024 presidential election.

Given the absence of sustained agitation against the status quo—no revolutionary newspapers or online publications, no credible activist organizations of significant size, and only sporadic, small-scale street demonstrations—it is evident that Che's "peaceful struggle" has not begun.

Nor is it likely to do so soon.

I wrote above that we should start by defining ourselves. What *is* the Left? A movement is a grouping dedicated to a set of political principles and goals. So the first step has to be to agree upon and publish a list of demands. *We want this to change. We want that to be abolished. We want this other thing to change from what it is now to something new, which we define as follows.*

What kind of demands? Reality being what it is, issuing a *revolutionary* set of demands, no matter how reasonable their content, would be premature because we do not have the ability to leverage force or the credible threat of force against the authorities. Revolution is the replacement of one ruling class by another; such a seismic event is not on the horizon as far as we can see. (Though it could happen tomorrow! But we cannot assume anything like that.)

We appear to be stuck with this system—the duopoly, its corporate masters, their media lickspittles and their awesome brutality—for the foreseeable future. Therefore, this is a *reformist* set of demands, albeit a radical one. It asks for changes and improvements that could take place without burning down the current political and economic system.

Communists asked: what is to be done? Here and now, before the next revolutionary moment, we should do the only thing we can do to prepare for a better future: undermine the system.

Schoolchildren are told they live under a government (and by extension a system) "by the people and for the people." Many adults know it's a lie. Too many do not. Even among those who grasp the truth—that the current American government does not, cannot, and will not respond to our needs and desires—most believe this "imperfect system" (in reality, our mortal enemy) can someday be reformed into one that cares about them. Our first task is to prove that we live under a system that exploits us for the benefit of a tiny elite and that this is not a failure or an error, but rather is inherent and intentional, and will therefore never, as far as we are concerned, improve.

We must expose the true nature of this system—to demonstrate that it does not care about us, that it does not want to help us more than it has to in order to avoid popular revolt, that the elites don't care about us.

Here, we troll the elites.

What's Left is a radical exercise. Because it makes demands that assume that the current system continues—albeit with better priorities—it is not revolutionary. (If you're interested in a revolutionary call for the overthrow of the state, refer to my *The Anti-American Manifesto*.)

What's Left does not demand that the ruling classes be toppled. Instead, it calls for the powers that be to surrender or relinquish their wealth and prerogatives so that everyone else can live decently. We know full well that the rich and powerful will never give up anything voluntarily.

What's Left is a provocation. It is a thought experiment: what if we ask for improvements in our lives? What if those requests are reasonable? What if the system can afford them?

What's Left asks for a lot. But it does not ask for too much. It asks the ruling class to do what's right and moral for their fellow citizens—us—within the existing parameters of this tax system and the current federal budget and institutions as they currently are. Theoretically, nothing would have to fundamentally change in order for most of the major problems that afflict us to be largely or completely resolved.

What's Left is a set of demands that the American government, its corporate owners and their news media propaganda mouthpieces should not refuse. Because they are oppressors, however, they will never grant us our wants and needs.

The bosses and the politicians and the media barons believe that they have the right, God-given and otherwise, to exploit us and extract our money and time and life force. They think they are better than us. They think we do not matter.

We will make these reasonable requests. *They will say no.* In saying no, they will be exposed as the monsters we know that they are. Then, those people who do not yet understand the true nature of the system, the moderates and fence-sitters, will no longer be able to turn away, distract themselves or make excuses for the ruling class. They will achieve class consciousness because, at long last, they will understand that they have enemies and who those enemies are.

All the ruling classes would have to do to address our wants and needs is listen, and care, and act.

If they care, if they act on that care, they might remain in power.

A MINI-MANIFESTO ABOUT MANIFESTOS

On October 31, 1517, the chairman of theology in the senate of the theological faculty of the University of Wittenberg nailed a list of demands to the wooden door of All Saints' Church in his town in eastern Germany. You probably know this very famous story.

What is famous (or, if you're Catholic, infamous) may or may not be true. It's possible that Martin Luther really affixed his thoughts to that church door. Martin Luther did write his demands, that part is certainly accurate, but there's a strong possibility they were delivered more prosaically, officially filed with the local senate and thus in keeping with protocol. Radical though the contents were, their delivery was more *The Hudsucker Proxy* than punk rock. It is fitting that the origin story of the Protestant Reformation, one of the most dramatic and most sweeping controversies of Western civilization, is itself a matter of dispute.

Structured as a scholarly discussion of the sale of indulgences and other contemporary controversies within the Roman Catholic Church rather than as a strident list of demands, Luther's *Ninety-Five Theses* was distributed via the then-novel technology of the printing press. Mass distribution and rapid adoption by disgruntled parishioners quickly imbued *Ninety-Five Theses* with the character of a manifesto. A dissident movement organized itself around Luther's writings, which he encouraged by expanding upon them the following year. The resulting crisis split the Church and shaped the form of Christianity in the Western world for the half-millennium to follow. While controversies over the sale of indulgences (penance reductions) have been resolved and forgotten, the schism remains.

It's hard to imagine the writings of one person, no matter how well-conceived and organized or how resonant, whether intended as a manifesto or not, making such a tectonic impact today.

One might point to *The Communist Manifesto* as further evidence of the power of the individual (well, two individuals) to popularize a list of political demands. But one would be mistaken. Published in 1848, the seminal and most famous work by the illustrious authorial pair of Karl Marx and Friedrich Engels initially appeared in only a few languages, and then in tiny print runs, and quickly fell into obscurity. The British historian Eric Hobsbawm has written: "By the middle 1860s virtually nothing that Marx had written in the past was any longer in print."

Then the tide turned. Marx's involvement in socialist organizations and parties—notably the First International and the Social Democratic Workers' Party of Germany—renewed interest in his work. Both were convened following the upheaval of the Franco-Prussian War and the 1870 Paris Commune, prompting publishers in thirty countries to reprint a revised and updated version of the *Manifesto*.

Social democratic parties rose in prominence around the world, including in the United States, achieving stunning victories that culminated with the Bolshevik Revolution in Russia in 1917. Marx and Engels' ideas captured the imagination of the political world only after their books were adapted by political organizations, specifically socialist and communist parties in the 19th and 20th centuries, and then were cited and disseminated by the official publishers of socialist nation-states like the Soviet Union and revolutionary China, where they became required reading material in public schools and universities.

In the modern postwar era, manifestos written by individuals tend to be relegated to the role of historical curios until and unless they are embraced by and inspire an organized political movement. Ted Kaczynski's 1995 *Unabomber Manifesto* (with the official title "Industrial Society and Its Future"), a critique of industrialization with its roots in the idea that pollution and climate change are the inevitable results of settled civilization, is hardly read today save by a tiny subset of readers who seek it out—its ideas are outside the mainstream of the environmental movement despite being pretty much spot-on. Should a militant ecological movement catch fire sooner than planet Earth, Kaczynski's tome may go viral. My

2010 *Anti-American Manifesto* urged immediate revolt over gradual organizing.

I argued that the problems facing us could not await grassroots organizing that might or might not happen before the climate crisis and other issues spin out of control. Its relevance stems from its adoption by the Occupy Wall Street movement, which coincidentally sprang up shortly after its publication.

A revolutionary manifesto, my little red-and-white book was disseminated by the thousands to hundreds of encampments, where it was studied and dissected by activists interested in leaderless organizing and motivated by a sense of urgency. After Occupy was savagely busted up by local police coordinated by the Obama Administration's Department of Homeland Security, scraps of my yellow-lined book were washed away with firehoses; its readership faded away too.

The manifestos of our current era, those that enjoy widespread discussion and whose bullet-points get discussed in mainstream corporate media, are exclusively the policy platforms of the two major American electoral entities, the Democratic and Republican Parties. The duopolistic dominance of American electoral politics by this pairing has implied the assumption that a list of political demands is something that ought to be crafted and issued by elites and distributed to the proletariat. Like the Ten Commandments carried down from Mount Sinai by Moses, American political party platforms are not by the people for the people. They are, at best, sets of guidelines or promises and, at worst, diktats. These days, for better or worse, they are empty words destined to go unfulfilled and forgotten by all concerned.

Elites publish laws and regulations and, if we're lucky, they promise to improve things in the hope that we'll remain compliant. Until, of course, our attention wanders and we fail to demand that they make good on their promises.

A true manifesto is the work of and in service to those who are excluded from influence. Only an outsider has the independence of thought and the necessary objective perspective to critique laws, rules and customs everyone else takes for granted.

Therefore, a party platform can never be a manifesto. A manifesto is a list of demands issued from outside the corridors of power, which may or may not confront the fundamental assumptions of an existing system. The author's mentality matters more than social status or its absence—Luther examined the Church through an outsider's lens though he was a church official. (Not for long, since he was excommunicated. Think like an outsider and you will be condemned to become one.) A manifesto can also, as this work attempts to do and Luther's *Theses* did, call out the internal inconsistencies and hypocrisies of a power structure and demand that it reconcile these contradictions and adhere to its self-professed principles, knowing full well that the powers that be are neither willing nor able to follow their own rules.

Which is the whole point.

As the bishops and cardinals of the 16th century learned, a set of words that comprise a reformist manifesto can be a powerful weapon. Hypocrisy and graft are not flaws. They are foundational features of many systems, including the late-stage American capitalism under which we live, suffer and thrive today. Issuing a set of demands that leaders could grant, if they chose to, puts them on the spot. If "our" elected officials—in a system that calls itself a "representative democracy"—deny our needs and wants, even though those demands are eminently reasonable, our leaders are exposed as our enemies. If, on the other hand, the politicians whom we elect choose to make concessions, they risk losing many of the privileges they acquire from systemic corruption, including wealth, status and power. A well-crafted popular manifesto corners politicians in a brutal checkmate: they must choose between legitimacy and greed. I hope this qualifies.

Even if we had faith in some as-yet-unfounded viable political party and its plenary officials to conceive and articulate a radical platform of proposed laws and regulations directed at meaningfully improving our lives, there is at present neither such an organization nor the prospect that one will come together any time soon. The constitutional requirement that a winning party must win 270 votes in the Electoral College makes it all but impossible for a "third party" to gain traction in the U.S. electoral system. The two major parties deploy money and lawsuits to kick newcomers and independents off the ballot. The news media's refusal to cover non-Democratic and non-Republican contenders condemns them to obscurity. The suppression of socialist and communist voices—even on the non-Democratic Left—nearly eliminates any chance of a truly Left party emerging within the system. If and when such a Left party were to arise, moreover, it would likely be torn apart by the same kinds of internal rifts that fractured the New Left in the late 1960s and early 1970s, when the militant Weather Underground split off from the relatively moderate Students for a Democratic Society. Ideological divisions are inevitable when organizing efforts precede the development of a platform of demands around which people can coalesce.

If you want to change the world, you don't begin by building your revolutionary organization. You start with a set of ideas. Float them, keep what works and ditch what doesn't, refine and adapt them.

Ted Rall
May 2025

1

WHAT IS "THE LEFT"?

"While there's capitalism, there'll be socialism, because there is always a response to injustice."
—Ed Miliband, Leader of the UK Labor Party 2010-2015

What I want, or what I think those of us to the Left of the Democratic Party should want, is not the central thesis of *What's Left*.

What matters is what the people want. The people must declare what they want.

What I really hope the people will pick up from this book is this: there should be an organized *structure* and *format* for any list of demands. Right now, we just have a bunch of people chattering on social media and in the comments sections of online opinion pages of legacy media.

Just as crucially, I hope the Left will draw inspiration from the boldness of these demands and proposed solutions.

Go big or go home.

Mainstream politicians, educators, pundits, and other propagandists repeatedly tell us Americans the United States is a conservative country. They argue the fifty-yard line of politics lies well to the right of Western European representative democracies. Our political culture derives from these democracies and is most often compared to them.[1]

Many commentators, often self-servingly, cite Donald Trump's second victory as proof of America's inherent conservatism. These commentators, typically Democratic or Republican conservatives themselves, also cite his first win, Bush's pair of wins (despite losing his first election), and every Republican White House victory.

But this country is *not* conservative. Obviously, many people do vote Republican. But that's because both major parties are conservative (by Western European standards) and there's no Left party on the ballot to vote for—not a "real" party that is allowed to fully participate in electoral politics, to be taken seriously, to be covered by the media, to have its ideas considered fairly, and thus might have a chance to win.

In fact, the Left represents a substantial double-digit plurality of eligible voters over the age of eighteen.[2]

There is a gaping chasm between the policy orientation of the two major parties that receive media coverage and the leanings of the American people whom these two "mainstream" "normal" entities purport to represent.

Who Are the Left? How Big Is It?

The latter question is surprisingly difficult to answer.

To start our investigation, let's define the Left. Though the terms "Left" and "Democrats" are often conflated, they are not the same.

And who are Leftists? Mostly, Leftists are socialists and/or communists—people who subscribe, whether they know it or not, to a Marxist class analysis of politics. For our purposes, the Left is everything and everyone to the left of Democratic Party politics.

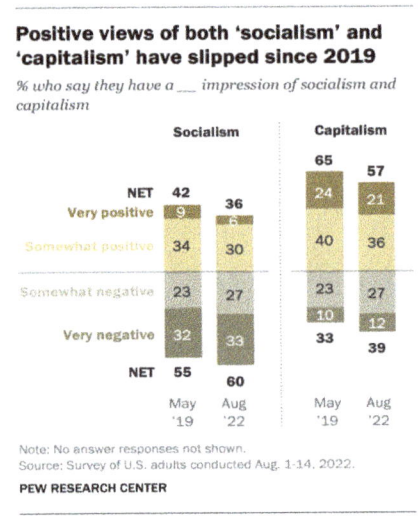

Pew does not track separate categories of those who approve of socialism only, capitalism only, and those who approve of both. Even people who approve of socialism and capitalism should be considered open to socialism.

So how many Leftists are there in the United States? As Cody R. Melcher noted in *Jacobin* magazine, "Unfortunately, no contemporary major survey of Americans actually bothers to ask respondents if they identify as socialist—much less what socialist-identifying Americans actually think. Instead, American surveys typically stick to the liberal-conservative, two-dimensional scale of political ideology. Are you 'very liberal' or 'somewhat conservative'? This, it is alleged, encompasses all meaningful ideological variation among Americans."[3] Nevertheless, there are data-based indications that there is plenty of life to the Left of the Democratic Party.

The most recent Pew Research Center poll on the subject, conducted in 2022, finds that 36% of the public views socialism favorably, though this reflects a decline from the 42% who felt the same way in 2019. (Positive views of capitalism fell even more during the same interval.)[4] As in other polls, support for socialism is greater among young people.[5]

Gallup's long-running poll of basic ideological leanings consistently finds that four of ten Americans have a positive view of socialism.[6] (There is overlap. Half of Americans are also favorably predisposed toward capitalism. How to explain this contradiction is less important for our purposes than to take note of the fact that far more space exists to discuss and propose socialist policies than most people are aware of.)[7]

The more you try to measure the American Left, the more likely you are to conclude that corporate journalists, think tanks and academic institutions don't quantify it because it's far bigger than they want you to think.

Four in ten Americans view socialism favorably? In a country with two Red Scares to its name in the last century alone? This number reflects suppression, intimidation and marginalization.

Imagine how many more Americans might embrace the real Left if its history, achievements, beliefs, and long-suppressed influence on mainstream liberalism were taught in schools, covered by the news media and woven into popular culture.

A predisposition to socialism—or mere openness to a vague concept—might be brushed off as theoretical. But when this surprisingly significant and consistent subset of American citizens (forty percent!) is given a chance to demonstrate that they like socialism, which is not often, they often rise to the occasion. They show up to rallies. They vote.

Senator Bernie Sanders, a self-described "democratic socialist," won 43% of the Democratic primary popular vote in 2016[8] and 26% in 2020[9] (and consider how much higher those numbers might have been had the DNC not rigged the process against him).[10] Four members of the Democratic Socialists of America are members of Congress.[11] Despite a century of Cold War reactionary suppression and McCarthyite propaganda,[12] U.S. voters have moved *more* left since the heyday of the old Socialist Party of a century ago, whose four-time presidential standard-bearer Eugene V. Debs peaked at 6% in 1912.[13]

During the 2020 campaign, when democratic socialist Sanders was waging his second run, 76% of Democrats and 45% of independents told Gallup they would vote for a socialist president.[14]

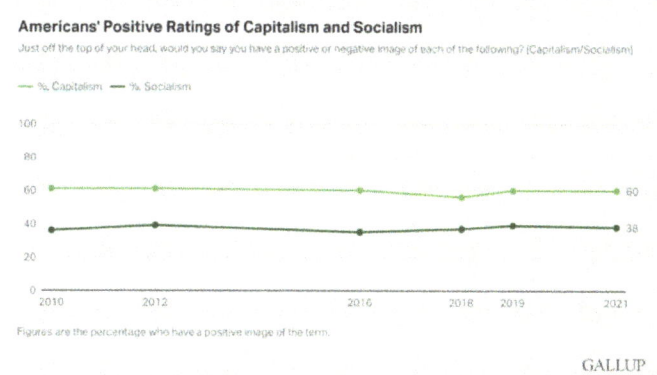

History is punctuated by periods of protest that reveal Americans' yearning for a world with greater economic equality, a merciful justice system, increased individual rights and the prioritization of human needs over corporate profits: the Black Lives Matter demonstrations and riots of 2020, Occupy Wall Street in 2011, marches against the 2003 invasion of Iraq, the 1999 Battle of Seattle, etc., etc., all the way back to the women's suffrage and abolitionist movements at the dawn of the republic. These leftist movements were ruthlessly crushed by state violence and marginalization by the media before, in some instances, ultimately achieving their goals.[15] Whether successful or not, and whether they vote or not, the point is that the American Left—the real Left to the left of the Democrats—is important. We are a substantial plurality. We may be mocked and ignored and disrespected. But we exist. We are an untapped consumer market in the marketplace of political ideas, a sleeping giant that will surely be awakened someday.

The Democrats and Republicans keep pretending we don't exist or that, if we exist, we don't matter. Like disused streetcar tracks that keep reappearing as the asphalt used to pave them over continuously erodes, the fundamental human cravings for fairness and equality always reemerge.

I write this at one of those times between spasmodic uprisings, when the presence of the Left in Americans' lives feels irrelevant, certainly as an organized force. (We're talking here about the actual, socialist/communist-influenced electoral Left of the sort we find in Europe, not the corporate "liberal" Democratic Party.)[16] Older readers have witnessed such constructions as the Soviet-aligned Communist Party USA and its perennial presidential candidate Gus Hall fade into the mist. So has the once fairly formidable Socialist Workers Party. The Revolutionary Communist Party has devolved into a cult of personality around Bob Avakian, who no longer even lives in the United States. New York's Working Families Party, once a Left-leaning alternative to liberals, lingers as a ballot line mirroring the Democrats' candidates. The Green Party, the nation's biggest Left party, received 0.2% of the vote in the 2020 presidential election; it did not appear on the ballot in some states, including New York, in 2024 when Jill Stein, the Greens' standard-bearer in 2024, scored 0.5%.[17]

There are no sustained street protests about any issue, including the right-wing Supreme Court's repeal of abortion rights. The anti-Trump Women's March, billed as a monthly event, happened once in earnest, then again a year later in muted form, before vanishing.

Israel's war on Gaza sparked one major antiwar demonstration (over 100,000 attendees) in Washington, matched in size by a pro-Israel counter-march. Notwithstanding Sanders's post-election *cri de coeur* taking the Democrats to task for abandoning the working class, he and his fellow democratic socialists have been swallowed by the Democratic Borg.[18]

We can't identify any group or party that speaks for the Left. American leftists are bereft of leaders. We have no presence in the media. We have no realistic prospect of having our positions aired, much less seriously considered and debated or enacted into law.

Though unorganized as a party, the Left includes tens of millions of Americans, as polls show widespread openness to its ideas.

Sanders's massive campaign rallies, drawing tens of thousands of attendees in numerous cities, proved we are able and willing to mobilize when we feel hopeful. Our record of taking to the streets to fight racist cops, warmongers, strikebreakers, and gay bashers shows our revolutionary spirit. We do this despite formidable risks to our personal safety and public reputations.

A 2020 Harvard-UCLA study of French voters found the "bandwagon effect" isn't limited to sports, where winning teams attract more fans than losing ones. "We find that many elections are swayed by a relatively small fraction of voters following their preference to be on the winning side, rather than substantive differences between candidates," the researchers wrote. "Our findings indicate that voters' actual preferences may themselves depend on others' behavior."[19] Being declared the frontrunner in the polls bestows a French presidential candidate with an additional six percentage points of support that he or she would not otherwise have enjoyed.

Why, Thomas Frank famously asked in his book *What's the Matter with Kansas?*, do many working-class, liberal-minded voters vote Republican, i.e. against their own economic and cultural interests? A 2015 study published in the *European Journal of Political Economy* answers Frank's question.

The power of the bandwagon effect in electoral politics is striking: "It is worth noting that bandwagon behavior may stem from a willingness of voters to vote with the majority even when their private preferences are with the minority (or to abstain and let the majority win).

Minority voters might wish to support the majority in two ways: by voting directly for the majority or by abstaining. They do so because they aim to support the choice that benefits the most voters, even at a personal cost.

Such an explanation makes intuitive sense. That is, in almost all naturally occurring elections and in experimental work a particular choice is more likely to win when it is supported by the majority, thus there is almost perfect correlation between providing support for choices that benefit the majority of voters (which would be other-regarding behavior by the minority) and bandwagon behavior."[20]

Winning begets winning, not only because it's fun to be on the winning team. We are social creatures. Social cohesion relies on consensus. We want our group to be happy, so much so that some of us are willing to vote with them against our individual opinions and interests. When we sense that the majority wants a change, some of us go along or stand aside.

Forty percent of Americans view socialism favorably. Many more would probably join a socialist party, if they thought it might possibly win.

List Our Grievances

How do we confront the rich, who are hogging the resources we all need, and the powerful, who enforce laws, regulations and propaganda mechanisms that deny us access to those resources?

In this pre-revolutionary moment, lacking an organized mass movement, we're left to do what medieval peasants did: petition our rulers—Congress, the President, and the media—to address our grievances.

We list our grievances and explain how they can be addressed. We do not demand that our sovereigns step down (not yet) for two reasons: first, they will not do so willingly and we are not (yet) in a position to force them to do so, and second, we will appear reasonable to the fence-sitters who are not yet radicalized.

As it happens, many of our worst problems could be resolved within the existing system. They won't be—because, as we've seen for decades, the ruling class does not want to. But they could be, in theory. So we will not demand (yet) to change the existing structure one iota. For this exercise, we accept the system as it currently exists.

This book is a list of complaints and suggestions for fixing them. N.B.: my purpose is not to tell anyone what to care about or what to want. I am in no position to lord anything over anyone. I'm just a 61-year-old guy with chronic respiratory issues, still listening to CDs, wearing skinny jeans, collecting political buttons, and raised as an only child by a single mom, a high school teacher in southwestern Ohio.

If and when the time comes for an organized Leftist party or other organization to issue demands of the elites, that Leftist entity should and will compose its demands after discussion, debate and compromise within its ranks. It should not be created by any one person or small group of people.

However, I do—after a half-century of sentience—have a pretty good idea of the major issues the workers of this country have been dealing with.

So I've enumerated some of them here in hope that people who read this will be inspired to agitate. The details are up to the people.

Confront the Ruling Classes with an Aggressive Opening Bid

Anyone who has experience haggling at a flea market has intuited the basics of negotiating. If a seller offers the item you want at a fire-sale price that you're unlikely to find elsewhere, don't counter. Smile, pay the asking price and walk away before they change their mind. If the seller's asking price is many times higher than you're willing to pay, just walk away. Stratospheric pricing pretty much eliminates the odds that you'll be able to come to terms. Your time is better spent haggling with another vendor. In other cases, in between these extremes, offer a low-ball rate and work toward middle ground. Be ready to compromise but also to walk away.

American liberals tend to ignore these time-tested strategies. They negotiate against themselves. Instead of pushing for bold change, Democrats start with an incremental approach, preempting their conservative opponents' counteroffer and working from there. Since the Right is aggressive, they push back hard, to the point that the resulting change is a smaller improvement that in many cases is so tiny 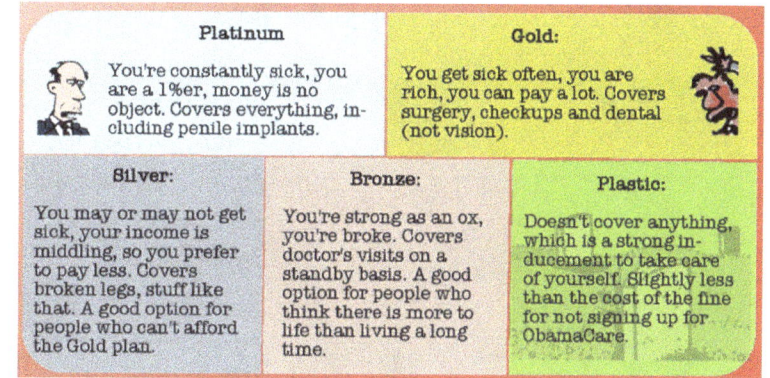 as to be a rounding error. Obama's opening gambit in the healthcare reform debate illustrates this phenomenon.

We know what we wound up with: Obamacare. Originally developed by the right-wing Heritage Foundation,[21] it's a free-market scheme that prioritizes insurance-company profits. It relies on economies of scale and assumes robust competition will reduce costs.[22] (In practice, the healthcare business is de facto monopolized to the extent that there is little downward pressure on prices.[23] The industry has little incentive to join the public sector, so only a small fraction of health plans available individually or through private employers can be bought on the ACA's online marketplace.[24])

The point here is how the ACA as we know it came to pass. Obama, wielding considerable political capital at the start of his first term, decided to make healthcare reform his first major legislative priority. The public, long struggling under high costs for medical care and prescription pharmaceuticals, was supportive across party lines.

WHAT'S LEFT?

Straight out of the gate, Obama negotiated against himself. Though he'd promised during his campaign that the ACA would include a "public option"—i.e., the right to join what Bernie Sanders called Medicare for All—Obama dropped it from the bill because, Democrats explained, they lacked one Senate vote.[25] Joe Lieberman, a right-wing independent senator from Connecticut, which is not coincidentally home to the corporate headquarters of many of the nation's major insurers, threatened to scuttle the measure via a parliamentary filibuster maneuver.[26]

Obama could have forced Lieberman and his Republican allies to go on the record as rejecting a popular bill on a major issue. Instead, he dropped the public option. Obama noted that the public option had "become a source of ideological contention between the Left and Right."[27] Anyway, he lied, "I didn't campaign on the public option." Good news: the ACA passed. But the lack of a public option was so unpopular (88% of Democrats wanted one) that it was a significant factor behind Bernie Sanders' campaign.[28] Rather than a landmark achievement, Obamacare is widely seen as a disappointment. Most Americans say its failure left healthcare unresolved.[29]

Shortly before he left office, Obama tacitly admitted his error and suggested that Congress add a public option to the ACA.[30] This is what happens when you negotiate against yourself.

The four out of ten Americans who oppose capitalism—socialists, communists, left libertarians and others to the Left of the Democratic Party—should take careful note of the Democrats' repeated refusals to seek big changes and the subsequent failures that have followed as a result. Unlike the Democrats, who negotiate in Congress against Republicans who share their basic political values and assumptions on the relationship between workers and their labor, militarism and social priorities, we on the actual Left are fighting to overturn the system entirely.

Though revolution is our aim, we lack the organization to pursue it now. There is no viable leftist political party with a revolutionary orientation, no well-funded highly distributed media outlet to disseminate news and opinion with our point of view. We have, even accounting for the so-called progressive "Squad" in the House of Representatives, zero elected representatives who seek to abolish capitalism and prioritize the needs and desires of the people. Absent these basic structures or an as-yet-undeveloped Internet-driven strategy that bypasses traditional grassroots organizing and agitation, emancipation by revolution will remain out of reach.

First, the Left Needs to Describe a Better Future

Some reviewers criticized my *Anti-American Manifesto* because in it I called for revolution, or more precisely for opening rhetorical space for revolution as a viable political option, without laying out a step-by-step path for organizing a revolutionary organization.[31] Whether that was an error is for others to judge; my explanation (not a defense) is that my omission was no accident. It was intentional.

Allowing ourselves psychological access to the R-word must precede organization. That was my goal in writing my *Manifesto*. I wanted to make revolution something people might think about thinking about, which was not and still is not the case in a political environment where "the left" has been downgraded by being equated to the Democrats, "the right" are the Republicans and "politics" is a silly carnival that occurs every two-to-four years on the first Tuesday after the first Monday in November.

Revolution must come from the masses, not an individual. In any case, I am not blessed with the gifts of a street-level organizer and wouldn't know how to begin to build a grassroots movement. Still, no doubt about it, we have a lot to do. We must agitate and confront and organize and work inside electoral politics and out in the streets.

But for what?

What do we want?

What should we fight for?

Karl Marx and his contemporaries would call the answer to these questions a programme—a list of demands and desires, like a political party platform of the not-so-distant past, which confronts the biggest problems facing us and lays out specific ways to solve them if and when we win power at the ballot box or seize power at the point of a gun as the culmination of a revolutionary movement.

We, the Left, need to express a coherent vision for the country. What is wrong? How should we fix it? Are our solutions realistic? What are our priorities? We must build credibility by demonstrating that we know what has people worried, terrified or merely annoyed; successfully identifying people's concerns shows that we get it, that *we get them*. We need solutions to their problems. We need to walk people through our ideas, listen to their thoughts and adjust our programme in response to their feedback.

So what is the Left?

The term originated during the early months of the French Revolution, when representatives who supported secularization and the replacement of the monarchy with a republic sat to the left of the speaker's dais in the National Assembly. Over the following centuries the umbrella term "Left" came to include the union movement, socialism, certain varieties of anarchism and libertarianism, as well as the struggles for civil rights, women's rights, gay rights, pacifism, environmentalism and many other political orientations.

What do these movements have in common? Put simply, those who belong to the Left subscribe to the idea that everyone is entitled to the good things in life by virtue of existing, that human beings should all enjoy equal rights and opportunities and that the basic necessities of life like food, shelter, healthcare, education and transportation should be guaranteed by the government.

In this, the richest nation ever—albeit with the widest wealth gap—we have the resources to provide these essential goods and services to everyone who needs them.[32]

But we will never accomplish much within the constructs of the electoral politics trap. Never has the dysfunction and uselessness of the duopoly been clearer than in the most recent election cycle, when most voters began the year by telling pollsters in overwhelming numbers that they wished that neither of the two major-party candidates were running. Yet they did. One won.

And no one expects the winner to keep his promises or make life better in the ways that matter to us.

Get the Ruling Classes on the Record, Make Them Say No to the People

As we build a mass movement, we must lay the groundwork for revolutionary foment. We must, within the constructs and limitations of the current capitalist system, expose the true nature of a government that claims to be by and for the people but is in truth nothing but a Ponzi scheme that extracts wealth upward from the poor and the working class up to the tiny few at the top point of the pyramid. We can and must accomplish this by exposing the system's internal, self-evident contradictions.

This begins by questioning the powers that be, who endlessly funnel billions into destructive nonsense—foreign wars, corrupt defense contractors, corporate tax breaks—while smugly insisting there's never money to meet basic human needs.

We know that when we demand that everyone has enough to eat, political elites will refuse or ignore us. We expect, when we demand that everyone be housed, that we will be told to go to hell. We understand, when we demand that a day of work should be paid fairly, that we are asking for something that they will never agree to—indeed, that they cannot because it would destroy them and their self-perceived identity in the power structure.

We make demands, not because we believe they will be achieved under this fake parliamentary-style democracy. We do so because they will be refused—unreasonably and without just cause. We want people to hear us ask, and hear them say no, over and over in order to expose them and the fundamental nature of their system.

We are not really negotiating. We are demanding. Those who demand should appear reasonable. But our demands should be aggressive enough that we would genuinely be satisfied were we to achieve them. They must never be so modest that there is a chance the ruling classes would ever seriously consider them.

Nothing less than a perfect world will do.

But, you may think in reply, everything feels hopeless. Like nothing will or can ever change for the better. The existing American system feels like it will last forever. And that's what our rulers want us to think. It isn't so.

West of Ashgabat in the former Soviet republic of Turkmenistan lie the ruins of Nisa. Nisa was the capital, the residence of the emperors of the mighty and fearsome Parthian Empire (247 BC – 224 AD). There is not much to see. It is not, by itself, worth a trip to Turkmenistan (though other things are).

When Westerners think of Parthia at all, it's as the one power ancient Rome couldn't conquer and deemed unconquerable. Ultimately, Rome's leadership accepted that, in Parthia, they had found the limits of imperial expansion. The Parthians were badasses. At their peak they ruled all of modern-day Central Asia. Yet all that remains of their Persian-related language today, aside from a few sandy walls and mounds at Nisa, are three thousand shards of pottery with writing found at a wine storage depot, a land-sale receipt, some graffiti and the fragment of a business letter found in modern-day Syria.

All empires fall.

Talking Points:

The Left needs an organized structure for demands, not just social media noise, to effectively challenge the conservative U.S. political landscape.

Despite claims of a conservative America, a substantial double-digit plurality of voters leans Left, unrepresented by the two major parties.

Polls show 40% of Americans view socialism favorably, indicating a larger, suppressed Left presence ignored by mainstream media and establishment voices.

The Left must list grievances and propose bold solutions within the current system, inspiring action without expecting immediate elite consent.

Without a cohesive vision or party, the Left relies on exposing systemic contradictions to awaken a revolutionary spirit among the masses.

2

IDENTITY POLITICS MUST DIE

> *"People can call themselves whatever they want, but the traditional Left was concerned with class issues."*
> —*Noam Chomsky*

When things are going smoothly and most people are doing well, there is space for incrementalism and gradual progress. This is not one of those times. This is an era of sociopolitical chaos, technological upheaval and ecological crisis. Yet leadership is glaringly absent.

Hundreds of thousands of our fellow citizens are homeless. Countless Americans suffer and die—literally uncounted because no one tracks them—because they lack health insurance or their plans refuse to honor medical claims. Most of our taxes go to killing innocent people in other countries and creating enemies who want to kill us. Our schools fail to prepare our children to succeed as adults. We are polluting our environment, killing our plants and animals, and poisoning our food and water. We are afraid of our police. Some of our elected representatives are corrupt; the rest turn a blind eye.

These problems are too vast and entrenched to be solved incrementally over time. This situation is too grave to tolerate any longer. We have radical problems. Radical problems require radical solutions.

Our radical problems stand no chance of being addressed by anti-radical, corporate bourgeois parties like the Democrats and Republicans. It's not that they cannot fix them. It's not that they're lazy. It's not because they don't want to.

They don't view our problems as problems.

Democrats: Useless, Hopeless, Enemies of the Real Left

The first thing that an American Leftist must accept is that there is no hope for the radical reform we need and want within the Democratic Party. This cannot be emphasized enough. Many liberals succumb, in this two-party system, to the siren song of the two-party trap: Democrats may not be perfect but they are not as bad as the Republicans, and only the Democrats can keep the Republicans out of power. To say the least, that argument is highly debatable. And I debate it often! But the point here is more holistic: the Democratic Party is where the Real Left goes to die.

The Democratic Party is wholly captive to corporate donors who pour hundreds of millions[33] of dollars into each election cycle—over $3 billion in 2024. The Democrats are not only not a potential vessel for a reformist or progressive insurgency, they oppose anything that looks as though it might threaten the privileges of the power elite.

A vacuous yet vicious cult of incrementalism rules the Democrats. The failed 2024 candidacy of then-Vice President Kamala Harris highlighted a key flaw. Asked by an interviewer what she would have done differently from the consistently unpopular president who dropped out, she replied, "Not a thing that comes to mind." This response cast a harsh spotlight on the reality that nothing—not even the risk of losing to an opponent she and many historians labeled a "fascist"—could push the Democrats to adopt bold changes to the status quo.[34]

Most Democratic voters lean significantly left of their party's leadership.[35] They have little power or influence within "their" party. But a majority is still a majority. So, rather than declare open war against Leftism and thus risk mass voter boycotts, the Democratic Party has stumbled into an effective new tactic to keep its progressive-dependent coalition under its big tent: deflection and distraction centered around the politics of personal identity.

It's so ironic. Identity politics was meant to free people. Now it's being wielded to keep workers shackled, diverting us from the broader reality of class struggle.

Identity Politics Have Been Co-opted by Elites

Emancipation struggles with historic weight and legitimacy—such as the feminist and civil rights movements, the fight for gay, lesbian, and transgender rights and efforts to ensure the disabled can access public facilities—movements born outside and to the Left of the party—have been co-opted by the Democrats and their media and political allies. They are used to displace and to replace the class warfare waged by union members and the working class to extract higher salaries, better

benefits and decent working conditions from their increasingly rapacious employers (many of whom are mega-corporations that buy Democratic politicians with their donations).

It was a natural de-evolution. In the 1960s and 1970s, when being a woman or an ethnic minority roughly doubled as a marker of economic disadvantage, class issues could be sidelined without abandoning the traditional class-oriented Left. True, not every Black American was poorer than every white American. Broadly speaking, however, there was a race-class correlation; most Blacks were poorer than most whites. Openly gay men, when they were not being beaten and even murdered, lived on the margins economically as well as socially. The fight for gay rights, then, was a form of class struggle. In general, to be socially disadvantaged was to earn a lower income and vice versa.

Championing ethnic and other underprivileged minorities served as a credible, if rough, proxy for pursuing class equality.

This is no longer true. Consider, for example, gay men. Joel Mittleman, a sociologist at the University of Notre Dame, published a 2022 study in the *American Sociological Review* that found that "on an array of academic measures, gay males outperform all other groups on average, across all major racial groups."

NBC News summarized: "Gay men are far more likely than straight men to have graduated from high school or college, with just over half of gay men having earned a college degree, compared with about thirty-five percent of straight men. Some six percent of gay men have a Ph.D., J.D. or M.D., a rate fifty percent higher than that of straight men. Mittleman found that gay men's markedly higher educational attainment persists even after accounting for differences in race and birth cohorts. What's more, gay men's college graduation rate dramatically bests even that of straight women, about one-third of whom have a bachelor's degree."

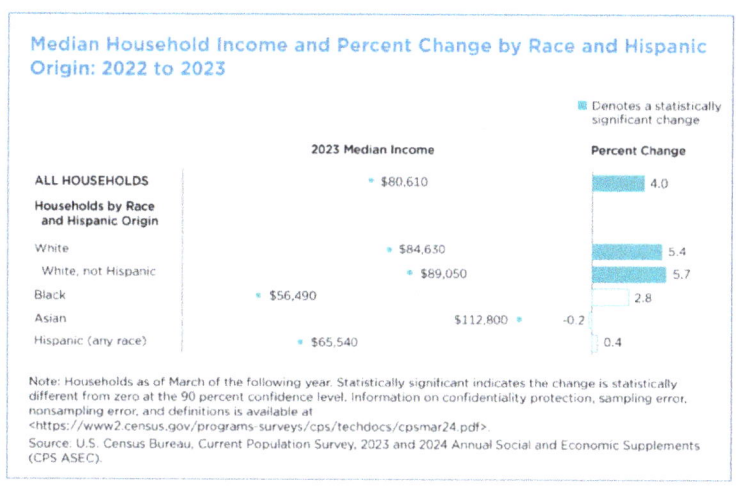

As the economic fortunes of gay men improved, they gained social currency and access to the corridors of power in Washington and corporate America. Former Secretary of Transportation Pete Buttigieg, for example, is on most analysts' short lists of presidential prospects. Not coincidentally, the rate of homophobic hate crimes directed against gay men has fallen over time.[36]

Similarly, women are far more likely than men to attend and graduate from college, paving the way for higher earnings in the years ahead.[37] As women earn more, their political power increases as well. A woman has been nominated by a major party to run for president not once, but twice. Abortion rights have become a top election issue (granted, after the Supreme Court took them away). Domestic violence against women declines each year.[38]

Asian Americans, not whites, have by far the highest median household income in the United States: about $113,000 annually in 2023, compared to $85,000 for whites.[39] This is a dramatic reversal from a century ago, when Asians were specifically excluded from immigration to the U.S. and suffered from widespread systematic discrimination and brutal poverty. Asian Americans have advanced so far that, perversely, many colleges and universities started discriminating against them, fearing they had become overrepresented.[40]

Discrimination against members of traditionally oppressed groups remains a problem. Still, sufficient progress has been achieved that discrimination by the rich against the poor as a discrete, non-identitarian issue has become a bigger problem than ever.

To the extent that meritocracy ever made sense—why should being talented and/or a workaholic make you worthy of praise or, for that matter, a high income?—the Horatio Alger striver ideal has been killed off by late-stage capitalism. This will come as a surprise to Americans, more of whom tell pollsters they think they have a chance of upward mobility into the upper income classes than their European counterparts. But the opposite is true. These days, it's easier to get ahead in "Old Europe" than in the New World.[41]

"[In the United States] the community you come from has a huge effect on your economic mobility," *The New York Times* confirmed in July 2024. "For centuries, this meant a tremendous advantage for white Americans, even those born into low-income families. But in a surprising shift, [a Harvard University] study suggests that advantage is not as large as it once was...Over the decade and a half of the study, the opportunity gap between white people born rich and those born poor expanded by roughly 30%." On average, it's still easier to be born white than another race. But, in the same way that the average speed of a motorist driving 60 and a pedestrian walking on the side of the road is slightly more than 30, we don't live in the average or the mean. We live as individuals. Your race isn't nearly as determinative to your destiny as your parents' income.

"Class is becoming more important in America" while race is becoming less so, Raj Chetty, the study's lead author, told the *Times*. None of this is to say that there still aren't disadvantages to being non-white, non-cis-male and/or disabled in the United States. There are, and those injustices must be constantly struggled against by the Left.

At the same time, the politics of "woke" slam into a dead end because they have nowhere to go: even if identity politics were to achieve total success, the basic structure of the capitalist system would remain intact, meaning that the idea that all human beings are truly created equal would not even be a goal of our society. Poverty, sickness, dysfunction, injustice would continue because they are intrinsic to the notion that there is nothing wrong with unequal outcomes.

But equality is everything. Any Leftist movement or party worthy of the name must restore the primacy of class struggle to our politics.

Barack Obama illustrates the problem of prioritizing racial tokenism over a class analysis. Obama's 2008 presidential campaign, primarily an appeal to identity politics, highlighted the history-making potential of electing the nation's first Black commander-in-chief. No one knew or cared much about the young Illinois senator's policy positions and he didn't much bother to share them. After he won, there was no way to hold him accountable from the Left since he'd already delivered on his promise: he was Black, he became president, and that was about it.

By contrast, Bernie Sanders' 2016 and 2020 insurgent challenges from the progressive wing of the party focused on a succinct trio of issues that the long-time independent self-described democratic-socialist senator from Vermont hammered on: student loan debt relief, increasing the minimum wage and upgrading national healthcare to a European-style model.[42] A product of the 1960s New Left, Sanders' issues centered around economic class. The fact that Sanders would have been the first Jewish president was scarcely noticed or mentioned.[43]

Had Sanders prevailed in a general election, there would have been clear benchmarks that he defined, against which to assess his success or failure.

A USA Today/Ipsos poll from March 2023 show a sharp turn against woke ideology, with only 56% of Americans viewing the term positively—down from earlier years—suggesting voters are fed up with its excesses. The sanctimonious woke crowd, once smugly dominant in elite circles, now faces a backlash. Even latte-sipping liberals are tiring of word-policing and guilt-tripping. By November 2024, a YouGov poll found just 17% of voters regularly use "woke" in a positive light, signaling a collapse of its cultural grip.

Identity politics is not entirely empty. It appeals to voters because symbolism really does matter. "When I heard last evening that Pennsylvania had gone for Barack Obama, I think I had an out-of-body experience," Representative John Lewis of Georgia, the civil rights icon left bloodied and nearly killed by racist cops in Selma, Alabama, recalled. "I jumped, and I shouted for joy. And my feet left the floor, and I just kept jumping. Something lifted me up, and I shed some tears. And I tell you, I have cried so much during the past few hours, I don't think I have any tears left."[44] Voice of America quoted a 36-year-old graphic designer from Harlem who was deeply moved as she took in the 2008 election results: "Now when your grandmother tells you that, baby, you can be the president of the United States, hey, you don't have to look at her doubtful now. You can say it is the truth." Who doubts, that after watching President Obama on their televisions for eight years, it became easier for hiring managers to imagine a person of color as an executive at their company?

Symbolic progress can and does spark meaningful change. Because it usually becomes tokenism, however, identity is also a trap.

Tokenism is a Dead End

Too often, the personal success of someone from a disadvantaged ethnic, racial or other group is later viewed as a letdown. Obama's years in the White House are a perfect example; not only did he fail to fight for and achieve much on the policy front, any pressure he might have felt coming from those who took him to task for not accomplishing more was suppressed by supporters who characterized the president's critics as racists. Obama's election made symbolic history but it did not create significant change or improvement for the average American voter, including people of color.[45] No doubt, Obama's failure to deliver helps explain why Kamala Harris' 2024 campaign failed to excite as many Black voters as analysts had expected.

Ruling elites, having learned that identitarian progress distracts from class-directed policies that might impact their bottom lines, have come around to embracing identity politics in order to avoid making concessions to working and poor people on workplace and other economic policies.

Lyndon Johnson, responding to a warning that pushing through the Civil Rights Act would be politically costly, famously asked: "What else is the presidency for?" In other words, what's the point of power unless you leverage it to improve people's lives? There was a big street party in Miami's "Little Haiti" neighborhood on the night of Obama's victory. Lucy Coma, a restaurant owner, echoed LBJ: "We don't vote for Obama because he is Black; we vote because we want change. That's everybody, white, Hispanic, Asian. All the things he promised, that is why we vote for him. We are so happy." Many people felt like Coma: they understood Obama's election as a historical moment, but first and foremost, a presidential election ought to be a chance to fix some of the nation's big problems.

People hoped for change in 2008. They were disappointed. By 2016, voters were so unhappy with the president that his Gallup poll disapproval rating nearly quadrupled, from 13% at his inauguration to 45% on Election Day 2016. Determined to send a message—a raised middle finger— to the elites, votes shocked the political world by snubbing Obama's anointed successor in favor of Donald Trump. Unlike the Democrats, Trump consistently spoke about downward mobility, particularly among the white working class in the post-industrial Midwest.[46] He made people who had long felt ignored and abandoned feel seen. He didn't follow up with meaningful action, of course. But acknowledging people's anger was better than nothing at all.

You might think Trump's 2016 win was considered by liberal elites to have been a political failure, a debacle that prompted Democratic Party leaders to conduct an after-action report that culminated in a change of course.

That would be misunderstanding their point of view. To leading Democrats like Obama and Bill Clinton, losing the White House to Trump was a personal victory. Obama joined Clinton and her husband on the lucrative speech circuit, where talking for an hour earned him $400,000.[47] Driven by appeals to liberals alarmed and furious at Trump's presidency, the party fundraised more than ever after the 2016 "defeat." Though they lost seats in the Senate, gains in the House in the 2018 midterms made the next election cycle a wash. The American Cancer Society would shut down were cancer ever to be cured; the Democratic Party is more of a fundraising scheme than a political party fueled by an ideology that it seeks to turn into reality by winning elections and passing bills.

Why Nothing Improves: Politics Without Politics

Obama perfected a model launched by Jimmy Carter and honed by Bill Clinton: politics without politics. Promise to do little and fail to deliver on the few promises you do make. If you lose, fundraise harder using the argument that you could have won if you had had more money. Focus on the politics of personality—celebrate Obama's youthful charisma, promote Hillary Clinton's potential to become the first woman president, push back against Trump's brutalist bigotry, use a pandemic to cast Biden as the nation's grandpa, double down on Kamala Harris's symbolism as a potential first woman-of-color president—and the press and the people will forget all about the idea that elections are supposed to be about legislative proposals.

To be sure, even though they succumb to electoral razzle-dazzle—look at that sex scandal! how cool is her ethnicity! can you believe he said *that?*—people still live their lives and still have their complaints. Resentments build. Candidates like Clinton and Harris fall to defeat, partly because some voters see through the bullshit. But there's no real pressure on the political system to address the real problems that keep those people awake at night—people who don't complain because they've given up, because they accept that there's no redress to be found by voting or by writing a letter to the editor or anything else. This in turn keeps the huge corporations and wealthy individuals who rely on the system remaining as it is—exploitative and cruel—and who donate the most money to political candidates, satisfied.

The federal minimum wage, stuck since 2009, is now worth $4.95 in real terms—more billions for McDonald's shareholders.

Democratic strategists advising Kamala Harris' campaign counseled her to focus on an Obama-type identity play, emphasizing her race and gender by implication rather than overtly, and to avoid saying anything of substance for as long as possible.[48] This was particularly remarkable given the truncated time frame of her campaign, just over three months. For her, this was too much time in the public eye.

"The longer the Harris campaign can portray her as a cultural phenomenon," *the Times* reported in late July 2024, shortly after she took over the Democratic nomination from Biden, "the longer she can avoid articulating details of her policy agenda that could divide her support…For now, the Harris team intends to skip some of the traditional markers of a presidential bid. While Ms. Harris released a host of policy papers during her 2020 campaign—some of which she has since disavowed—this time she plans to cast herself as a policy extension of Mr. Biden's administration."[49]

Politics without politics: "I think we are three weeks from knowing whether she can ascend the Obama ladder to where it's about her and not any specific policies she has," Rick Davis, campaign manager for John McCain, the Republican who lost to Obama in 2008, predicted. Forty days of her 107-day campaign passed before she finally sat down for her first short interview, in which she used a lot of words to say very little. That, it turned out, was her first and last chance to make a good first impression.

If a party-machine politician like Kamala Harris can become a contender for President of the United States without making specific policy promises, good for her. If she could have gotten elected the first woman president—the first woman-of-color president—the symbolic resonance would have been undeniably powerful. But we, as individual voters, have interests that go beyond making a symbolic change. We want to pay less for goods and services. We want/need to earn more. We need a safety net to catch us if something goes wrong, like we lose our job or get sick. We need clean air to breathe. We need our world to feel safe, without wars or threats of terrorism. We need privacy and equal opportunity and efficient transportation and care for our aging parents and a government that understands new technologies like artificial intelligence well enough to regulate them intelligently without stifling their potential.

We need so many things.

And, because our nation is rich, we can afford so many things.

And we deserve them. Our government, which we fund handsomely with our income and sales and property taxes, owes us those things.

You Don't Owe Your Vote to Anyone or to Any Party

"I'm with her," a Hillary Clinton campaign slogan adopted by Kamala Harris supporters, is the opposite of what representative democracy is supposed to be about.[50] A president should be watching our backs. A politician ought to be there for us, fighting like hell to improve our lives.

Like Harris, Obama ran like a rock star, long on charisma and short on specifics. Progressives and other leftists who gave him their votes quickly learned that being young, Black and cool enough to enjoy weed is no guarantee that a candidate will govern any better or differently than a boring old white guy.[51] As president, Obama was decidedly uncool. He did exactly what a Republican would have done. He declined to codify *Roe v. Wade*—despite a filibuster-proof Senate supermajority in 2009 at his popularity's peak, he deemed abortion rights "not the highest legislative priority"[52]—granted Guantánamo torturers full immunity[53], sent tens of thousands more troops to fight losing wars against Afghanistan[54] and Iraq[55], launched assassination drones[56] ten times more than Bush and backed the military coup against the democratically-elected, left-leaning president of Honduras.[57]

Obama's decision to bail out Wall Street[58] but not Main Street after the 2008-09 subprime mortgage crisis and to push through a for-profit healthcare bill originally conceived by a right-wing think tank drove pissed-off progressives to form the Occupy Wall Street movement[59] in late 2011. True to conservative form, Obama ordered his Homeland Security Department to partner with Wall Street banks, real estate firms, local police, and the FBI to brutally dismantle hundreds of Occupy encampments in coordinated, violent raids.[60]

Post-presidential Obama is still a rock star. But his presidency gravely wounded the Democratic Party. Obamaism led directly to Bernie Sanders' insurgent 2016 campaign—and an intraparty schism that contributed to Donald Trump's surprise wins.

The left-leaning Democrats who comprise the majority of the party's voters refused to get conned into supporting another Democrat In Name Only like Obama, Biden or Hillary Clinton.[61] So in 2024, progressives demanded a clear, coherent policy agenda for a potential Harris administration. "She is not Trump" was not enough. Nor was "we need a Black woman president." By those standards, we could have elected George W. Bush's hawkish secretary of state Condoleezza Rice. Democratic strategists thought Leftist voters were bluffing, that they would turn out for Democrats out of fear of a second Trump presidency.

There was no bluff. In one of the biggest voter boycotts in history, at least ten million Democrats who usually vote sat on their hands and refused to turn out for yet another empty suit, Kamala Harris. And it wasn't even organized.

Left-leaning Democrats knew too little about where the party— cagier than ever—stood on key issues.

The little that lefties learned about big issues like Israel's war against the Palestinians in Gaza (Harris supported Israel), universal healthcare (she was against it)[62] and the long-frozen minimum wage (she didn't talk about it) gave them little cause for optimism. So many stayed home.

Class Comes First

The Left is the political stance that prioritizes the state's duty to individuals, defining a set of rights every person deserves—regardless of circumstance—simply for existing or being a citizen.

Identity politics obscures and deflects the struggle to protect these existing rights and establish new ones. By dividing people into interest groups based on race, sex, and more—and then buying them off—identity politics weakens and waters down the workers' fight against the ruling class. Because workers cannot prevail against bosses if they are disunited, and because identitarianism takes up space in public discourse that would otherwise go toward economic conflict, identity politics is an enemy of the Left.

This is not to say that the Left should ignore fights for racial and gender equality, for LGBTQIA+ rights, and so on. The Left must always side with the oppressed. But these issues should never be allowed to replace or supplant class issues. While it is possible for an oppressed group to achieve emancipation by improving its economic position—as, for example, Asian Americans achieved over a past century—the opposite is never true. You can elect Black Americans to every public office in the country, but creating a sub-class of elite Blacks will not stop cops of any race from shooting Black motorists, or prevent employers from discriminating against them in hiring decisions. Economic issues, financial power, class—they are destiny. There cannot be social equality without financial equality. Class comes first, identity comes second.

When negotiating nuclear arms reductions with the Soviet Union, Ronald Reagan quoted a Russian proverb: "Trust, but verify."[63] When a leader asks you to trust her without offering any reason to do so, when she asks for a blank check, when citizens willingly suspend skepticism, when those who wish to wait-and-see are shouted down as party poopers in service to evildoers, you are observing a key component of fascism: blind trust in The Leader. Jason Stanley, a Yale philosopher, noted: "Truth is required to act freely. Freedom requires knowledge, and in order to act freely in the world, you need to know what the world is and know what you're doing. You only know what you're doing if you have access to the truth."[64]

What was the truth about the Kamala Harris campaign? No one knew. We were asked to trust in "joy" and a "new way forward." There was no way to verify, which was just as well since the campaign offered so few specifics.

In a democracy, no citizen should have to resort to Cold War-style Kremlinology to guess how a candidate for president would govern the country. The fact that a major political party ran a presidential campaign without issuing many specific promises is evidence that its leaders don't consider the U.S. to be a vibrant democracy. In this and little else, they are correct.

Until we can and will hold politicians' feet to the fire, representative democracy will be unaccountable and therefore worthless. When we give our votes away without any promises in return, we are reduced to speculation about what they might or may not do. Once elected, elected representatives do not represent us. They do whatever they want.

Leaders who promise nothing owe us nothing. Voters are worse off, and our system is worse, than people in a corrupt autocracy who sell their votes for money or, as in some countries, kitchen tools.[65] If we vote without demanding accountability, we are worse than those who sell their votes for a pot or a pan. We are suckers—we give our political leverage away in return for nothing.

If a leading candidate for high public office won't tell us what she thinks, or we don't like what she says, she shouldn't get our votes. They don't work for us. They work for their big corporate owners. The only thing they need from us is our vote. So we should only vote for candidates and parties who share our values.

Despite what they say, it is not our job to be interested in politics. People who don't vote should not be insulted as "apathetic." We should not accommodate ourselves to whatever policies "our" candidates and parties choose to promulgate. It's up to politicians to meet us where we are. To that end, we—as unashamed idealists dreaming and fighting for a better future—must issue specific demands outlining solutions to the problems we face.

Politics is the art of debate. Debate inevitably requires negotiation that results in compromise. Because the ruling powers that be have all the advantages—they enjoy massive powers of political and social inertia, control of the news media and culture and unlimited economic and military assets—our starting point in negotiations with the ruling class and the elected representatives they have purchased must be radical.

Incrementalism, that gutless creed of baby steps and half-measures, has sunk its claws deep into the Democratic Party, turning a movement of dreamers like FDR and LBJ into a pack of timid bureaucrats who'd rather polish the status quo than smash it. These sniveling worms worship at the altar of "pragmatism," churning out tepid policies so watered-down they don't inspire anyone. The party's vision has shriveled into a sad little footnote, drowned out by the drone of consultants preaching caution while the planet burns and the working class gets screwed.

Do not settle for token progress.

Do not waste your time, energy, money or vote on an anti-radical party promoting the dead-end politics of distraction.

Talking Points:

America faces radical crises—homelessness, healthcare failures, and environmental ruin—requiring bold solutions, not the incrementalism offered by Democrats and Republicans.

The Democratic Party, tied to corporate donors, stifles the Real Left, using identity politics to distract from class struggle.

Identity politics, once a stand-in for class issues, now serves elites, as marginalized groups gain ground but economic inequality worsens.

The Left must prioritize class over identity, demanding specific, radical changes from politicians who otherwise owe us nothing.

3

WHERE TO START? DEFUND THE PENTAGON

"No war can be undertaken by a just and wise state, unless for faith or self-defense."
—*Cicero*

Marx theorized that the struggle to build socialism must necessarily follow industrialization in advanced economies;[66] he argued that capitalism's inherent drive toward consolidation and self-interest would deepen the class divide, fostering class consciousness.[67] He also argued it's easier to advocate for wealth equality in a rich society than in a poor one where suffering is widespread.

The United States of America at the dawn of its semiquincentennial is a perfect illustration of the Marxist argument. The U.S. is one of the richest, if not *the* richest, nation-state in the history of the world. It also is the most unequal.[68] Many of its people live in misery and squalor. What good is it if a country has spectacular wealth, yet is unable or unwilling to provide a decent standard of living for its citizens?

Surely there is a better way.

We can and should redistribute our immense income and wealth. Until a revolution achieves that, though, we live under a U.S. government that gathers revenue and allocates it across various priorities—one that constantly claims to be of, by and for the people. If this is truly our government and exists to serve us, a question emerges: Why does so much of that money get spent on projects that so many disapprove of? Meanwhile, more urgent and popular needs remain unaddressed.

By far the largest and most glaring misuse of public funds is Pentagon spending. Whenever we are told there's no money for things we care about—fixing a run-down bridge, paying teachers more, building a new school, you name it—one of the first thoughts that springs to mind is: If that's true, why is there always money for the Pentagon's $800 toilet seats?

In the 2024 presidential race, voters across the spectrum voiced a concern: Why are we sending billions of dollars overseas to places like Israel and Ukraine? So many people need help here at home.

People ask that question or one analogous to it year after year.

No one, not in the political class responsible for how all our money is spent, ever answers. Because there is no good answer.

A pre-revolutionary Leftist economic plan, rooted in today's realities, should start with the federal budget.[69]

How are revenues collected, and from whom? How should that taxation regime change? How is the money being spent? How should it be spent instead? The Left should articulate a holistic approach to the federal budget we are all familiar with because spending priorities *are* ideological priorities.

According to the U.S. Treasury's website, the federal government rakes in tons of cash: "The federal government collects revenue from a variety of sources, including individual income taxes, payroll taxes, corporate income taxes, and excise taxes. It also collects revenue from services like admission to national parks and customs duties."[70] This came to $4.44 trillion in 2023. The biggest source of this cash bonanza was income taxes.

States and cities also collect about $2 trillion annually.[71]

$6 trillion is, to state the most obviously obvious thing in the world, a staggeringly enormous amount of money. (By way of comparison, that's the total value of all U.S. currency currently in circulation worldwide.)[72]

We Are Not Predestined to Live in a Shithole Country

Donald Trump famously called Haiti and some African nations "shithole countries" (as opposed to, according to him, Norway).[73] It certainly doesn't feel as though *we* live in a rich country with vast tax revenues flowing into its coffers. Nor does it look like one.

People sleep on the streets. Factories are abandoned. Schools are dilapidated. Hospitals are chaotic, understaffed and depressing. Storefronts are boarded up. Litter abounds. Bridges collapse, subways derail, doors fall off passenger airplanes, high-speed rail and free college and affordable healthcare are for other countries. How does China, with a budget half ours and a population more than four times larger, pull this off? They continually build massive new hydroelectric dams, suspension bridges and tunnels. Meanwhile, our urban centers are empty and boarded-up husks haunted by drug-addicted zombies.

It feels like *we* live in a shithole country.

It also feels like we're moving backward. Which we are. The Social Progress Index, "the most comprehensive measure of a country's social and environmental performance independent of economic factors," has found that the U.S. is one of only three countries (the others are Brazil and Hungary) of 163 countries to have slid backward.[74] We have the worst poverty among the world's 26 most developed nations. And now our life expectancy is falling.

Why can't we Americans have nice things? One can blame cycles and systems: late-stage capitalism, the duopoly, boom-and-bust, deindustrialization, the latest addiction scourge (opioids), the corrupt revolving door between businesses and the government officials who are supposed to regulate them. But many other countries that do a better job for their citizens face the same or equally serious challenges.

Fundamentally, the answer boils down to one simple fact: the American system of government has bad priorities. The people in charge would rather spend our money on the things that *they* care about than on what *we* want and need. They ship costly weapons abroad instead of feeding the poor, grant corporate tax breaks rather than treating young drug addicts, and build prisons instead of hiring social workers.

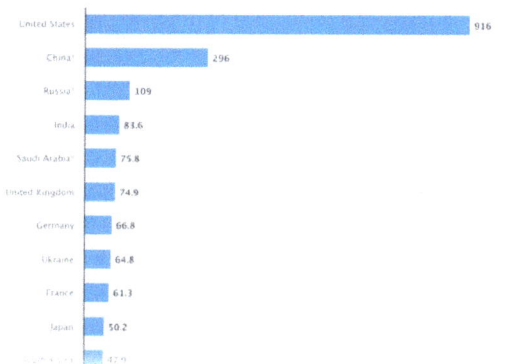

These figures represent current annual military spending only.

That's seriously fucked up. We need to take away money from stupid expenses and redirect it to human needs.

Reordering a society's social and economic priorities is a complex task. To keep things relatively simple, let's set aside the comparatively lesser and diffuse state and local budgets in order to focus upon the federal budget as the principal focus of the Left's proposed shift of the U.S. to a country that puts people first. Further to the goal of simplification, let's assume for the sake of this argument that overall revenues will remain flat in real terms adjusted for inflation—no major tax cuts or hikes, no significant changes in tariffs like a protracted trade war.

When we search the federal budget for money that could be better spent elsewhere, we can begin with either the stupidest waste of money or the biggest single item.

We do not need to choose.

The U.S. military budget is both our biggest and dumbest expense. Defund the Pentagon—it's way overdue.

Militarism Is Sucking Us Dry

The most recent fully-calculated U.S. military budget, for 2023, came in at $916 billion. It's by far the largest expense—exceeding all other federal spending combined. It is the biggest single expense of any government on planet Earth. And that's radically understating the real cost of militarism.

As the socialist journal *Monthly Review* calculates, when you include costs associated with medical and other expenses related to veterans, debt service on deficit spending for old wars and military aid to foreign countries, the amount doubles. So the actual 2024 total of military spending comes closer to $1.6 trillion.[75]

But we need to spend all that money to keep ourselves safe from our enemies, right? Not even a little bit.

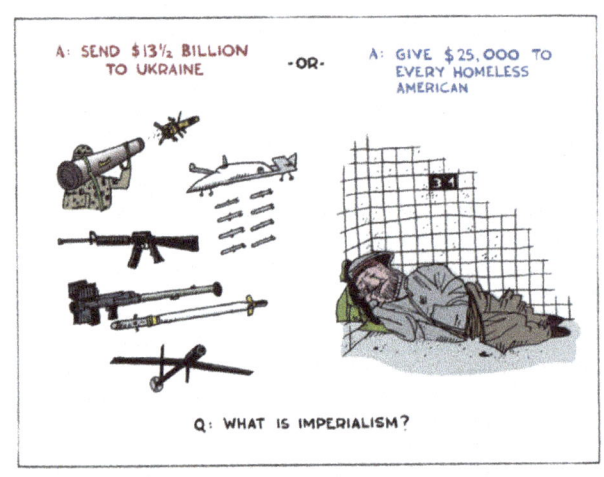

Tragicomically, America's over-the-top military spending is counterproductive. Nothing makes us less safe than a forward, aggressive military posture in which U.S. forces and proxies are stationed around the globe. Our troops are sitting ducks and provocateurs. Their presence does not keep us safe. It endangers us.

The number one job of the Defense Department is supposedly to protect the United States from invasion or attack. Over and over again, it proves itself incapable of fulfilling its function.

Consider these examples: hijacked planes flew around the northeastern U.S. for nearly two hours on 9/11. So-called "Chinese spy balloons" crossed the country unchallenged by air defenses. Swarms of drones appeared on the Atlantic seaboard in late 2024, unidentified, though officials assured us they posed no threat. Plainly, spending trillions of dollars on the Pentagon serves little purpose.

Not only does the military fail to keep Americans safe from foreign threats, it endangers Americans inside their own borders. The U.S. military is the world's top institutional source of greenhouse gases.[76] Military bases are contaminated with per- and polyfluoroalkyl substances (PFAS), also known as "forever chemicals." These chemicals are found in groundwater and soil around many bases nationwide.[77]

From the B-25 that crashed into the Empire State Building in 1945 to the January 2025 air disaster in which an American Airlines passenger jet was struck by a Black Hawk military chopper in Washington D.C., killing 67 people, military aircraft kill more Americans in the homeland than they have ever saved. The helicopter, which was flying above its permitted altitude at the time of the crash, was part of a unit that ferried congressmen and other dignitaries who wish to avoid D.C. traffic—"the V.I.P. taxi service of the federal government in Washington," *The New York Times* called it.

I call it bloat. It's a menace as well as a giant waste of money.

A Left worthy of its name is not reflexively pacifist or anti-military. It is, instead, pro-defense. The distinction is sharp. The Left favors a military apparatus designed to defend the U.S: no more, no less.

What do we really need to be safe? We need missile defenses, border protections, a naval force to protect our coasts, the kind of domestically-focused armed forces that could have effectively responded to the terrorist attacks of September 11, 2001. Given our uniquely secure geography—flanked by two vast oceans and bordered only by two friendly allies—we can secure genuine defense, not the hegemony we fund through the Department of Defense, for far less than we currently spend.

The U.S. military is bloated beyond belief. Chalmers Johnson, the academic and great critic of the American empire, once phoned the Pentagon in order to ask the press office for a list of its overseas bases; not only could they not produce such a list, they could only estimate the number within 100 or 200.[78] (It's 800, more or less.[79])

To say the least, not knowing your base count signals overreach.

Another indication that you may have too much on your plate, that you might be fighting in too many places, is the increasingly common reaction, when learning that one of your country's soldiers has been killed in combat in Chad or Burundi, of surprise that we were in that nation in the first place or of having to check a map to see where it is.[80] None of this makes sense. None of this keeps us safe. We should close every last U.S. military installation that is not in the U.S. and bring every last soldier and sailor home.

Brazil is about the same size as the United States.

What It Would Cost to Actually Defend the U.S.

How much do we really need to defend the U.S. homeland, nothing more?

A good example of a country that is doing it right, or at least better than us, is Brazil, a regional superpower bigger than the contiguous forty-eight states, with a military budget of $20 billion.[81]

That's a mere rounding error compared to our gargantuan "defense" budget, just 2.5% of what we spend. Of course, Brazil doesn't wage wars or plant bases on the opposite side of the planet—and neither should we.

Brazil defends its long borders, many of which are more perilous than ours. They deal with violence, drug trafficking, migration and border disputes with unfriendly countries, the latter directly with neighboring Uruguay and indirectly, between Venezuela and Guyana.

We can emulate Brazil. We can spend 2.5% of what we're spending now. We can spend the $1.6 trillion that we save on stuff that helps instead of kills.

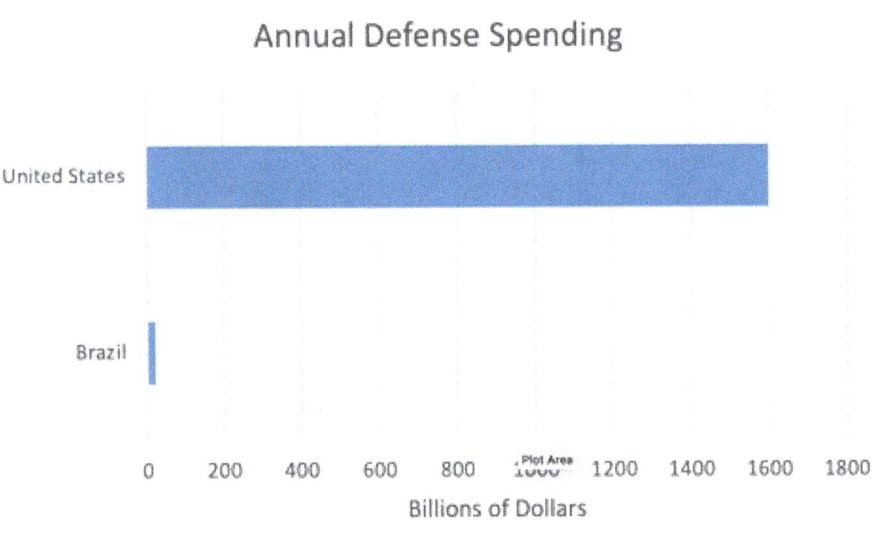

Political conditioning, the constant fearmongering instilled by the news media and politicians and popular entertainment that tells us everyone is always out to get us, makes that figure leap off the page. Two or three percent of the defense budget, sure, we could cut that much...maybe. No more! What if we got invaded?

Given numerous well-documented examples of Pentagon waste, some people might be able to get behind Representative Alexandria Ocasio-Cortez's and Senator Bernie Sanders' proposal[82] to reduce the military budget by 10%.[83] That's as far as mainstream "progressives" are willing to go—because even they, like their corporate Democratic and Republican colleagues, are trapped in a series of false assumptions and have been propagandized by the cult of militarism. A 90% cut in military spending? No way! 97.5%? That's crazy!

Except: it's not. What's crazy is what we're doing now, pissing away trillions of dollars for nothing while our people and our infrastructure are decaying.

The Bipartisan Cult of Militarism

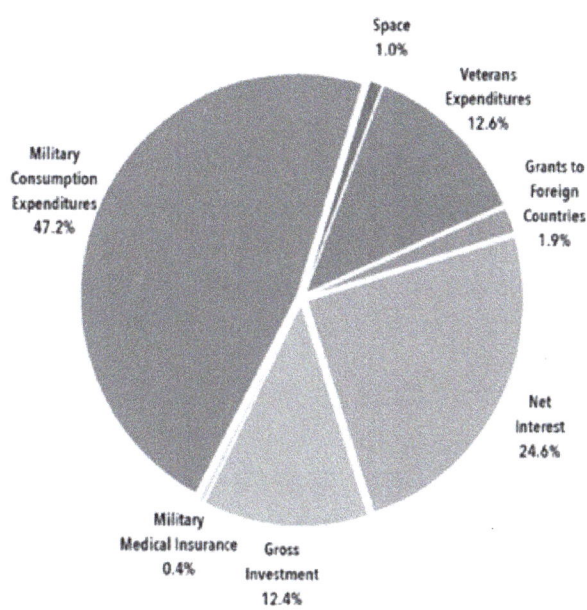
How Pentagon spending is currently apportioned

The United States is one of the most politically polarized countries in the world.[84] Because effective lawmaking requires bipartisanship and members of Congress are, like their constituents, at their most ideologically divided point in a half century, cooperation is in increasingly short supply.[85]

As a result, or, more precisely non-result, the U.S. Congress passes fewer bills every year.[86]

There is, however, one consistent area of agreement on Capitol Hill: defense spending.

For six decades, the sprawling National Defense Authorization Act—Washington's term for the military spending bill—has passed with strong bipartisan backing.

Defense appropriations are so sacrosanct that the press always describes the NDAA as "must pass."[87] It is routine for Congress to add in hundreds of millions of dollars of extraneous spending that the Pentagon does not want or request.[88] Such largesse, of course, does not extend to education, healthcare or the arts.

In the U.S. Congress, even "antiwar" voices support the cult of militarism. Obama's 2008 campaign was largely launched from his opposition to the U.S. invasion and occupation of Iraq.

Yet even his GOP opponent John McCain didn't care to call out Obama on the fact that, when Obama had six chances to vote on the Iraq War, he voted to send the money every time.[89] Obama wasn't yet in the Senate when it voted on the measure authorizing President George W. Bush to attack the government of Saddam Hussein. And when Obama got into the White House, he sent *more* troops to Iraq.

Bernie Sanders repeatedly voted to fund the military and send weapons for wars being waged by U.S. proxies like Israel and Ukraine.[90]

The idea that military expenditures are "must pass" relies on the assumption that the U.S. faces existential threats to its safety and/or sovereignty.

This is bullshit.

We Are Safe

21st century Americans are as safe as human beings anywhere anytime have ever been.

As Stratfor's classic 2011 assessment of the United States and its geopolitical position noted: "The American geography is an impressive one."[91]

Consider, by contrast, the Russian Federation. Russia has thousands of miles of land borders, most of it without significant natural barriers like mountain ranges or large bodies of water to deter a potential invader, millions of square miles of flat grasslands that can quickly and easily be traversed, and is surrounded by numerous neighbors that are hostile and have invaded Russia in the past. Given its perilous situation, Russia's rulers have traditionally relied on maintaining friendly buffer and vassal states around its perimeter. It has precious little access to the world's oceans.

On the other hand, "The U.S. Atlantic Coast possesses more major ports than the rest of the Western Hemisphere combined," Stratfor observed.[92] "Two vast oceans insulated the United States from Asian and European powers, deserts separate the United States from Mexico to the south, while lakes and forests separate the population centers in Canada from those in the United States. The United States has capital, food surpluses and physical insulation in excess of every other country in the world by an exceedingly large margin." Canada and Mexico, the U.S.' only two border nations, are friendly vassal states.

Red Dawn was just a movie. Gun nuts who think they will need AR-15s to arm a Resistance against foreign invaders are delusional. No one wants to invade us. No one wants to take away our freedoms.

Calm down. Breathe.

We Americans are freaking out like hippopotami. Hippos are the most dangerous land animal on the planet, killing five hundred human beings every year. Big and dumb and mean, they're nervous and high-strung because they rapidly evolved from a much smaller creature that made easy prey. Poor things! They don't realize that they've become huge, that they've grown fearsome teeth and no longer need to be aggressive and territorial. Like the hippo, the U.S. started out small and vulnerable to aggressors like England, which re-invaded in 1812 following the War of Independence. But things have changed for both the hippo and us. Can't we become smarter and less reactive than a hippo?

Like other countries, the U.S. has faced raids, like the Pearl Harbor attack and cross-border incursions from Mexico during the 19th century. In a now largely-forgotten episode, two of the Aleutian Islands were occupied by Japan during World War II, before Alaska became a state.[93] Non-state terrorists have struck the contiguous forty-eight states, as on 9/11. But those were minor events. None of these incidents, though violent and disturbing, presented anything resembling an existential threat. Most countries, faced with attacks of such small scale, would not feel traumatized. They would merely be annoyed.

No enemy army or navy has posed a substantial threat of territorial invasion since 1815. There have been two actual invasions of the U.S. by armed troops, a two-week retaliatory border incursion by Mexico into Texas in 1846 during the Mexican-American War (which we started) and the War of 1812 (we started that one too). To paraphrase Walter White in *Breaking Bad*, we are the ones who invade. The U.S. has invaded 68 countries and has dispatched combat troops to 191 out of the 194 countries recognized by the United Nations.[94] (The three exceptions are Andorra, Bhutan, and Liechtenstein. I'm sure we'll get to those sooner rather than later.)[95]

In the 21st century, the U.S. confronts two primary threats to national security: terrorism and cyberattacks.[96] These concerns are addressed by, respectively, the Department of Homeland Security and mostly the FBI. We don't need a fleet of ships lining our coastlines or a perimeter of military bases to fend off the Germans or the Japanese or the Chinese or the Russians. Which is good, because we don't have them. The "Defense" Department doesn't defend the U.S.; it attacks and disrupts other countries and non-state entities abroad and, far less frequently, defends U.S. allies against internal uprisings, rival factions and hostile neighbors.

Given our enviable security situation, it is entirely likely that the U.S. could get by eliminating its military budget entirely, as have countries like Costa Rica, Panama and Iceland, all of which have abolished their army, navy and air force and yet have not been invaded.[97] Could it be that, much as you are likelier to be shot by a gun if you own one, an unarmed nation is less likely to be attacked because its neighbors no longer view it as a threat?[98]

Donald Trump and his Republican lackeys are bellowing the right tunes about putting America's military defense first, thumping their chests with "America First" bravado while saying they want to end foreign wars—yet their track record reeks of hollow swagger. Look at March 2025, when Defense Secretary Pete Hegseth talked about slashing $50 billion from the budget to refocus on U.S. soil, only for GOP hawks—

like influential Senator Roger Wicker—to squawk for a "generational" spending hike to flex muscle abroad. The GOP's 2024 platform called for a missile defense "dome" to shield the continental United States, but congressional Republicans threw a tantrum over whispers about withdrawing from NATO. They love to play global cop. They chuck red meat to their party's populist base, but whether it's Democrats or Republicans doing the talking, it always means bigger bases overseas and a massive war budget.

Defense should be about defense, i.e. defending our own borders.

Anything more is not defense at all.

Talking Points:

The U.S. is a rich but unequal nation where wealth redistribution could thrive, yet government priorities favor militarism over people's needs.

The U.S. collects $6 trillion annually, yet misallocates it, with the $1.6 trillion military budget dwarfing spending on crumbling infrastructure and social services.

Military spending is wasteful and counterproductive, failing to defend against real threats while endangering Americans through pollution and reckless operations.

A Leftist budget should slash the Pentagon to Brazil's $20 billion level, redirecting $1.5 trillion to human needs like healthcare and education.

America's geographic safety and lack of existential threats expose the bipartisan cult of militarism as unnecessary, propping up a bloated, aggressive empire.

4

WE WASTE $3.8 TRILLION.
LET'S SPEND IT ON PEOPLE.

"Don't tell me where your priorities are. Show me where you spend your money and I'll tell you what they are."
—James W. Frick, Educational Philanthropist

When Americans think of "defense," the first thing that comes to mind is soldiers and military hardware called up to fend off an invading army. But a country can be brought down by any number of internal or external threats that look very different than that: environmental catastrophe, disease, a cyberattack, biological warfare in the form of an intentionally disseminated pandemic, economic sabotage, etc. History shows that more great empires have collapsed due to internal contradictions and crises than have succumbed to a foreign invasion. Ancient Rome spent its final four centuries telling itself it was a republic at the same time it expanded its empire, rationalizing that imperialism was a temporary state even as its institutions solidified to prop up its political reality. The Soviet Union couldn't reconcile its lofty founding mission as the world's premier socialist experiment with its authoritarian governance and privileges for elites.

The United States system has a major internal contradiction. It was established as a representative democracy that claimed all men were created equal. Yet, at the same time, it legally allowed people to own human beings. That hypocrisy culminated in the Civil War, which nearly destroyed the country, and continues to consume its energy through the scourge of systemic racism.

Now, an analogous problem threatens to destroy America. We are an empire that claims to be exceptional. We host the United Nations, effectively decide which countries gain international recognition or can develop nuclear weapons, and enforce our laws even in other countries. We claim to be and are extraordinarily rich, yet our own people live poorly compared to those of other countries. Life expectancy is falling, largely because we have the worst healthcare system of any developed country.⁹⁹ Key metrics like infant mortality, education, and personal safety, as well as addiction to illegal narcotics, show us failing. Like the freedom-loving U.S. during the slavery period, the U.S. as a world-controlling empire with citizens suffering from poverty is a contradiction. This has fueled political instability and could easily tear us apart.

Swear Off the Cults of Militarism and "Inflation Fighting"

But it doesn't have to be this way. Budgetary priorities can be changed. We can swear off the cult of militarism. We can put people first.

The $1.6 trillion we waste each year on the Pentagon is an irresistible target for Leftists looking to redirect funds toward human wants and needs currently neglected and ignored.¹⁰⁰ As we saw in the last chapter, almost all of that money is completely wasted.

So let's redirect Pentagon spending to something more worthwhile than slaughtering innocent people around the planet—e.g., anything else. But while we're scrounging around under the sofa cushions of the U.S. federal budget, why stop with the military?

The budget is full of poor spending choices and waste created by bureaucratic inefficiency.

One big item you might not immediately think of as flexible is interest on the national debt, which amounted to $659 billion in the 2023 fiscal year.¹⁰¹ That derives from past spending. We don't have a time machine, so what can be done about that?

Quite a lot, actually. Unlike an individual who has no choice about the interest rate charged by Visa or Mastercard, the U.S. government sets the rate on its own debt obligations. The national debt for 2023 reflects an increase of $184 billion, or 39%, from the previous year. It is nearly double that for the 2020 fiscal year.¹⁰² The main culprit behind that massive spending spike is the Federal Reserve Bank's optional, unnecessary, totally reversible, anti-worker decision to repeatedly raise interest rates following the Covid-19 lockdown.

Americans have experienced the trope of the Fed as the government's first line of defense against runaway inflation for so long that it doesn't occur even to many Leftist economists to question its underlying assumptions, factual basis or efficacy. When inflation rises, the Fed raises interest rates to make borrowing more expensive and slow down the economic activity they say is "overheating" the economy—i.e., causing higher prices and wages. Those higher rates, however, are primarily directed at wages because salaries and benefits are the biggest expense for most businesses. They do indeed have the effect of reducing inflation—but not as much as they do of benefiting capital and employers over labor and workers by weakening the latter's ability to demand improved wages and working conditions. Ever notice that a recession quickly follows a labor shortage? Capitalists declare a recession when workers get uppity, impose layoffs and austerity and get workers to fall back in line. "Recession fighting" is a ruse, union- and labor-busting in disguise.

In our globalized economy, moreover, the Fed can't take on goods inflation anyway. Most of the driving forces behind goods inflation are overseas and therefore out of the control of Fed policy. As Representative Ayanna Pressley, a Massachusetts Democrat, pointed out at a 2022 hearing with Fed chairman Jerome Powell: "the root causes of the inflation we are seeing are supply chain disruptions outside of the Fed's control, whether it's Covid-19 lockdowns in China or the Russia-Ukraine war, which is why this knee-jerk response to raise interest rates is so alarming. The Fed cannot control the factors causing inflation, but this policy choice would plunge millions of people back into unemployment, dampen wage growth, and tip the economy into a recession." As Pressley pointed out, there are more precise tools available, like direct credit regulation, which would set different rates for different types of businesses. "This would allow the Fed to regulate the availability of credit in the specific sectors of the economy experiencing high inflation without impacting other sectors."[103] Congress could direct the Fed to go that route—but that wouldn't be as beneficial to big corporations trying to crush workers.

The Fed raised returns on government-issued Treasury bonds and notes that finance the national debt. This was to fight a spike in inflation after the economy reopened. That spike probably would have eased without any action by monetary regulators. That, after all, is what happened the last time the national government put the economy into a deep freeze during a pandemic; after the Spanish flu, the Harding Administration rode out inflation without resorting to government intervention and everything worked out fine. Pent-up consumer demand was released, production capacity caught up to demand and prices leveled off. And, despite some modest rate cuts as of this writing, these unnecessary interest hikes are only going to continue over time. The Congressional Budget Office projects that interest on the debt, which currently amounts to two percent of GDP, will rise to six percent by 2030. Mainly, this will be more about keeping labor undervalued than about fighting inflation.

American taxpayers would have saved $184 billion had the Fed chosen to leave well enough alone, stop attacking labor and refuse to increase interest rates. Which, if our society valued labor as much or more than capital, it would not have. Not only is the Fed's obsessive fear of inflation a paranoid[104] and anachronistic vestige of a 1970s economy that no longer exists[105] and in any event was not nearly as bad[106] for workers as we've been told, it repeatedly leads them to risk recession because, in the worst-case scenario from business' vantage point, layoffs and wage cuts rein in the power of labor,[107] which amounts to about two-thirds of the expenses of a generic U.S. corporation. Historically, a recession typically follows Fed rate hikes by about 18 months.[108]

A Leftist government would direct the Fed to avoid rate increases as a matter of policy. It would also abolish the present official goal, repeated with the blind fervor and lack of logic of a religious fanatic,[109] of a two-percent annual inflation rate.[110] It would not squander $184 billion a year on the altar of phony inflation-fighting.

Shaking Billions Out of the Sofa Cushions

That's not the end of the waste. The federal government issues about $250 billion[111] per year in overpayments made in error to individuals and corporations that objectively do not qualify for any subsidies, including $1 billion a year to dead people. The government does not bother to cross-check payments against death records, so the funds get mailed to survivors of the deceased and deposited in dead people's old bank accounts.

Nearly $2 billion per year goes to maintaining 77,000 empty buildings.[112]

Then there's the revenue side—or lack thereof. In 2021, the last year for which statistics are officially available, the Internal Revenue Service failed to collect $688 billion in unpaid taxes because it didn't send dunning letters or conduct audits of wealthy individuals or corporations.[113]

That's not even mentioning the fact that income taxes can and should be increased on high-income individuals and corporations.

We should abolish other expenses that are arguably wasteful, like most of the $103 billion budget of the Department of Homeland Security, the $70-billion-a-year foreign-aid[114] budget and outlandish headline-grabbing projects like federally-supported studies of how Russian cats walk[115] and how the fur color of Labrador retrievers affects their internal body temperatures. (Not that the results of such studies aren't interesting.) Taxpayer money should never be squandered. But to be as effective as possible, let's search for the biggest reservoir of foolishly-spent money, not the latest headline-grabbing Bridge to Nowhere boondoggle, which cost relatively little.[116]

When you add up all the federal government's wasteful spending, bureaucratic inefficiencies and failure to collect all the revenues that it should, at least $3.8 trillion per year is being frittered away for no good reason whatsoever. Meanwhile, Americans live in terror because they are one or two paychecks away from economic ruin, don't know what they would do if they were diagnosed with a terrible disease and are going into insane amounts of debt in order to send their kids to college.¹¹⁷ It's a ridiculous situation analogous to where I live in New York City, where officials ask residents to take shorter showers at the same time 15% of the city's water supply is lost to leaky pipes.¹¹⁸

Currently, families don't pay Social Security withholding taxes on income over $250,000 per year. Eliminating the highly regressive cap would bring in an additional $100 billion per year.¹¹⁹

Imagine if large corporations and wealthy individuals were made to pay their fair share of taxes. Six out of ten voters say they resent how low taxes are for the rich and big companies.¹²⁰ And they're right. The Tax Policy Center finds: "The United States raises less revenue from all corporate income taxes as a share of GDP than all other countries in the G7 and almost all other countries in the Organization for Economic Co-operation and Development (OECD). In 2021, total federal, state, and local corporate income tax revenue as a share of GDP was 1.6% for the U.S., compared with the 3.2% average for the other 37 OECD countries."¹²¹

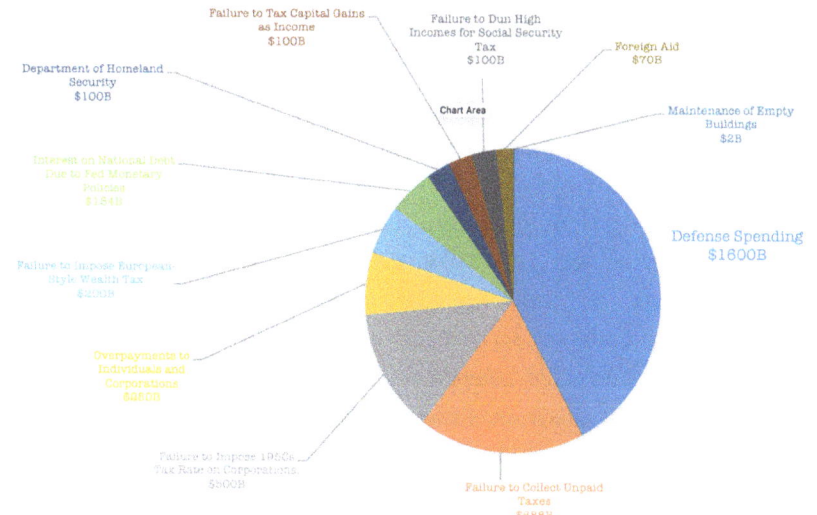

A 2% or 3% wealth tax on people worth more than $50 million ¹²² —a tax on assets rather than income, as other developed countries have—would bring in at least $200 billion annually.¹²³

Taxing capital gains at the same rate as income would bring in an additional estimated $100 billion a year.

Corporate income taxes as a percentage of GDP have steadily fallen since 1950, peaking at 6% during the Korean War, hitting 3% in 1970 and plunging to 1% during the Reagan years, where they are now. Companies are sponging off the greatest consumer market on earth; they should be made to pay if they want to continue to play. If we returned to that 3% rate, when the economy was booming by the way, the Treasury would bring in an additional $500 billion annually.

All told, we are looking at roughly $3.8 trillion per year. $3.8 trillion a year that could be used to alleviate hunger, house the unhoused, treat the sick, build infrastructure, educate the young, and retrain older workers.

So much money, so little imagination!

Electoral Two-Party Politics Are Not Real Politics

The 2024 presidential campaign highlighted the small-bore thinking that dominates electioneering and journalistic punditry. Trump and the Republicans called for eliminating taxes on tips; Harris and the Democrats followed suit. If enacted, however, this change would have a negligible effect, only affecting 2.5% of wage earners.[124] GOP vice presidential candidate J.D. Vance suggested a $5,000 increase in the earned income tax credit; Harris called and raised to $6,000. Again, this change wouldn't do much. Only 13% of taxpayers qualify for that benefit.[125] Harris wanted to pay a subsidy to first-time home buyers.[126] This might have helped a lot of people since it would have applied to roughly one out of four people buying a house or condo in the next few years. But the idea didn't stand a chance in Congress because neither party wanted to get behind it.

Major-party candidates keep tinkering at the margins of big systemic problems like unaffordable rents and mortgages and ignoring others, such as the existential threat to humanity presented by climate change (we'll get to that later).[127]

The political system is unresponsive to our wants and needs, and we know why. Lobbyists and big corporate donors with a vested interest in the status quo pay to install cooperative candidates who promise that nothing will fundamentally change (in Biden's infamous phrase) and to oppose and remove those who resist them and their interests.[128] Educational institutions purge and blacklist teachers who challenge the dominant corporatist narrative.[129] The news media are loath to challenge the half-dozen corporate leviathans that own them and do not hire investigative reporters or rebellious outsiders who threaten to rock the boat.[130] Citizens, surveying this bleak landscape of conformity and corruption, have rightly concluded that the situation is unlikely to improve any time soon. Voters feel trapped; forced to choose between two nearly identical unpalatable parties, they opt out entirely or cast spite votes against the party and candidate they despise most.[131]

As with so much else, there could be a better way.

You know it. I know it. Odds are, you've discussed, through gritted teeth, the inability and unwillingness of Congress and/or the system writ large to get things done. Why does it have to be this way?

It doesn't have to be.

Americans who travel abroad and witness how politics is a part of everyday life in other countries can't help but notice the contrast here. We consume politics passively. During election campaigns, people who take an interest in politics tune in to check what the two major parties and their candidates have to offer. If we're *really* engaged, we're one of the five percent of voters who volunteer to phone bank and talk to our neighbors on behalf of a contender.[132] If we're part of a tiny minority of voters, we may make a donation.

But here in the U.S., where our citizens have one of the lowest rates of civic engagement of any developed Western nation, we don't exert actual political pressure.[133] What passes for politics in the U.S. is a section of the newspaper, a subject link on a website or app, or a headline passed along to "friends" (for articles we might not read ourselves). It's a form of entertainment delivered like sports, traffic, weather, and streaming movies. It is not something we live and breathe.

It is different in many other countries. Protest marches, national strikes and other forms of direct action in the streets are not considered outlandish alternative forms of politicking outside the normal system, as they are here. These aggressive tactics, which can shut down cities and might even bring down a government, are legitimate forms of confrontation that can force significant reforms that an ossified electoral democracy would otherwise never consider. At their most effective, demonstrations and

other forms of street-level protest are so seemingly dangerous that the mere fear of provoking a riot can sometimes prompt the ruling class to yield to the people's demands without anyone having to draw up a picket sign or throw a Molotov cocktail.

Without a revolutionary Leftist organization, the periodic spasms of spontaneous activism we see in the United States—Black Lives Matter, Occupy Wall Street, the Battle of Seattle, campus protests over American military support for Israel's war in Gaza—rarely result in lasting improvements in people's conditions. They make a splash. Then they are quickly suppressed and co-opted.

We desperately need such an organization. Such a Left organization would, as they do in other countries, compile a list of demands that it would use in order to recruit members and set standards for what changes the elites would need to concede and enact should they desire to remain in power with the active consent of the governed. But there are currently too many obstacles in our duopolistic political culture to allow such a formation to gain traction.

So let's start with our demands.

The first step of radical organizing is to examine society and its current structure and to reimagine them from scratch, without consideration for legacy politics. A useful comparison is technology. Computers use the QWERTY keyboard, designed to minimize jammed type bars in typewriters in 1874, because people are used to it. It's a legacy. If the computer were invented today without a precedent, its keyboard would be configured differently.[134]

If we were looking at ourselves from the outside, objectively analyzing how the U.S. economy could be reordered and the fruits of our workers' labor redistributed in a fairer, more equitable and more just way, we would ask ourselves: What and how much do we have? How are we spending and dividing these items? How could we do it better?

What should be clear to everyone is that the current rubric, in which we send billions of dollars to foreign countries at the same time American citizens sleep out on the street and go bankrupt from paying medical bills and can't attend college because it's too expensive, is stupid, rotten and ridiculous. The fact that neither major political party and no major presidential candidate is willing or able to even begin to think about a different set of policy priorities that addresses the everyday concerns of the vast majority of people is the ultimate evidence of their illegitimacy.

Talking Points:

Empires like the U.S. collapse more from internal contradictions—like wealth disparity amid poverty—than foreign invasions, threatening national stability.

The U.S. misallocates $1.6 trillion yearly on militarism, neglecting human needs, despite claiming to prioritize its citizens' welfare.

The two-party system offers trivial reforms, ignoring systemic issues, while a revolutionary Left must demand radical budget reprioritization.

5

OCTUPLE THE MINIMUM WAGE

"In the 1960s, a minimum wage job would keep a family of three afloat."
—Elizabeth Warren

When Gallup pollsters ask Americans what causes them the most stress and worry,[135] personal economic concerns—cost of living, lack of money, the gap between rich and poor, difficulty finding a job, or, if they're employed, low wages—consistently come in first, so much so that they can't imagine saving for the future.[136] General economic issues like poverty, hunger and homelessness come in next. In a capitalist country with decades of rising income inequality[137] and a modest safety net, these findings come as little surprise.[138]

The rent is too damn high[139]; buying a house keeps getting more and more out of reach.[140] We're living paycheck to paycheck,[141] expenses rise faster than salaries, and bosses, who can fire you at will[142] even if you've been working hard and following the rules, have absolute power in a country where only 10% of workers belong to a union.[143] No wonder we're worried sick. Literally! Stress kills an estimated 120,000 Americans a year. 83% of Americans say they suffer from work-related stress; 65% say that stress is a major factor in their lives.[144]

In a capitalist society with a skimpy safety net, there is no bigger worry than fear of losing one's job and being unable to pay the bills, or that the job you hold won't pay enough so that you can sustain yourself and your loved ones. So it's no surprise that economic insecurity is America's biggest political issue.[145] Yet neither of the major parties campaigns on it. At most, they'll refer to it obliquely, as when a candidate will note that higher prices are a hardship. The president might send out a $300 stimulus check. When nativists call for reduced immigration, sometimes they argue that new arrivals take away jobs from the native-born. But no politicians from either of the two big parties fight for higher pay so that people can afford to pay their higher bills.[146]

Many of the other problems that keep people up at night are partly or fully grounded in economic insecurity. Crime and violence, perennial worries in urban and rural regions alike, are more pervasive in poor neighborhoods[147]; courts are better-staffed and more efficient in wealthy areas. Patients worry about being able to afford to see a doctor and pay for medications at least as much as they do about the quality of healthcare. Racial tensions tend to dissipate in places where incomes are high for all demographics and during periods of prosperity.

We need a raise.

The failure of bourgeois electoral democracy to address the nation's biggest political issue, economic insecurity, specifically the need for higher worker pay, is tailor-made for the agenda of the Left.

The ultimate goal of Leftists is to overthrow capitalism. This greed-based system views inequality and monopoly as inevitable at best and laudable at worst. It rests on the worst possible assumption of any ideology or economic system: we are all created *unequal*, and nothing should be done to change that.

Leftists want to replace capitalism with a socialism that provides equal access to the basic necessities of life and equal opportunity to achieve more. But Revolution is not like a cake; there is no recipe to follow that reliably results in the overthrow of one class of ruling-class elites by another. All the conditions must be ripe, and—frustratingly for the revolutionist—whether those conditions exist can only be confirmed after success.

One predicate for Revolution is a well-organized grassroots movement. It is foreseeable that such an organization or group of organizations would agitate with street demonstrations, strikes, sit-ins, sabotage and other militant actions centered around a Left programme that begins with an increase in the base pay for the lowest-paid, most disadvantaged working people.

Such a movement would also likely demand a maximum wage, a salary cap on CEOs and other top income earners, in order to shrink the gap between rich and poor and redistribute funds more fairly. The idea isn't outlandish; in 1942 President Franklin D. Roosevelt proposed a marginal tax rate of 100% on annual incomes over $25,000 (the equivalent of about $500,000 today) in order to discourage profiteering during World War II and force wealthy people to do their part. Cuba had a longstanding maximum wage of $20 per month for almost every job.[148] But, with the exception of schemes like British politician Jeremy Corbyn's 2017 proposal for a CEO-to-worker pay ratio of 20:1 (in which CEOs could keep their high salaries if they raised those of their employees), soaking the rich doesn't inherently benefit the working class.

Never has the public been more predisposed to the argument that government ought to intercede on behalf of those who are having trouble making ends meet, or fear that unemployment might put them into such a position.[149] People's buying power has been ravaged by inflation, corporations are again turning the screws after a brief period of liberalization driven by the post-pandemic labor shortage, and it has been sixty years since either major party proposed a federal anti-poverty program (LBJ's Great Society).[150]

Some bourgeois political analysts, particularly in the progressive wing of the Democratic Party, identify the vacuum in the dialogue space of economic injustice. But neither party will ever be able to meaningfully address issues like poverty and homelessness for a simple reason: they are capitalist parties. Whatever room existed for the reformist impulse within capitalism vanished after the postwar period yielded to the beginning of America's late-capitalist decline. For the plutocrats and their minions, admitting out loud that capitalism leaves millions behind, and that it's intentional and not an oversight, is unthinkable. They certainly won't use legislation to try to fix the problem.

We, the Left, have the signature issue of economic justice all to ourselves, provided that we do not obsess over identity politics to the exclusion of class divisions.

Money Changes Everything

Wages are at the top of our list of economic concerns. Money may not solve every problem. But money does buy more and better education. It buys more and better healthcare. It buys security and safer neighborhoods. If you do nothing else, putting more money into people's pockets will do more to improve their lives than anything else ever could.

The federal minimum wage, stuck at $7.25 an hour since 2009, is an affront to human decency. It is, by definition, a poverty wage: a full-time employee on the minimum wage earns $15,080 a year before taxes. Without accounting for taxes, that is exactly $20 a year more than the poverty rate for a one-person household. For a two-person household, like a single parent with one child or a couple, the poverty rate is equal to $9.83 an hour.[151]

Mississippi, the state with the lowest cost of living,[152] has an average rent of $1,480 a month, or $17,760 a year.

An increase in the minimum wage tends to exert upward pressure on higher wages, particularly for those near the minimum threshold. A 2014 study by the Brookings Institution found that an increase in the minimum wage would positively affect "up to 35 million workers—that's 29.4 percent of the workforce."[153]

Conservative arguments that raising the minimum wage causes inflation have been repeatedly debunked;[154] even a big minimum wage hike might not increase prices.[155] It might even reduce unemployment.[156]

A day's work ought to pay enough to pay for rent, a car and other necessities. If the federal minimum wage had kept up with inflation since 1970, it would currently be $30 an hour.[157] The official inflation rate, however, undercounts the actual increase in prices. Several times since 1980, the Bureau of Labor Statistics has changed the way it calculated inflation so that it can, for example, pay a lower annual cost of living increase to older people who receive Social Security. The average worker is twice as productive as in 1970,[158] so fair compensation equivalent to 1970 levels, when gas was 36 cents a gallon, a dozen eggs cost 53 cents and Harvard charged $4,000 a year, would double that to $60—which is still less than adjusting the rate using the 1980 method of calculation.[159]

The Minimum Wage Is Shockingly Low

For a full-time worker a revised minimum wage, one that's the same as 1970 and adjusted to account for increased productivity, would be $120,000 a year. (And 1970 wasn't a perfect time for workers.) $60 is a start. We deserve and demand better than that. The Left should think of $60 an hour as the *bare minimum* necessary to live decently in the United States, and push for *more* for skilled labor.

Think that's unrealistic? If so, and this is understandable, you may have been corrupted by the torrent of capitalistic propaganda that constantly devalues labor. Or, more likely, you've been beaten down by the capitalists' pet media and have learned to accept reduced expectations. In 2024 Donald Trump not only refused to consider a rise in the federal minimum wage but wondered aloud whether it ought to be reduced. Kamala Harris issued vague wishes for a raise while failing to articulate how much, if any, she would raise it if it were up to her.[160] Bernie Sanders and the Democrats' progressive "Squad" are still struggling to raise the federal minimum from $7.25 to $15.00—that's what passes for progressive nowadays![161]

There is a tendency for wage-increase demands to be diluted as inflation erodes earning power during negotiations. Progressives' push to increase the minimum wage to $15 is more than a decade old—today's $15 is no longer worth anything close to that old $15—yet they keep asking for the same $15. A recent example: strategist James Carville advised Democrats trying to regroup after Harris's loss to Trump: "While Democrats have next to no chance of passing a bold, progressive economic agenda in the next four years, what we can do is force Republicans to oppose us. We must be on the offensive with a wildly popular and populist economic agenda they cannot be for." So far, so good. But then he concluded: "Let's start by forcing them to oppose a raise in the minimum wage to $15 an hour."[162]

No. $15 wasn't high enough when it was proposed two presidencies ago and it's woefully inadequate now. As time passes, agitators should adjust their demands to account for inflation. It's accurate. And it disincentivizes dithering.

You know who thinks $60 is the bare minimum you need in order to survive? Landlords. In New York, where I live, you can't qualify for a rental apartment unless your annual salary is 40 times the monthly rent.[163] You need $120,000 to be considered for a $3,000 per month apartment; good luck finding housing cheaper than that, even in the slums. It's not that landlords want to discriminate against working-class tenants. They've simply learned from experience that people who earn less than $120,000 are far likelier to fall behind on the rent until they have to be evicted, costing building owners and managers money.

Is $120,000 too much? According to a 2024 study by Smart Asset, "the average salary needed to live comfortably in a major city is $96,500 for one person and roughly $235,000 for a family of four."[164] It's not like everyone can move to the country; more than 80% of American workers live in urban areas because that's where the jobs are.[165]

The federal minimum wage, measured in real terms, no longer reflects the reality of the labor market in most of the country. As of now, thirty of the fifty states have raised their minimum wage above the federal rate.

Any minimum-wage increase must apply without exception. The minimum base pay for tipped employees at workplaces like restaurants is an insanely low $2.13, whether or not they actually receive any tips from customers. Worse still, numerous bosses steal their workers' tips.[166] Under the current law, workers with disabilities, young people under age 20 and full-time students may legally be paid an oxymoronic "sub-minimum wage." Farmworkers, people who work at seasonal recreational establishments, newspaper deliverers and fishermen are among the long list of Americans exempted from minimum wage requirements.[167] These exceptions must be abolished.

Be reasonable. Demand the impossible: Though there is room to discuss adjusting this figure for areas where the cost of living is low, we begin with a demand for a $60-an-hour minimum wage.[168]

Talking Points:

Economic insecurity—low pay, high rent, job loss fears—dominates Americans' stress, yet both major parties sidestep it, leaving the Left an opening.

Capitalism's rising inequality and weak safety net amplify economic worries, priming the public for a Leftist push against greed-driven systems.

The federal minimum wage, frozen at $7.25 since 2009, traps workers in poverty, far below the $60 hourly minimum required to live decently.

A $60-an-hour minimum, reflecting 1970's value and doubled productivity, is the Left's starting demand to match urban living costs.

The Left must demand a universal $60 minimum wage, ending exemptions, to force a reckoning on economic justice and inequality.

6

PAY EVERYONE

> *"The dictatorship tries to function without resorting to force so we must try to oblige it to do so, thereby unmasking its true nature as the dictatorship of the reactionary social classes."*
> —*Che Guevara*

Wages high enough to cover one's basic expenses are essential to modern life. For the Left, obtaining the mere right to subsist (which is fiercely resisted by the vicious forces of capital) is only the beginning of any serious war against economic insecurity.

We must fight for workers' rights on the job, as well as a robust social safety net to protect people when they find themselves unemployed or underemployed. Americans suffer the worst labor benefits of the major developed countries;[169] U.S. workers are tied with Botswana, Iran, Mexico and Pakistan.[170] Our social safety net comes in dead last.[171] In this age when disruptive technologies like artificial intelligence are expected to eliminate many jobs, we must guarantee everyone an adequate income, whether or not they work.

Give Labor a Fighting Chance Against Management

There is an unspoken assumption on the part of capitalist economists that, when workers negotiate for salaries and benefits with their potential or existing employers, there is an even playing field where give and take apply equally to both sides. This is not close to true. For as long as anyone can remember, the balance of power between labor and management has been radically tilted in favor of bosses. While federal law has made it illegal for a boss to fire you for joining or trying to form a union, these provisions are hardly

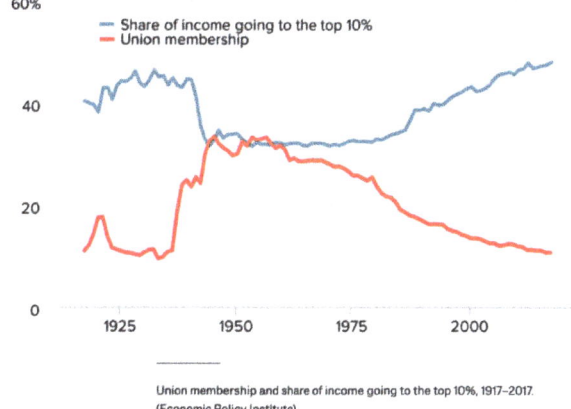

Union membership and share of income going to the top 10%, 1917–2017. (Economic Policy Institute)

ever enforced. As a result, nine out of ten workers are not members of a union[172] despite the fact that six out of ten would join one if given the chance.[173]

Employers, on the other hand, form cartels in the form of business associations and secret collusion in order to set prices for labor. Corporations also enjoy outsized influence in Washington and state capitals through campaign contributions to politicians that dwarf those from labor unions.[174]

Globalization has exacerbated this imbalance. An apparel company like Nike may manufacture goods in low-wage, anti-union countries like Vietnam or Indonesia.[175] It then ships them to high-income markets like Europe or the United States on container ships subsidized by taxpayers there.[176] However willing a worker might be to abandon family and cultural ties for higher wages in places like Norway or Qatar,[177] obtaining work permits—let alone citizenship—is nearly impossible. Significant language and cultural barriers make it tough to move overseas for higher pay. Plus, there's the daunting prospect of being stranded far from support networks if things don't work out with a foreign employer.[178] Business, on the other hand, can easily overcome foreign regulations and transportation issues. Globalization is a misnomer, at least as far as the labor side of the labor-management equation is concerned.

Capital is highly fluid; labor is stationary.

Employers have been rigging the system to limit workers' bargaining power. They require even low-wage workers like those in fast food to sign noncompete agreements. Companies cut anti-poaching deals with their rivals so that workers can't play bosses off against one another. Corporate consolidation means that many workers really only have one possible place to work near their home. Workers are encouraged to specialize, reducing the number of employers where they might apply. Tying benefits like health insurance to employment discourages people from seeking new jobs or careers.[179]

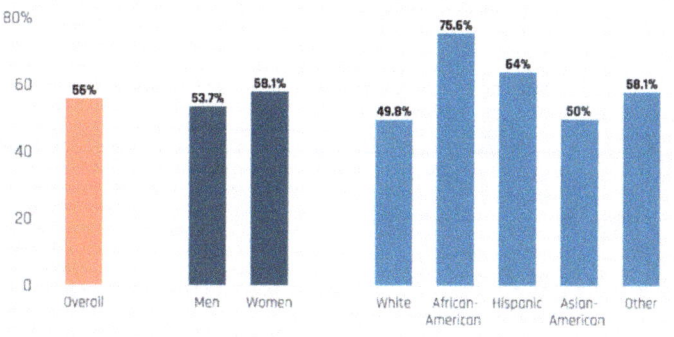

Majority of nonunionized public-sector workers would vote to join a union

Share of nonunionized workers in the U.S. public sector who would vote for a union, by sex and race, 2024

Source: The State of the Public Sector Workforce Survey, 2024.

After a Revolution, the Left would create a system that prioritized workers and turned many of them into government employees. In the meantime, the Left should work to level the playing field between labor and management under capitalism so that, when they sit down to discuss wages, working hours, benefits, conditions and so on, both sides must compromise to the same degree.

U.S. labor laws are breathtakingly skewed in favor of capitalist employers over the employees who add the value that creates profits. Employment is legally "at will," meaning workers can be fired for any reason except discrimination based on race, sex, sexual orientation, or other legally protected classes. Yet violations of these civil rights laws are typically remedied only through lawsuits, which involve uncertainty, high legal costs and long court delays.[180] Since employees are disposable, at-will is a license for companies to over-hire during booms and impose mass layoffs whenever the economy cools down, as we saw tech companies do after the Covid-19 pandemic.[181] It allows bosses to grant themselves raises while firing workers—many of whom uprooted their lives, sacrificed other opportunities, and bear no blame for management's decisions.

At-Will Employment Is Wage Slavery

At-will must go. Unless you did something seriously wrong and that act can be proven, your boss should not be able to fire you. An employer who wants to fire an employee should be required to prove to a special Department of Labor tribunal that either the layoff is due to company finances or the employee did something wrong to merit dismissal. Financial layoffs should occur only after upper management takes pay cuts to the level of the company's lowest-paid workers and stockholders have lost all dividends for a significant period.

For misconduct, employees should be entitled to a hearing before an impartial court established to arbitrate labor-management disputes.

Workers' leverage relies first and foremost on the right and ability to withhold their labor if and when contract negotiations break down. Therefore, every American who works for a company with ten or more employees ought to be legally guaranteed the right to join a union—even if they are the only member of their company's workforce who wants to sign a union card. Existing laws that prohibit employer retaliation against union organizers and members,[182] which are weak and rarely enforced,[183] must be strengthened to the point where it is nearly impossible to fire someone for standing up for higher wages and working conditions. State "right to work" laws that allow workers in union shops not to pay union dues while still receiving negotiated benefits undermine labor solidarity and should be repealed.[184]

Laws like the Taft-Hartley Act of 1947,[185] which ban solidarity strikes and strikes by the military[186] and other public-sector workers[187] and have been expanded by courts and presidential executive orders to include supposedly "essential" workers like coal miners[188] and rail workers,[189] go far beyond the rights of employers in other developed nations and must be annulled. If workers like firefighters and postal workers are truly essential to the functioning of the nation, they should be remunerated accordingly. In the case of exceptional categories of employees deemed essential in matters of life and death, which should be sharply limited, their loss of their right to strike should be compensated by guaranteed raises pegged to the inflation rate.

Workers are divided into arbitrary classifications designed to allow corporations to treat them like dirt. I work at least forty hours a week as a cartoonist and columnist yet my syndicates (and they are typical) misclassify me as an "independent contractor."[190] Same for Uber and Lyft drivers, though there's nothing independent about a job which specifies everything about your tasks down to the model of car you must drive, though you pay for it yourself.

The distinction between a full-time Form W-2 worker and a Form 1099 independent contractor is random and arbitrary. When I lost my W-2 job as a syndicate executive, I qualified for unemployment even though I had only worked half-weeks. If my syndicate cans me as a cartoonist and writer I do not, though I work longer hours for them.

For the Left, all work is work, all work has value and all workers must be protected. The "independent contractor" loophole should be closed. A twenty-hour-a-week job should come with at least half medical benefits. A third of U.S. citizens are self-employed; they should qualify for unemployment benefits when work dries up, just like people who work for other people.[191]

And work *will* dry up. Because boom-and-bust cycles are intrinsic to capitalism, the Left should agitate for a safety net that reflects this reality.[192] Jobless benefits should be far more generous than they are now. Unemployment checks should end when you find a new job, not after the six-month limit set by most state legislatures. By way of comparison, countries like Denmark, France, Italy, the Netherlands, Norway, Portugal and Spain provide up to twenty-four months of unemployment payments. Iceland gives thirty. There should be no time limit at all.

"Get a job!" That's the clichéd response to panhandlers and anyone else who complains of being broke. But what if you can't?

That dilemma is the crux of an evolving silent crisis that threatens to undermine the foundation of the American economic model.

Two-thirds of gross domestic product, most of the economy, is fueled by personal consumer spending.[193] Most spending is sourced from personal income, overwhelmingly from salaries paid by employers. But employers need fewer and fewer employees.

You don't need a business degree to understand the doom loop. A smaller labor force earns a smaller national income and spends less. As demand shrinks, companies lay off many of their remaining workers, who themselves spend less, on and on until we're all in bread lines.

Assuming there are any charities still collecting enough donations to pay for the bread.

Civilian labor force is the portion of the work-eligible adult population that either holds a job or is actively seeking one.

Jobs Are Vanishing. We Still Need Income.

The labor force participation rate has already been shrinking for more than two decades, forcing fewer workers to pay higher taxes. 2.5% of Americans in the labor pool have been unemployed so long that they've given up looking for a job. They're not counted as officially jobless. Yet they represent a far bigger problem than short-term unemployment between jobs. It's about to get much worse.

Workers are already being replaced by robotics, artificial intelligence and other forms of automation. Estimates vary about how quickly new technologies will kill American jobs as they scale and become widely accepted, but there's no doubt the effects will be huge and that we will see them sooner rather than later. A report by MIT and Boston University finds that two million manufacturing jobs will disappear within the coming year;[194] Freethink sounds the death knell for 65% of retail gigs in the same startlingly short time span.[195] A different MIT study predicts that "only 23%" of current worker wages will be replaced by automation, but it won't happen immediately "because of the large upfront costs of AI systems."[196] Disruptive technologies like A.I. will create new jobs. Overall, however, the McKinsey consulting group believes that 12 million Americans will be kicked off their payrolls by 2030.[197]

"Probably none of us will have a job," Elon Musk said recently.[198] "If you want to do a job that's kinda like a hobby, you can do a job. But otherwise, A.I. and the robots will provide any goods and services that you want."

For this to work, Musk argued, idled workers would have to be paid a "universal high income"—the equivalent of a full-time salary, but to stay at home. This is not to be conflated with the "universal basic income" touted by figures like Andrew Yang. UBI is a nominal annual government subsidy, not enough to pay all your expenses.

"[The age of A.I.] will be an age of abundance," Musk predicts.

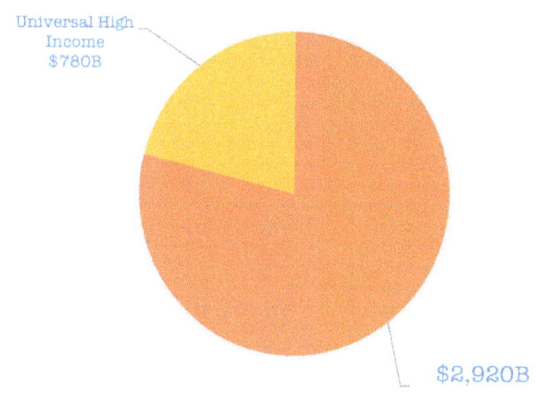

The history of technological progress suggests otherwise. From the construction of bridges across the River Thames during the late 18th and early 19th centuries that sidelined London's wherry men[199] (boatmen who ferried passengers and goods), to the deindustrialization of the Midwest that has left the heartland of the United States full of boarded-up houses and an epic opioid crisis, to Uber and Lyft's decimation of the taxi industry that now has drivers committing suicide,[200] ruling-class political and business elites rarely worry about the people who lose their livelihoods to "creative destruction."[201]

At a bare minimum, the government should provide jobs counseling and cover the tuition and other expenses for people who seek retraining, whether in the form of vocational training or formal education, in order to move into a different field of work.

Whether you're a 55-year-old wherry man or cabbie or an accountant who loses your job through no fault of your own other than having the bad luck to be born at a time of dramatic change, you always get the same advice: pay to retrain in another field. Hopefully you have savings to pay for it; hopefully your new profession doesn't become obsolete too! "Embrace a growth mindset."[202] As if that will put food on the table. Use new tech to help you with your current occupation—until your boss figures out what you're up to and decides to make do with just the machine.[203]

Look at it from their—the boss's—perspective. Costs are down, profits are up. They don't know you, they don't care about you, guilt isn't a thing for them. What's not to like about the robotics revolution?

Those profits, however, belong to us at least as much as they do to "them"—employers, bosses, stockholders. Artificial intelligence and robots are not magic; they were not conjured up from thin air. These technologies were created and developed by human beings on the backs of hundreds of millions of American workers in legacy and now-moribund industries. If the wealthy winners of this latest tech revolution are too short-sighted and cruel to share the abundance with their fellow citizens—if for no better reason than to save their skins from a future violent uprising and their portfolios from disaster when our consumerism-based economy comes crashing down—we should force them to do so.

An economic model in which you need a job in order to have health insurance, to pay for shelter, to eat—to *survive*—breaks down in a situation where it becomes impossible to secure employment.

Thus, we must ensure everyone receives a livable income, whether they can work or choose to. Average individual income is $65,000, so paying a universal high income, or simply replacing lost pay, to the 12 million people expected to lose their jobs to A.I. and other forms of automation will cost $780 billion a year. This subsidy would create upward pressure on wages for those who keep their jobs.

The ultimate manifestation of economic insecurity, the abject poverty that leads to homelessness, hunger and death, ought to be impossible in this wealthiest of all countries in history. Even if they "want" to do so, the Left should not allow people to sleep outside because they don't have a job (a job they may not be able to find!), for the freedom to die in the cold is no freedom whatsoever.

Talking Points:

The Left must fight for high wages, workers' rights, and a strong safety net to combat economic insecurity in a job-scarce future.

Capital's dominance over labor—via at-will employment and anti-union tactics—demands reform, including banning at-will firing and union rights.

Automation threatens millions of jobs, requiring a universal high income of $65,000 yearly to sustain the 12 million displaced by 2030.

U.S. workers endure the weakest labor benefits globally, necessitating robust unemployment support and retraining funded by tech profiteers.

Survival should not be tied to employment.

WHAT'S LEFT?

7

HOUSE THE HOMELESS

"It didn't take me long to go from financial stability to fearing homelessness."
—Stephanie Land, Author of "Maid: Hard Work, Low Pay, and a Mother's Will to Survive"

Homelessness is the single most powerful indictment of capitalism, the embodiment of human disposability, the ultimate expression of callous cruelty. In this nation, where one out of sixteen[204] rental homes sits vacant at any given time, at least one in six hundred[205] Americans (550,000) sleeps outside.

An additional 3.7 million people, the so-called "hidden homeless"[206]—one out of ninety of our sons, our daughters, our brothers, our sisters, our fathers, our mothers—are doubled up in other people's homes because they can't afford their own place.

I rely on the 550,000 number because it has more or less held firm in recent years. It is, however, a figure that bears close watching. The U.S. Department of Housing and Urban Development reported a dramatic spike in homelessness between 2022 and 2024, reaching 770,000 people.[207] The increase, officials say, is jointly attributable to a series of climate-change-related natural disasters like a hurricane that struck North Carolina and wildfires on the West Coast, as well as the Biden-era admission of millions of migrants across the U.S.-Mexico border.

Biden shut down the border in his last year, a policy persisting under Trump, so it is likely that many if not all of the new arrivals will find homes rather than remain homeless. Climate change, on the other hand, will not only continue to have an impact but is expected to worsen and accelerate. I'm going with the older, more conservative number rather than the higher one that may turn out to have represented a short-term phenomenon. But it may not.

"You look out the window of the White House and see the ragged and pathetic figures huddled over the steam grates of the Ellipse," President George H.W. Bush told an audience of insurance agents in 1989, calling homelessness "a national shame." He said it was "an affront to the American dream," and he was right.

Bush promised to do better. Yet, because not even a president can singlehandedly change the fundamental nature of an economic system, nothing improved. Marx's theory of capitalism includes a reserve army of the unemployed as a core feature;[208] a reserve army of the unhoused propping up demand for real estate is a modern-day corollary. As power and wealth gravitate from the many to the few due to capitalism's inherent trend toward monopoly,[209] and real estate interests have increased their wealth and political influence,[210] housing has become increasingly unaffordable[211] and homelessness has increased.[212]

Because the Left (as always, we're talking here about the real Left outside the Democrats) is the only political orientation in the U.S. not beholden to capitalism or the privileges of the ruling classes, only the Left can fix it. Indeed, dedication to the destruction of capitalism is the single defining characteristic of the Left.

Of the many ways America fails its citizens, the country's failure/refusal to ensure that everyone has somewhere warm and safe to sleep at night is an especially stark example.

Unless you are lucky enough not to be born into poverty, and lucky enough to avoid succumbing to addiction or some other dysfunction to which you may be genetically predisposed, and lucky enough not to suffer a debilitating physical or mental illness, and lucky enough to have the charm and the education and the experience that an employer happens to need, and lucky enough that the economy is not contracting at that time, and lucky enough to find an employer at the exact moment he happens to need someone exactly like you, sooner rather than later you may find yourself sleeping on the street or a subway platform or on a park bench or a steam grate across the street from the White House.

That's a lot of luck to ask from life.

Such a society, in which life and death, housing or living out in the elements comes down to stupid luck, cannot credibly claim to believe that every life is precious. It cannot criticize the way other societies handle their affairs.

It has zero moral standing.

Homelessness Affects Everyone

Empathy should be enough reason to want to put a roof over the head of a human being who does not have one. But self-interest also applies.

Chronic homelessness creates problems that impact housed people as well. Responding to calls about public drinking and trespassing diverts the police from dealing with serious crimes.[213] Areas with a high homeless population suffer significantly reduced property values, which lowers assessments and hurts municipal budgets.[214] Because homelessness is associated with chronic health conditions, mental illness and substance abuse disorders, homeless people's frequent visits to emergency rooms—where they account for a third of all patients—clog up the healthcare system and cost hospitals an average of $18,500 per year per person, unreimbursed due to lack of insurance.[215] Those expenses are passed on to the rest of us.

Homelessness is closely tied to street crime. Mentally-ill people are thirty-five times more likely to commit a crime if they are homeless, compared to the mentally-ill domiciled. They are also much more likely to become victims.[216] Though some people lose their homes due to mental illness, it has become clear that homelessness causes mental illness,[217] especially schizophrenia,[218] and that the single most effective way of treating it is by providing housing.[219]

Our national epidemic of homelessness is a luxury we cannot afford. The National Alliance to End Homelessness estimates that one chronically homeless American costs the taxpayer an average of $35,000 per year.[220] That comes to about $20 billion for the Americans now living outside.

Fear of falling is a powerful motivating force. Catching a glimpse of one of America's caste of untouchables attempting to shelter outdoors has an insidious downward effect on wages and living standards for us, the housed. It reminds you: this could happen to you. Better, perhaps, not to risk asking your boss for a raise.

The best answer to the present state of homelessness is "re-housing." We give homes—not shelters—to the people who don't have them. If they don't have enough money for rent, make up the difference with stipends. We don't differentiate between "deserving poor" and others. We get everyone inside.

Most cities keep doing what we know does not and cannot work: providing dangerous shelters that are only open overnight with no path to housing. Homeless people are denied shelter because of drinking, using drugs, having a criminal record or acting out. These failed policies have the homeless preferring to take their chances outdoors, forcing them to wander the streets, cutting off their access to government assistance and virtually eliminating the possibility of positive intervention like anti-addiction programs. Rather than learning from our mistakes, the U.S. government worsens our current, long-standing, dreadful situation by criminalizing homelessness and poverty—conditions no one chooses. In the recent case of *City of Grants Pass v. Johnson*, the U.S. Supreme Court ruled 6-3 in favor of an Oregon town that issues fines and jail sentences to the homeless. Thus, cities can create and enforce laws that prohibit homeless people from sleeping outside even when there is no shelter available.[221]

The current system is cruel, self-perpetuating and counterproductive.

Real homes, not shelters, help people get off drugs and alcohol because most people who abuse substances do so at least in part to numb the misery of their situation.[222] As Pope Francis mused about those who use generosity in order to control people, "There are many arguments which justify why we should not give these alms: 'I give money and he just spends it on a glass of wine!' A glass of wine is his only happiness in life!"[223]

The question is: Where can we find these homes?

Whenever homelessness or the shortage of affordable housing is discussed in American news media, the topic inevitably turns to the need to ease paperwork and zoning restrictions in order to make it easier for real estate developers to build more homes. Even community activists believe this. The assumption is: if there is a shortage of housing, if rents and purchase prices are too high, the problem must be due to the law of supply and demand. We need more supply.

Truth is, we don't need to pour more money into the developer-industrial complex. Renovating an old home costs about $100 per square foot; building a new one runs $150 per square foot. The construction business emits a whopping 39% of total energy-related carbon dioxide emissions—four times more than cars.²²⁴ Why add more? Before we build a single new house, we ought to use what we've already got.

As it happens, we already have more than enough homes to solve homelessness once and for all, and then move on to add lots of affordable housing. 15 million homes are sitting vacant right now.²²⁵ 550,000 of these 15 million homes, one each for every homeless American citizen, should be seized. City and state housing authorities should be granted the right and the funding appropriations necessary to seize vacant housing units under eminent domain for conversion to housing for the homeless, with fair market compensation to be paid to those deprived of their properties.

Use Vacant Homes

Let's begin with abandoned units and those that have remained without a tenant for years. While some neighbors of these houses and apartments may feel trepidation about a formerly homeless person living next door, a renovated housing unit will be a major improvement over a boarded-up eyesore that attracts crime and drugs and drives down property values.

Who owns those 15 million empty homes we'll target to fix the

housing crisis? Three out of four are investment properties.²²⁶ Many are owned by predatory venture capital companies that are converting homeowner neighborhoods into hubs of transient rental units²²⁷ with algorithmically inflated rents,²²⁸ particularly in middle-class, diverse areas.²²⁹ Most of these are vacation homes, timeshares and hunting cabins that sit empty well over 95% of the year.

Florida and Hawaii, both popular vacation destinations, have more vacant second homes than other states. But the vacation-house mentality also afflicts cities with high densities—or that used to have them. In the 2005-2009 American Community Survey, 102,000 of the 845,000 apartments and houses in Manhattan were identified as vacant. One out of 25 units in the nation's cultural, media and financial capital was occupied less than two months out of the year. "In a large swath of the East Side [of Manhattan] bounded by Fifth and Park Avenues and East 49th and 70th Streets, about 30% of the more than 5,000 apartments are routinely vacant more than ten months a year because their owners or renters have permanent homes elsewhere," *The New York Times* reported in 2011.[230] It's gotten worse since then.[231]

Interestingly, the number of vacant units in New York lines up almost exactly with the city's estimated number of homeless men, women and children: 100,000.

Every single person who shivers on the sidewalks of the Big Apple does so within a few dozen feet of a heated, insulated, empty apartment with running water, a place that no one uses. It's obscene. It's piggish. And it needs to be fixed. A real estate speculator's right to invest in a housing market is not as important as a homeless person's need to sleep inside. A bourgeois family's desire to winter in Florida and summer in New York must take a back seat to the human right of a homeless person not to die.

You can build a nice house, but what if some homeless people don't want to move into it?

Rapid re-housing can and should be mandatory; no one should be allowed the "freedom" to live outside and succumb to the elements. Few things are more important than free agency or personal freedom, but America's homelessness crisis is not driven by romantic early 20th century images of hobos, tramps or vagabonds who prefer to live outside polite society. These are desperately sick, poor people. Homelessness should be illegal, meaning not that the homeless should be punished as in Grants Pass, Oregon, but that the government should have a legal mandate to provide high-quality housing to every homeless person and that, in cases in which a person sleeping outside clearly cannot make good decisions for themselves, they are brought to that housing and properly cared for whether or not they consent.

Housing First

Rehousing, as advocates for the homeless call a policy of housing first, should be done free of traditional preconditions like employment, income, absence of criminal record or sobriety. Each person's needs, whether addressed by physical rehabilitation, job or language training, therapy or other services, should be carried out by a team of social workers and other experts, not the police. Housing first, *The New York Times* reported in 2022, rests on a reality-based approach: "When you're drowning, it doesn't help if your rescuer insists you learn to swim before returning you to shore. You can address your issues once you're on land. Or not. Either way, you join the wider population of people battling demons behind closed doors."

Houston, the nation's fourth-largest city and not one known for progressive social policies, has succeeded with housing first. It moved 25,000 people directly into apartments and houses between 2011 and 2022, reducing its homeless population by an impressive 63%.[232] Denver, another housing first city, saw arrests of homeless people drop 95% and dependence on government cash-benefit programs fall by 80% after housing first was enacted.

According to the National Alliance to End Homelessness, "supportive housing" costs an average of $12,800 per person per year. That comes to $7 billion for the outdoor homeless population, or $55 billion if you also include the so-called "hidden homeless" who bounce around from place to place.

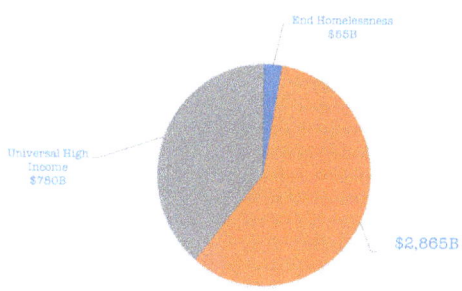

The higher figure is 1.4% of the $3.8 trillion a year the U.S. is currently wasting on wars and other garbage. Subtract the $20 billion we currently spend annually on policing and hospitalizing the homeless, and it's 0.8%. Or we can reallocate the funds currently going to arrest, jail and hospitalize the homeless to maintain homes seized under eminent domain until their new occupants get jobs and can begin covering their own expenses.

So we can afford to declare and win a war on homelessness.

The roughly half a million Americans who are chronically homeless and nearly four million more "hidden homeless" who are imposing on friends and family for a place to stay that may or may not remain available in the future are suffering needlessly. Cities are blighted, families are shattered, children are traumatized, talent and potential are wasted.

The economic outlook is grim, with jobs stagnating, inflation gnawing at wallets, and the Fed's 2024 rate hikes choking the life out of any faint hope for a soft landing. We are staring down a recession barreling in like a freight train. Evictions are spiking—there was a 15% jump in filings in cities like Phoenix during the last quarter of 2024—and tent cities are metastasizing from coast to coast. Every percentage point the economy tanks drags down more Americans. The next downturn's body count will be measured in sleeping and body bags.

Homelessness is a moral and economic crisis as well as a failure of leadership.

The United States signed the Universal Declaration of Human Rights, which recognizes housing as a basic human right, in 1948.[233] The UDHR was codified into a treaty, the International Covenant on Economic, Social, and Cultural Rights in 1966. Because the U.S. signed the ICESCR, it is obligated to uphold its "object and purpose." Nearly eighty years after our nation committed to ensuring that everyone has a decent and secure place to live without fear of eviction, our country should make good on its commitment to international law.

Talking Points:

Homelessness reveals capitalism's cruelty, leaving 550,000 unsheltered despite available vacant homes.

Climate disasters and migration caused homelessness to surge to 770,000 recently.

Capitalism maintains an unhoused population to boost real estate demand and prices.

Chronic homelessness burdens taxpayers with $20 billion in healthcare and crime costs.

Seizing vacant homes offers a practical fix for homelessness.

8

FREE HEALTHCARE FOR ALL

"The U.S. has the most dysfunctional healthcare system in the industrial world, has about twice the per capita costs, and some of the worst outcomes. It's also the only privatized system."
—Noam Chomsky

Liberals are more likely than conservatives to believe that a compromise that gets us closer to a goal is better than no progress at all.[234] But compromise can lead to the dead end of dilution and a false sense of resolution.

Unlike food, a consumer sector in which there exists a wide variety of options, medical care is a product in which the purchaser has little to no choice whether or not to buy. Left untreated, a relatively minor health issue can become a matter of life and death. My mother ignored a cold that worsened into bronchitis then pneumonia. It spread to her chest, attacked her liver and left her with chronic viral hepatitis which later mimicked dementia and caused the fall that ended her life.

Healthcare is a sector in which competition scarcely exists. Sick people have neither the inclination nor the time to shop around for the cheapest doctor. Time is of the essence. Because we don't have a national database of Americans' medical records, it makes sense for most people to stick with the physician who knows them and their history. Inertia wins.

Pricing is opaque. Patients cannot obtain a reliable price quote for medical services or medications before ordering them. This makes comparison shopping impossible. Finally, consolidating private doctors' offices into insurer-owned or -affiliated groups reduces competition and raises costs. This stymies the few patients who might overcome the systemic barriers mentioned earlier and try to shop around for a cheaper deal.

Doctors and hospitals sell a service you have to buy. It's not surprising that they can charge pretty much whatever they want.

The healthcare industry (though its concerns soon proved unfounded) worried about losing precious profits after the Affordable Care Act passed. In fact, their profits increased dramatically after the government ordered millions of uninsured people to buy private insurance plans or pay a fine.[235] (The penalty was later repealed.) Instead of the ACA's state-by-state, county-by-county online healthcare "marketplaces," patient advocates would have preferred a European-style, fully socialized system in which doctors and nurses are government employees. Leftists believed the ACA would nudge the system toward socialized medicine. So, they set aside their reservations and supported the Obama Administration. They reasoned that something is better than nothing and that moving the ball further down the field would be easier later.

We now know that the ACA has failed to fix the problems it was supposed to address. Competition was expected to drive down prices for doctor's visits and prescription medications, but in many American counties (health plans are assigned and sold by county) competition has basically been nonexistent because the local online government "marketplace" has just one or two plans to "choose" from.[236]

America's Healthcare System Is a Disaster

The system is expensive and low-quality. The only high-income nation without universal health coverage, the U.S. spends far more on healthcare, both per person and as a share of GDP, than other countries.[237] Yet we still have the lowest life expectancy at birth of the OECD countries, the highest death rates for avoidable and treatable conditions, the highest infant mortality rate, the highest rate of people with multiple chronic conditions and an obesity rate nearly twice the OECD average.

Prevention is the best cure, but health insurance bureaucracy hampers our access to the preventive care that would save lives and reduce costs. Only about 8% of Americans get routine preventive screenings.[238] The U.S. loses an estimated $55 billion each year due to missed prevention opportunities, amounting to 30% of all healthcare costs.[239]

Premiums and co-pays are high, and many plans have huge annual deductibles, so we see physicians less frequently than patients in most other countries. In 2022, for example, 38% of Americans said they or a family member skipped or delayed medical care, according to an annual healthcare poll by Gallup.

A whopping 650,000 Americans go bankrupt each year due to healthcare bills, accounting for 60% of all personal bankruptcies.[240]

Americans are extremely dissatisfied with the cost and access to healthcare, a fact that became shockingly evident by the public reaction when Brian Thomas, the fifty-year-old CEO of United Healthcare, the nation's biggest insurer and its eighth-largest corporation, was gunned down on a Manhattan street as he walked to an investor conference.[241] Scorn and ridicule rained across the Internet as patients rage-shared their stories

of attempting to navigate a health insurance system whose profit model relies upon the routine denial of valid claims for treatment and medications ordered by doctors. More than 90,000 users reacted to United's Facebook announcement of the killing with laughing emojis.[242]

A poll showed that 41% of respondents supported the killing or were neutral about it; 67% of young adults aged 18 to 29 said the same thing.[243] *Sorry, the bullet in your chest is out of network* was a typical remark. Ironically, the Mt. Sinai hospital to which Thomas was rushed had recently been removed from United's approved network.

I can't recall the demise of any public figure being greeted with as much glee and dark humor, including the killing of Osama bin Laden. Which makes psychological sense. If you believe that someone is trying to kill you, you hate them.

Health insurance companies are trying to kill us.

While Americans were shocked and some traumatized by the 9/11 attacks, most didn't feel *personally threatened* let alone harmed by Al Qaeda. On the other hand, an insurer like United, which is reported to deny a whopping 32% of in-network claims,[244] wields the power to overrule doctors' orders,[245] harasses sick people at their most vulnerable,[246] and, given the sky-high health costs in this country, puts medical treatment—the ultimate non-discretionary expense—out of reach.[247] Rare is the health-insurance customer who can't tell a horror story of being unfairly turned down for reimbursement for a doctor's visit or procedure, usually after being put on hold for ages, given misinformation and the runaround over pre-authorizations, procedural codes, doctors erroneously listed as in-network, and other Soviet-style nonsense.[248]

Sometimes health insurers decide that people—people like you[249]—shouldn't receive life-saving care.[250] Patients die every year due to the health insurance industry's sinister profit model,[251] which heavily relies upon quotas for automatic[252] and in many cases automated denials.[253]

A microscopic 12% of Americans believe the healthcare system is handled extremely well. The number drops to 6% when they're asked about prescription drug costs, the quality of care at nursing homes and mental health care.[254]

Even when health insurance works as advertised, it feels like a scam. You pay a monthly premium, yet even when you file a legitimate claim, you probably won't be able to collect a reimbursement due to high deductibles that can exceed $10,000 a year.[255] Insurers' online directories of in-network health providers are typically years out of date; most of the doctors listed no longer accept the company's insurance (or never did), have moved their practices, or are retired or deceased.[256] "In a 2023 analysis, researchers surveyed nearly 450,000 physicians in the Medicare provider database that appeared in online physician directories for UnitedHealth, Elevance, Cigna, Aetna, and Humana," *Jacobin* reported.[257] "They found that only 19 percent had consistent addresses and specialty information across all the directories in which they were found."[258] (Failing to keep these lists up-to-date is illegal under the 2022 No Surprises Act, but this federal law is not enforced.)[259]

There ought to be a difference between the experience of being uninsured and that of having insurance. And there is: when you're "insured," you fill out more forms.

Health insurance companies create misery that feels intensely personal. A procedure or medication ordered by your physician can be overruled. This physician knows you and has examined you personally. Yet, an anonymous individual—who has never seen you—can override it in a completely opaque process. That can be maddening. And getting them to pay for covered procedures is hard. According to the Patient Advocate Foundation, it takes an average of 27 phone calls to customer service before an insurance company finally cuts a check.[260] 90% of patients give up and pay out of pocket.

Insurers want to make more money. They don't necessarily want you, the patient, to suffer. But profits are king. To keep and add to profits, they are willing for you and your loved ones to suffer great pain, and perhaps even death. The drive to keep raking in billions of dollars a year in profits comes ahead of all else.[261] This is why the profit incentive is inherently incompatible with healthcare.

This system will not change unless we force it to. "Our role is a critical role, and we make sure that care is safe, appropriate, and is delivered when people need it," UnitedHealth Group CEO Andrew Witty reassured employees in an internal video following Thompson's killing.[262] "We guard against the pressures that exist for unsafe care or for unnecessary care to be delivered in a way which makes the whole system too complex and ultimately unsustainable." Witty, who "earned" $23.5 million in 2023, hasn't learned a thing. Or maybe he has. He knows Congress is in his pocket.

Witty's argument, of course, is bullshit. Companies like UnitedHealthcare are leeches, a net negative to the patient experience. No one believes they are "guarding" us against any danger whatsoever. They aren't fighting "complexity;" they *are* the complexity. They add an additional, unnecessary layer of bureaucracy between sick people and healthcare providers, with only one goal: profits.

The Solution: Medicare For All

The obvious solution is to abolish the medical insurance industry and join the 69% of the world's population that has some form of universal healthcare.[263] For now, however, huge donations by the health insurance lobby to both Democrats[264] and Republicans[265] make it highly unlikely that a solution like Medicare For All, popular among voters of both parties,[266] will be enacted anytime soon.

A decade and a half after the ACA passed, Americans hate the system. Yet there is no indication that politicians of either party are inclined to propose a legislative improvement. Nevertheless the need is acute. The right to affordable—no, free—healthcare is a basic human right. Without it, after all, people quite literally drop dead.

If we *must* keep the current for-profit health insurance system, federal regulations are acutely needed. Medical insurance companies should not be allowed to deny claims, period. There should be no requirement to obtain preapproval for medical procedures or medication. There should no longer be such a thing as an out-of-network physician; if you go to see a licensed doctor, your health insurance should pay. (Until we abolish those stupid networks, you should be covered if you see a doctor who is listed on your provider's website as in-network.) This, after all, is how it was in the 1970s.[267] And there were plenty of profitable health insurance companies.

Health insurance is a middleman. It adds no value. It denies care and reduces rates paid to doctors. And it collects the profits. It's a giant leech and it should be abolished.

Instead, we need socialized medicine or something like it.

According to a 2020 estimate by the nonpartisan Urban Institute, Bernie Sanders' Medicare For All plan—the most thoroughly thought-out, frictionless plan on the drawing board that salvages as much from the existing network as possible—would cost the U.S. about $3 trillion per year.[268] However, a Yale study concluded that the government would save about half a trillion each year "by improving access to preventive care, reducing administrative overhead, and empowering Medicare to negotiate prices."[269] Working net cost: $2.5 trillion per annum.

Medicare For All would replace our current, highly wasteful system. "We're already paying as taxpayers for universal basic automatic coverage, we're just not getting it," economist Amy Finkelstein says. "We might as well formalize and fund that commitment upfront." Finkelstein points to the fact that the federal government currently pays $1.8 trillion a year for Medicare, Medicaid, veterans' services and other government-funded healthcare costs—some of which would vanish after they were replaced by a holistic

Medicare For All scheme.[270] Third-party programs, which are often government-funded, and public health programs, eat up an additional $600 billion per year.

Medicare For All would save the lives of the 45,000 Americans who die annually due to lack of insurance.[271] The IRS would collect an additional $1 billion a year in tax revenues from the people who would live instead.[272]

Going with a high estimate that excludes savings on those currently covered by Medicare and related programs, the net cost of treating everyone who needs medical care is about $1.7 trillion per year, which is just about 45% of the $3.8 trillion we're currently wasting on wars and other things that make our lives worse.[273]

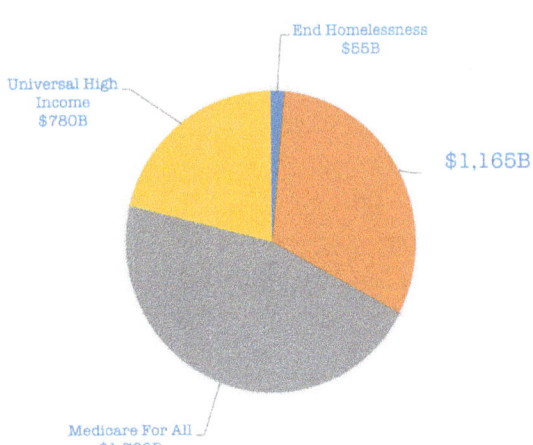

Most analyses of Medicare For All focus on how the plan would cut patient costs.[274] Even if enrollees had to pay higher taxes, this is indeed true. For liberals, such an improvement might be triumph worth celebrating in and of itself.

The Left, however, must be as ambitious as possible, even under bourgeois electoral democracy. Healthcare, a basic human need every bit as essential to life as food and clean water, should be provided by the government, gratis. The good news is we can afford it.

Because a medical financing system centered around affordability, access and preventive care requires a nationally integrated network of medical care providers, Medicare For All would be more efficient and effective than our current system. In 2022, during a postmortem of the coronavirus pandemic, *The Washington Post* examined how America's "fractured healthcare system" hindered our Covid-19 response.[275] Seeking to answer the question of why the pandemic continued despite and after the miraculously rapid development and distribution of mRNA vaccines, the *Post* homed in on organizational systemic shortcomings, citing the need for "improvements on the delivery side." One expert called for "increasing staffing and funding for local health departments, many of which have been running on a shoestring. Officials in some local health departments still transfer data by fax." Both observations are true. I am still asked to fax my records to hospital facilities where many nurses and doctors continue to rely on pagers.

Nowhere in the *Post* piece, however, was there any mention of what the United States is missing that most other countries in the developing world enjoy: a unified national healthcare system like the United Kingdom's National Health Service.[276]

Medicare for All is popular with voters. A YouGov poll from January 2023 showed 63% of voters—liberals and conservatives alike—approving. Even Republicans, typically allergic to anything smacking of "socialism," are on board, with a Hill-HarrisX survey from April 2020 finding 46% in favor of a single-payer system. Liberals, as you'd expect, have long been in favor, with KFF's October 2020 poll pegging 77% of Democrats ready to ditch the current patchwork mess of private plans. Pew's September 2020 data shows 63% of all adults saying healthcare ought to be the government's job. Medicare For All isn't a fringe fever dream. It's a scream for sanity.

Medicare For All Could Stop the Next Pandemic

Law-enforcement agencies can access criminal records from other jurisdictions via the FBI's National Data Exchange system. Similarly, public-health officials should have 24-hour access to a real-time, constantly updated source of every disease report—whether known or novel, paid in cash or covered by insurance, diagnosed by a country doctor, walk-in urgent-care center, or giant urban hospital system.

A fully-integrated national healthcare database would be a key benefit of a system like Medicare For All. Such a system would require treatment providers to access a patient's records in various situations. These include whether the patient lives in the state where they're treated, has transitioned to a different gender, has changed insurance or hospital groups, or is conscious and able to provide information about themselves.

The nation's top epidemiologists at the Centers for Disease Control are flying blind, relying on algorithmic models that estimate what's going on rather than providing the accurate, precise situational awareness that can give them a heads up about a disease outbreak as quickly as it occurs.

I tested positive for Covid-19 on December 30, 2020. I notified my doctor's office on January 1, 2021 but due to the federal holiday didn't hear back until January 3, 2021. Were New York City authorities and/or the CDC notified about my case and, if so, when?

Several friends and friends of friends tested positive using home tests. Many, probably most, didn't tell their doctor. Official numbers were significantly underreported.

If we had had a national healthcare system instead of a medical Wild West in which the ailing were jostling against each other fighting over $24 testing kits like shoppers scrumming into Best Buy on Black Friday, Covid testing would have been handled through clinics and doctor's offices in coordination with the federal government, which would have quickly compiled the results.

A national healthcare database could include "visualization tools to graphically depict associations between people, places, things, and events either on a link-analysis chart or on a map. For ongoing investigations, the subscription and notification feature automatically notifies analysts if other users are searching for the same criteria or if a new record concerning their investigation is added to the system…

[allowing] analysts to work with other analysts across the nation in a collaborative environment that instantly and securely shares pertinent information."

Is this about a medical database? No. I lifted that last quote from an FBI description of their national police database. Crime kills only a small fraction compared to the number of Americans who die from disease.[277] Why not prioritize our health instead?

HIPAA regulations governing the privacy of patient records would need to be modified by Congress for any of this to happen, but consider the potentially lifesaving

benefits even when there is no longer a pandemic.[278] According to a 2018 study by Johns Hopkins, more than 250,000 people in the U.S. die annually because of medical mistakes caused by insufficiently skilled staff, errors in judgment or care, and issues like computer breakdowns, mix-ups with the doses or types of medications administered to patients and surgical complications that go undiagnosed. Medical mistakes are the third leading cause of death after heart disease and cancer.[279]

Americans' support of privacy rights, though laudable in many arenas, should no longer extend to medical records. There is nothing inherently shameful or loathsome about illnesses or diseases; a person who contracts, say, a sexually-transmitted infection not only has not done anything wrong—they were merely the unfortunate victim of a virus or bacteria—they are part of the overwhelming majority of Americans, almost all of whom will get one at some point, even if they are not sexually active.[280] (You can catch STIs like herpes, syphilis, and HPV through contact with bodily fluids, such as saliva. You can catch chlamydia, HIV, and Hepatitis B & C through contact with infected blood.)

Embarrassment over a medical condition is a vestige of the Victorian era and should not be tolerated today, especially when it leads to reduced quality of care because doctors can't access all the relevant information about their patients. Discrimination due to health conditions, regardless of the type, should be banned under federal law, such as when insurance companies use pre-existing conditions to deny coverage.

Clay Shirky, the tech futurist, argued that in the near future, almost everyone would have a nude photo online,[281] thus reducing the chance that you might be blackmailed over such an image. In the same way that we recognize that everyone is nude under their clothes and that most of us have minor variants on the same parts and that that awareness makes nudity normal at a nude beach, the deprivatization of patient records would destigmatize the idea that anyone ought to feel ashamed about what ails them. Moreover, as we know from the 2013 Edward Snowden revelations, there is no privacy. The government uses and abuses our "confidential" data as they see fit. We might as well accept reality and put medical data to good use.

Decentralized private recordkeeping is anathema to public-health. If you live in Wyoming, there is no good reason that your medical records shouldn't be accessible to first responders driving the ambulance that responds to a call after you collapse and lie unconscious on the floor at a mall in Florida. As soon as you are identified—something that could be facilitated by a national healthcare ID card that you carry in your wallet or as an app on your smartphone or biometric data like fingerprints—EMS workers could use your patient history to identify any chronic conditions. They could avoid a medication to which you might be allergic or feel confident in administering one thanks to the knowledge that you are not. Privacy is dead. There's no need for you to risk death in order to protect it.

Recent studies have highlighted the cost savings of preventive care compared to the reactive nature of the dysfunctional U.S. healthcare system, where patients typically seek medical attention only after symptoms arise. Preventive care—encompassing regular check-ups, screenings, vaccinations, and lifestyle interventions—aims to detect and address health issues early, reducing the need for expensive treatments later. A 2023 study published in Health Affairs found that every dollar invested in preventive measures, such as managing chronic conditions like diabetes or hypertension, saves approximately $3 to $5 in long-term healthcare costs. This contrasts sharply with the U.S.'s reactive model, which spends nearly $4 trillion annually, much of it on emergency interventions and late-stage disease management.

The reactive approach often leads to higher costs because conditions like heart disease or cancer, when caught late, require costly procedures—surgeries, hospitalizations, or prolonged medication regimens. Preventive care mitigates these expenses by promoting early detection and healthier lifestyles. For instance, a 2024 report from the Commonwealth Fund showed that routine screenings for colorectal cancer reduced advanced-stage diagnoses by 30%, slashing treatment costs by nearly 40% per patient.

Universal healthcare systems in countries like Denmark, Japan and Canada exemplify the benefits of prioritizing preventive care. Denmark's system, with its focus on free annual check-ups and public health campaigns, spends roughly half per capita what the U.S. does, yet achieves better health outcomes. Japan's emphasis on mandatory health screenings and diet education has lowered obesity-related costs, while Canada's universal coverage ensures access to preventive services, reducing emergency care expenditures. These models demonstrate that proactive investment in health not only improves public health but also alleviates the financial burden on healthcare systems—a lesson the U.S. could adapt to curb its spiraling costs.

We can and should change the healthcare system. Focus on more prevention to avoid illnesses later on. Take high expenses and predatory for-profit companies out of the equation. Demand true parity between physical and mental health. Drop the arbitrary distinction between dental, vision and other kinds of medical treatment. Nationalize medical data so that any medical professional can treat you effectively anywhere, anytime, and give public-health officials a leg up on emerging threats. Make healthcare a basic human right, not a privilege or a luxury as it is now.

Talking Points:

Liberals favor healthcare compromises like the ACA, but it diluted reform and failed to fix costs.

U.S. healthcare lacks competition, driving up prices and opacity.

The ACA increased insurer profits but didn't lower costs or improve access.

High costs and denials cause 650,000 bankruptcies yearly, fueling public rage.

Medicare For All would save lives and money.

9

MAKE HIGHER EDUCATION FREE

"The higher amount you put into higher education, at the federal level particularly, the more the price of higher education rises. It's the dog that never catches its tail. You increase student loans, you increase grants, you increase Pell grants, Stafford loans, and what happens? They raise the price."
—Bill Bennett, Secretary of Education, 1985-1988

Learning is a societal and individual good. Educational attainment contributes to economic growth. Several studies estimate that each year of schooling within a workforce accelerates GDP by around 0.7% per year.[282]

Given that they make more money when more of us are well-educated, you'd think that American businesses would pressure their pet congressmen to heavily subsidize secondary education and to make higher education as affordable as possible, even free. It's like the old model of gambling cities like Las Vegas. Hotels were cheap and food was virtually free; the goal was to lure gamblers into the casinos that separated them from their money. However, American businesses are greedy as well as shortsighted. Vegas hotels are expensive now; so are restaurants. And the slots aren't any looser.

Similarly, we have weaponized higher education, which trains our high-end workers, into a profit center. Colleges and universities are an overcredentialization racket that coerces millions of young people to borrow hundreds of billions of dollars in tuition, room and board, often to study subjects in which they have little interest, for the chance to be hired for a job. To add insult to usury, the diploma for which young students sink into high-interest student loan debt often reflects an education with no useful application to the position where they land.

Meritocracy, a system that rewards talent and hard work, is deeply problematic. Talent is inherently subjective. So is hard work. Then there's the broader question of why someone should earn less because they're deemed to have less talent or to not have a strong work ethic. The college-admissions rat race and subsequent jockeying for status and social positioning based on the supposed merits of one's education play into the fictions of a meritocratic system that is dubious on its face and corrupt within its own constructs, as with "legacy" admissions of the dimwitted scions of wealthy alumni of Ivy League colleges.

Until the Revolution, however, there will almost certainly never be the space to reconsider the pros and cons of meritocracy. The college racket and the role of a college diploma in seeking employment will remain in place for the foreseeable future. All we can do is make it fairer.

It is tempting, from the standpoint of the Left, to dismiss the soaring price of college tuition, usurious student loan interest rates and overcredentialization as a first-world problem afflicting privileged middle-class suburbanites who, after struggling after graduation, will soon enough pay off their debt and enjoy a significantly higher income than workers with high school degrees. But a proper class analysis worthy of the Left cannot focus on the poor and working class to the exclusion of the bourgeois strivers who help form the intellectual vanguard of the future Revolution and, more immediately, are linchpins of radical change during a revolutionary crisis.

No society can afford to ignore the plight of its most highly-educated ambitious young people who, as the influential 20th century European historian Crane Brinton reminded us in *The Anatomy of Revolution*, are an essential catalyst to radical political change. History shows that a generation of educated upstarts who find their paths to professional advancement cut off and their ambitions dashed at an early age is a generation that may help spark a violent uprising.[283] Colleges are hotbeds of political activism, as we saw recently when pro-Gaza solidarity encampments spread across campuses during the spring of 2024. College students are a diverse lot. Nearly half are people of color and more than 60% are women. Despite the problems within higher education, especially affordability, America has no bigger engine for upward economic mobility.[284]

The Incredible Shrinking College Income Premium

Part of the problem is that the "college income premium"—the difference between the average salary of a college graduate and that of a high school diploma holder—only accrues to those who finish all four years and obtain their bachelor's degree. This includes very few poor and working-class people. 15% of students from the lowest quartile of wage earners complete a four-year education after they begin one, compared to 61% of those in the top quartile. The 85% who drop out before graduating find themselves not only devoid of necessary credentials, but also in debt. As for the 15% who make it, many of them major in subjects that do not improve their appeal to prospective employers enough to cash in on a college-income premium.

Share of Americans in the middle class has fallen since 1971
% of U.S. population in each income tier

Lower income ■ Middle income ■ Upper income

Year	Lower	Middle	Upper
2023	30%	51	19
1971	27	61	11

Note: People are assigned to income tiers based on their household incomes in the calendar year prior to the survey year, after incomes have been adjusted for the number of people living in each household. Shares may not total 100% due to rounding.
Source: Pew Research Center analysis of the Current Population Survey, Annual Social and Economic Supplement (IPUMS), 1971 and 2023.
PEW RESEARCH CENTER

Too many companies are lazy. They don't sort job applicants from a broader pool, like those with a high school diploma or a year or two of college. Instead, they demand all comers have college diplomas, even when the job doesn't require that education or training. It's their way of culling the herd. "More than half of Americans who earned college diplomas find themselves working in jobs that don't require a bachelor's degree or utilize the skills acquired in obtaining one," according to CBS News.[285]

Requiring a superfluous degree discriminates against the poor, widening the ever-growing class divide. Under a Left government, economic disadvantage would become a protected legal class alongside race, age, sex, gender identity, physical disability and so on. Workers should be able to report job listings that seek overqualified workers to a federal bureau in the Department of Labor, which would have the power to impose substantial penalties, including fines and compensation for applicants who are discriminated against because they don't have a degree they don't really need.

"Nearly two-thirds of American workers do not have a four-year college degree. Screening by college degree hits minorities particularly hard, eliminating 76% of Black adults and 83% of Latino adults," *The New York Times* reported in 2022.[286] Nevertheless, 44% of employers required at least a B.A. or B.S. for all their openings.

Because they are classist and lazy, bosses are turning away excellent candidates. A 2017 Harvard Business School study found that "60% of employers rejected otherwise qualified candidates in terms of skills or experience simply because they did not have a college diploma."[287]

Stop Requiring Unnecessary Degrees

Requiring employers to do the right, logical and fair thing, and hire qualified high school graduates, dropouts and GED holders, will allow more Americans to avoid college-debt traps, incentivize companies to train workers, give working-class families more opportunities to get ahead and reduce the high-intensity competition for college and university acceptance.

More fundamentally, the college income premium that forms the basis of young Americans' decision whether or not to borrow tens of thousands of dollars in pursuit of a degree is shrinking at an alarming rate. Wages for all Americans have been stagnating for half a century. Young workers are no exception. So it's decreasingly likely that a student who borrows to attend college will earn a high enough income for them to be able to repay their loans.

College student loans have exploded into a $1.7 trillion for-profit business that gives lenders ultimate leverage: no matter what they do or how legitimate their inability to pay, distressed borrowers cannot even discharge their college debts in bankruptcy.[288] At this writing, the average interest rate on student loans is

6.9%.²⁸⁹ The highest rate at which banks borrow money, however, is 5.5%—and the borrowing rate for the much longer terms consistent with student loans is lower.

Young scholars are bright, vulnerable citizens with endless potential, not a profit center for transnational lending institutions—well, they are, but they ought not to be. If we *must* have a for-profit system of post-secondary education and student loans to afford it, those loans should be at zero profit to banks or anyone else. Student loans should be able to be discharged in bankruptcy, just like any other debt.

Because college dropouts do not enjoy the college income premium, their loans should be fully forgiven or heavily discounted.²⁹⁰ This would put pressure on college administrators to work harder to keep young people in school instead of dropping out.

The role of Leftists is not merely to tinker at the edges to make a troubled system fairer or more efficient. Leftists look at a situation and ask: do we need a complete overhaul? If we were inventing any entrenched system—like America's higher education system—from scratch, is what we have now anything close to what we would come up with? If not, what is it? What would we change?

It's hard to imagine that anyone, regardless of their general political orientation, would say that we have created the best possible way to educate young people and prepare them for the future of work and life in general. Employers complain that college graduates know little to nothing about the "real world." Kids are so poorly prepared that "adulting," or learning how to navigate modern life, is a thing…for adults.

All this cluelessness and inexperience comes at a high price. The average household with student loan debt owes $55,000.²⁹¹ Over a 10-year term at 6.9%, the total due, including interest, is $76,000. That's the cost of a starter home in many parts of the country, and much more than students and their families spend in virtually any other nation.²⁹²

Thirty-nine nations offer free or low-cost college. These include European powerhouses like France and Germany, less prosperous ones like Greece and Portugal, plus socialist states like Cuba and Brazil.²⁹³

We can and should do the same.

Students and parents borrowed $95 billion in the 2021-22 academic year. Going forward, replacing every penny borrowed of student loans with a free federal grant would cost the government about $100 billion—a tiny portion of that $3.8 trillion a year we're currently wasting on the military and other misbegotten budgetary priorities.[294]

My grades and test scores were good enough to get into an Ivy League college. Presumably, I was smart. But I was still a 17-year-old kid who didn't know much about the world. In 1981 I didn't know you were supposed to tip your barber, that your major field of study might have no bearing on your future career, or that Manhattan and Long Island were different places.

So signing a student loan agreement committing to repay thousands of dollars from a salary derived from some imaginary job in a mysterious future was a surreal experience.

I sat next to my mom in the lobby of a big bank building in downtown Dayton, feeling nearly as clueless as I actually was. All I knew was that I had to sign a sheaf of incomprehensible documents if I wanted to attend college and escape my dying Rust Belt town before the

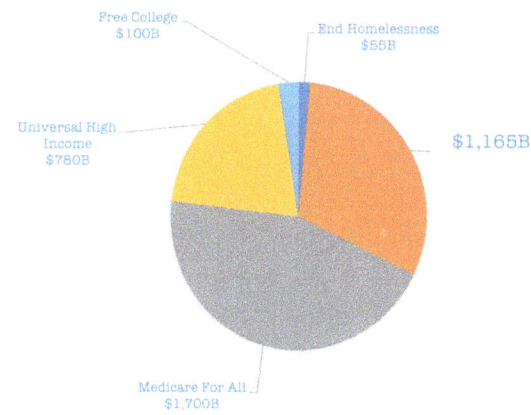

Even after establishing socialized medicine, guaranteeing an income to make sure no one dies of poverty, making college free and eliminating homelessness, there would be more than $1 billion left over from what we currently waste on defense et al. We can reduce taxes by that amount, or invest in something not mentioned here, or throw one hell of a party!

last factory closed. As my guidance counselor and teachers and parents had repeatedly warned, without a college degree I would be doomed to subsistence-level fast-food or manual labor—and even crappy jobs were getting hard to find.

Don't forget to initial each page.

Shouldn't I read these? No time.

How much would I earn after graduation? What would be my monthly payment? How does compound interest work? Was 9% a reasonable rate to pay? When would interest begin to accrue? What if I became unemployed—would I still have to pay my loans? I didn't know and if the banker satisfactorily explained this stuff it didn't stick to my hippocampus. I invisibly shrugged to myself, hoping that I'd somehow muddle through.

I return to my state of mind forty years ago whenever I hear someone deplore the ethics of the 15% of student loan borrowers who are in default at any given time.[295] Worthless brats! They took the money; why don't they pay it back? Is an obligation you don't understand when you agree to it an obligation at all?

Honoring commitments is important. If you borrow, you should repay. (I did.) But lenders have responsibilities too. As we saw during the subprime mortgage crisis of the late 2000s, the economy suffers when banks recklessly issue loans to borrowers who don't understand the terms or won't have enough income or collateral to repay, which is the case for most college loan borrowers. They're kids. The very same banks wouldn't issue them a credit card. Banks ought to take a hit when they lend out money willy-nilly instead of being supported by the federal government.

Forgive Student Loans

Student loans are a huge burden on our young people. 62% of Democratic and 57% of Republican voters aged eighteen to twenty-nine told a Harvard Institute of Politics poll that they consider student loan debt to be one of their biggest problems—a problem they think about when they pay their bills every month.[296] You may be older and not care. Maybe you never went to college. Or you did and paid them back (when it was much easier). But what if you want to sell your empty-nest house as a starter home to a young couple? You'll have trouble finding a qualified buyer among twenty- and thirty-somethings drowning in college debt. Impoverishing the young does not benefit the old.

Canceling student loans across the board would have a low multiplier effect and thus do little to stimulate the economy.[297] Still, there would still be advantages for everyone, not just borrowers.

Freeing a generation from debt slavery would provide flexibility and capital for new entrepreneurs and allow do-gooders to pursue work in helping professions with low wages, like joining an NGO.[298] Student-loan forgiveness would add liquidity to the nearly half of Millennials who report that their loan debts forced them to delay buying a first home by an average of seven years.[299] You may not have gone to college yourself yet you may get to retire earlier because you'll sell your home to a young couple at a higher price.

In no small part because student "consumers" can and must borrow huge sums to attend them, college expenses in the U.S. are too damn high. We have the most expensive system of higher education in the world after the U.K. on paper,[300] but Britain's are cheaper than ours when adjusted for grants and government-imposed price controls.[301] We're number one! When half of American borrowers continue to owe an average of $20,000 some twenty years after beginning as a freshman, reform is called for.[302]

There is also an argument for nationalizing public and/or private institutions of higher education. A college education, after all, will remain essential for a significant segment of the population even if we convince employers to stop requiring needlessly-high levels of education attainment.

Goods and services like credentials that are essential for contemporary human existence are, by definition, too important to be left to the fickle whims of a boom-and-bust marketplace. A college education surely qualifies. Higher education is too expensive a cost for cities and states to absorb. For the feds, however, it's not that big a deal.

We know because it's done in 46 other countries.[303] Finland, for example, covers 96% of college expenses for its students. The trade-off is it's harder to get in; only 33% of applicants are admitted.[304] Despite the country's economic challenges, Spain provides free college for its own citizens as well as those of the European Union. Even other international students pay less than $1000 a year.[305]

A federal takeover of colleges and universities would create economies of scale and countless efficiencies, such as the ability to negotiate discounted prices for textbooks and equipment, plus the ability to transfer professors and personnel throughout the system in accordance with educators' desires and regional needs. It might also be possible to create a seamless way to transfer from one institution to another, which would be useful when a student needs to move from one state to another.

If college education were made free in the United States, the economy could experience profound shifts, both positive and challenging. Eliminating tuition costs would likely increase enrollment, particularly among low- and middle-income students. A more educated workforce could boost productivity, innovation, and economic growth. A 2023 study from the Georgetown University Center on Education and the Workforce suggested that free college could raise GDP by billions over decades as graduates enter high-skill industries like technology and healthcare.

Models from countries like Germany—where tuition is free—suggest economic benefits offset costs over time. Germany's system, funded through progressive taxation, supports a historically robust economy with a low unemployment rate, partly due to its skilled labor pool.

Short-term disruptions might include workforce shortages in trades, as more individuals opt for college over vocational paths. Yet, long-term gains—reduced income inequality, a more competitive global workforce, and lower poverty rates—would outweigh these. The U.S. economy, historically resilient, could adapt, potentially mirroring Nordic nations where free education correlates with high living standards and economic stability.

As long as employers continue to insist on a college diploma before considering a job applicant, obtaining that diploma ought to cost as little as possible.

Talking Points:

Colleges profit from overcredentialization, burdening students with debt for often irrelevant degrees.

The college income premium is shrinking away, leaving graduates with debt and stagnant wages.

Forgiving student loans and nationalizing colleges would ease burdens and boost mobility.

10

CREATE A FOREIGN POLICY FOR PEACE, NOT WAR

> *"I'm not one of those critics that believes U.S. foreign policy is confused, or stupid, or misinformed, or well-intentioned but it goes awry. I think it's a brilliant policy filled with many brilliant, terrible, horrible victories."*
> —Michael Parenti, Political Scientist

Every country needs a coherent foreign policy. Since it's impossible to overstate the influence of the United States' military and diplomatic posture, we have an exceptional responsibility to the rest of the world to pivot away from our current, aggression-based approach to one designed for our country to establish and maintain friendly relations with every other country and to encourage them to get along well with one another too.

The U.S. has the world's second-largest[306] and most sophisticated nuclear arsenal (after Russia),[307] exclusive and comprehensive command over the oceans,[308] ideal geography,[309] nearly a thousand military bases[310] overseas and is by far the biggest dealer of weapons[311] and ammunition. And it uses them a lot: we have been at war throughout all of our history[312] since independence from Britain.

The U.S. relies on "hard" power to disrupt and overthrow governments, destroy infrastructure and economies, and wreak havoc and mayhem. Bolstered by military might, it wields "soft power" through cultural and linguistic hegemony. This established English as the world's lingua franca over the last century—something Great Britain couldn't achieve despite its vast empire.[313]

In a rarely questioned oddity, the U.S. determines whether up-and-coming nations are "permitted" to join the "nuclear club" or whether they may be recognized as sovereign countries by the United Nations and other international organizations.[314] It controls a vast array of intelligence operations (including those purporting to work for other countries) and non-governmental organizations, which pull the strings of foreign-based media outlets. The U.S. even hosts the U.N.[315]

Our military, economic, cultural and diplomatic power is incalculably formidable—and our reach is infinite.

In an ideal world, the U.S. would disarm in every respect. Rather than view the rest of the planet as full of people who threaten us and resources to plunder, we would assume our rightful place as one of a couple hundred nations, no better or more worthwhile than any other, nor any worse or less valuable. No matter what your teacher or the TV news or the president says, we are not exceptional.

History has brought us here, however, so we must deal with the fallout and try to undo our forefathers' errors as much as possible. In the interim, we are militarily dominant.

We have an awesome duty to exercise our massive power responsibly, intelligently, with restraint, and in service of the greater global good. Sadly, the opposite has been true more often than not.

If and when the Left were to take over control of the nuclear missile silos, the defense budgets and the embassies circling the globe, everything would change radically.

Nothing is foreordained. President Jimmy Carter hinted at what was possible for the U.S.'s interactions with other countries when, as the first president to do so and so far the last one, he promised to prioritize human rights in foreign policy.[316] Though he fell woefully short of his self-professed ideal, Carter propped up brutal dictatorships. These included the Shah's torture regime in Iran and Indonesia's massacre of the East Timorese. He also armed the far-right anti-Soviet jihadis in Afghanistan. Still, it's worth noting that the U.S. did not launch any wars or proxy conflicts during the late 1970s.[317]

Even had Carter lived up to his promises, our military infrastructure and culture would have remained unchanged.

Defense for Defense

First and foremost, the U.S. must adopt a fully defensive military posture. American troops should only be deployed, and then aggressively, in the event of an

invasion or armed incursion of U.S. soil by an enemy nation-state—or imminent threat thereof, as defined under international law.[318]

The U.S. must never enter into any treaty or mutual-defense arrangement under which it might be legally or otherwise obligated to assist or intervene as the result of a conflict to which it is not a party. For example, we should cancel our membership in NATO, a mutual-defense pact whose member states treat an attack on one as an attack on all, *Three Musketeers*-style.[319] As the lead state that created NATO, we should move to dissolve it because—despite NATO's Article 8 that requires member states to certify that they don't have conflicting treaty obligations—it is a perfect example of the type of dangerous interlocking alliances that triggered World War I.[320] Under Article 5, an armed attack on one member is deemed an attack on all. It doesn't take a vivid imagination or a paranoid personality to worry about the possibility of a border skirmish sparking a nuclear confrontation.[321]

A defense-only defense policy will allow the "defense" budget to shrink to a small fraction of current levels.[322] This will free up trillions of dollars. Those funds can address urgent, long-neglected domestic needs like fighting poverty and improving our schools.[323] It will end misguided foreign adventurism like the invasions of Afghanistan and Iraq, covert participation in regime-change "color revolutions,"[324] support of coups such as those that transformed Libya and Honduras into failed states, and the proxy war against Russia in Ukraine as well as our support of Israel's war against the Palestinians and Lebanon.[325]

Countless lives will be saved and improved after we withdraw our military and weapons from other countries and deploy them to protect our own borders. We will acquire fewer enemies, reducing the possibility of future terrorist attacks. At home, we will see fewer hate crimes directed at those who seem to somehow to be affiliated with whatever nation-state or ethnicity we happen to be designating as our enemy at any given time.

A key component of a comprehensive swords-to-plowshares strategy is to close all of our hundreds of military bases around the planet and bring our troops home where they belong. This will bring an end to the perverse practice of stationing soldiers in a place where they are likely to provoke an attack, as in Niger in 2018,[326] only to then double and triple down on our presence in order to protect the previous force. Smarter not to station them there in the first place.[327]

A foreign crisis or conflict might seem to require military intervention. This could be to restore law and order, stop genocide like in Rwanda in the 1990s, or serve another benevolent, selfless reason. U.S. involvement should be reluctant and carefully considered. It should be voted on directly by the American people, not our elected representatives. Then, should the U.S. choose to be involved, any such action ought to be coordinated by the U.N. in conjunction with a coalition of other member states. The U.S. is neither the world's policeman nor its mob enforcer; it ought not to pretend otherwise.

What about the perils of isolationism? Every schoolchild learns that Americans' reluctance to get involved in a second world war encouraged the rise of Nazi Germany and imperial Japan in the 1930s. But what we've learned isn't necessarily true. There is no evidence that the Axis powers looked at the U.S. and interpreted its military posture as a green light for territorial expansion. Steven Hadley, the neoconservative national security advisor to George W. Bush, articulated the argument against anti-imperialism: "[Isolationism and protectionism], when turned into policy, are particularly inappropriate now because we need to be able to sell goods overseas as we try to get our economy going. International engagement is also crucial in keeping the homeland safe from terrorist attacks."[328] The U.S. could sell its goods and services internationally without wasting half of every federal tax dollar on defense. China doesn't have any trouble moving widgets despite its smaller military and the fact that it does not maintain a constellation of foreign military bases far from home. Israel's Mossad is a formidable intelligence agency that doesn't need to express its military forces to the far side of the earth in order to conduct effective counterterrorism operations. Isolationism is not weakness.

As the world's foremost arms developer, dealer and distributor, the U.S. is uniquely positioned to leverage its lead in weapons development in order to initiate and organize a bold new era of arms control and de-escalation.

A Leftist U.S. will unilaterally point the way forward by methodically dismantling its nuclear stockpile, while encouraging others to do the same. Many countries, like China, Russia and North Korea, spend money they don't have to build nukes for fear of a U.S. first strike. They would welcome a statement from the U.S. that it would never fire nuclear weapons first and that they no longer need to try to compete with us.[329] We should join the international treaty banning the use of landmines.[330] Similarly, we are far ahead of other countries in the development of lethal drones.[331] We should forswear the manufacture, deployment and use of unmanned drone weapons, and ask the world to join us in a global convention prohibiting assassination drones.

Friends Wanted

A Left country prioritizes peace. Thus it is absolutely imperative that a Left-governed United States establish and maintain full and, to the fullest extent possible, friendly diplomatic relations with every other country, no matter what. Because we value and respect each nation's right to self-determination, it is not the place of the State Department to pressure or sway any country's politics or governance.

Whether or not we agree with a foreign state's ideological, economic, religious or cultural attitudes is irrelevant; a Leftist diplomatic corps will always be willing to talk to anyone about anything and to remain available to assist U.S. nationals traveling or living in other countries. In keeping with this open-minded approach, the United States will end any and all economic and other forms of sanctions against all foreign governments, and promise never to deploy them in the future for any reason whatsoever, no matter how seemingly justified. Sanctions are coercive gangsterism. As the stubbornly resilient socialist government of Cuba plainly proves, they don't work anyway.[332] And sanctions only affect ordinary people, never the elites.

The U.S. should not wield trade policy as a cudgel, such as imposing tariffs against imports from one producer but not another. While trade policy should always prioritize the protection of American companies and workers, tariffs and regulations should be applied uniformly to all imported goods without favor or disfavor to one or any group of producers.

Mainstream American political leaders regularly argue that the United States adheres to, defends and promotes a "rules-based international order." What's that? It's rarely defined.

The best summary I've found was articulated by John Ikenberry of Princeton University, introduced by *The Financial Times* as "an influential scholar whose former pupils populate the American government," in 2023.[333] "I think the rules-based order has a history that predates the U.S. and even predates 1945 and the great order-building efforts after World War II," Ikenberry said.

He continued: "But if you were to try to identify what open rules-based order is, it's a set of commitments by states to operate according to principles, rules and institutions that provide governance that is not simply dictated by who is most powerful. So it's a set of environmental conditions for doing business—contracts, multilateral institutions—and it comes in many layers. At the deepest level it's really the system of sovereignty. It's the belief that the world has a kind of foundation built around self-determined states that respect each other. On top of that, you have these layers of treaties and institutions culminating really in the United Nations system, building rules and principles around aspirations for the inclusion of all peoples and societies. Everybody gets a seat at the table that has a membership based on statehood. And then on top of that, even more work-oriented rules and institutions that came out of World War II that are based on problem-solving, regulating interdependence: the IMF, the World Bank, the WHO."

If this is the rules-based international order, the U.S. is working overtime to undermine it.

At the core of an arrangement in which "self-determined states…respect each other" is formal diplomatic recognition. In this system, countries open embassies and consulates on one another's territory, exchange ambassadors and issue tourist and work visas so their citizens can visit one another. Most essentially, they acknowledge each other's territorial integrity, right to exist and right to govern their populations as each sees fit.

At present, the United States neither maintains nor seeks diplomatic relations with North Korea, Syria, Iran, or Afghanistan. As the more powerful potential partner, the bulk of the blame and responsibility for the lack of ties lies with the U.S. Beginning in the 1950s, for example, the U.S. unilaterally imposed crippling economic sanctions against the DPRK for having committed the sin of refusing to lose the Korean War.[334] U.S. sanctions against Iran date to the 1979 Islamic Revolution which overthrew the American-backed dictator, the Shah. After negotiating its withdrawal from Afghanistan with the Taliban, the U.S. closed its massive embassy in Kabul, ending consular services. (The U.S. also does not have formal diplomatic relations with isolationist Bhutan, but ties are friendly.)

The U.S. seems to view the establishment of diplomatic relations as a reward for good behavior.[335] This stance is insulting and patronizing. In fact, the purpose of diplomacy is to maintain means of communications to resolve conflicts and keep one another informed as needed. If the U.S. wanted diplomatic relations with the aforementioned countries, it could and should have them (except for Bhutan, perhaps).

For "everybody [to get] a seat at the table that has a membership based on statehood," the goal is a world in which every person on the planet has citizenship of an internationally-recognized nation-state. Nevertheless, millions of people live in places that, as far as the U.N. and other international governing bodies are concerned, might as well not exist, like Kashmir, Palestine, Taiwan and post-Soviet frozen-conflict zones like Abkhazia, South Ossetia and the Transnistria. Along with stateless people like the Roma in Europe, the Galjeel of Kenya and Burkinabé living in Côte d'Ivoire, the U.N. estimates that 4.4 million people on the planet don't have a legal home and live in diplomatic purgatory.

The U.S.'s geopolitical policy of regional disruption—divide and conquer, or at least divide and keep weak—helps to maintain this state of affairs. The U.S. keeps favorable economic and political ties with smaller nation-states that feel threatened by their larger neighbors all over the world, especially outside Europe. Though the U.S. does not recognize Taiwan as a sovereign entity and officially maintains that it belongs to China, America sends billions of dollars a year in cash and weapons to Taiwan to try to keep China off-balance.[336] U.S. military aid props up the government of Ukraine, which stripped many residents of the eastern, ethnic-Russian Donbas of citizenship, rendering them stateless until Russia annexed the region following the start of the war in 2022.[337]

"We do not expect diverse countries to share the same cultures, traditions, or even systems of government," Trump told the U.N. General Assembly in 2017. "But we do expect all nations to uphold these two core sovereign duties: to respect the interests of their own people and the rights of every other sovereign nation." It goes without saying that the U.S.'s claim to respect national sovereignty is selective and self-serving. It invaded Liberia in 1997, Afghanistan in 2001, Iraq in 2003, Haiti in 2004, Libya in 2011, Syria in 2014, Yemen in 2015…the list goes on. None of these violent interventions were justified or legally approved by Congress.

Further to the U.S.'s bullying other countries, it routinely weaponizes institutions it controls, like the International Monetary Fund and World Bank. In 2014, for example, President Barack Obama ejected Russia from the G8 group of the world's biggest economies—now it's the G7—to punish Russia for its annexation of Crimea, despite reports by international observers and Western pollsters that the Crimean plebiscite was free and fair.[338] The IMF kicked out Russia from consultation meetings after the 2022 Russo-Ukrainian war began but those talks are now reportedly set to resume.[339] And Russia was banned from the 2024 Paris Olympics. These sanctions stemmed from Russia's 2022 invasion of Ukraine. If invading another country is just cause for trying to turn a country into a pariah, however, what could be more ridiculous than these efforts being led by the U.S., which has invaded ten countries over the last twenty years, most of them distant from its own borders?

Mahatma Gandhi, when asked what he thought of Western civilization, is reputed to have replied: "I think it would be a good idea." A rules-based international order? It would be a good idea—if there were some way for the U.S. to stop trying to kill it in its crib.

To the world, we say: we wish to be your friends. And if we cannot be friends, we will at least do everything in our power not to turn ourselves, as we have done so often in the past, into your enemy.

Talking Points:

U.S. foreign policy should shift from aggression to fostering global peace and friendship.

America's vast military power demands responsible use, not disruption of other nations.

A Left-led U.S. would adopt a defense-only stance, closing overseas bases.

Diplomacy must prioritize universal friendly relations, ending sanctions and interference worldwide.

Disarming nukes and drones would lead to global de-escalation, saving lives everywhere.

11

POLICE CAN DO SOMETHING NEW: THEY CAN HELP PEOPLE

> *"There is not one single police officer in America that I am not afraid of and not one that I would trust to tell the truth or obey the laws they are sworn to uphold. I do not believe they protect me in any way."*
> —Henry Rollins

The killing of 20-year-old Daunte Wright by a Minnesota police officer during a traffic stop was, at the time, the latest of a long string of high-profile shootings to have sparked widespread protests.[340] It was not the last. As often occurs after these terrible incidents, politicians and editorial boards floated ways to try to turn Robocop into Officer Friendly. To protect and serve. Instead of terrorizing us.

Aside from the fact that reform efforts tend to fizzle out as the body of the cops' latest victim cools, the main trouble with mainstream proposals to fix the police is an absence of ambition. They nip at the edges of a systemic problem, assuming that the cabal of powerful police unions was to allow their implementation. Bad cops are not "a few bad apples" spoiling an otherwise benevolent organization. Nor is it enough to urge the "good cops" to betray the Thin Blue Line and rat out the proverbial bad apples.

Cop culture suffers from deeply-rooted systemic problems. Who wants to become a cop? Aggressive people, mostly men. Who do police departments recruit? Aggressive, authoritarian people, mostly men, disproportionately ex-military. How are cops trained? They're told to prioritize their own safety and that of fellow officers over citizens.[341] Suspects, many cops believe, deserve whatever happens to them for getting into trouble. Some even think that behavior that indicates a citizen is afraid of cops suggests guilt.[342]

Nothing short of destroying existing police departments and their methods can fix policing that is authoritarian, predatory and violent to its core. If Americans seriously want to free people of color (and everyone else) from the abject terror they feel each time flashing lights appear in their rearview mirror, we must radically reinvent the purpose, personnel and posture of police officers.

Many killings of Blacks by police followed stops or detentions over trivial matters. Brooklyn Center police said Wright was pulled over for an expired registration.[343] Wright called his mom and told her the cop had an issue with an air freshener hanging from his mirror, a classic "pretextual stop" in which the police use a minor infraction as an excuse to search for drugs or run plates for outstanding warrants.[344]

The Texas state trooper whose arrest of Sandra Bland led to her death in jail three days later had a long history—a shtick—of zooming up behind cars to force a lane yield and then ticketing them if the flustered motorist forgot to signal, as with Bland.³⁴⁵ George Floyd, whose videotaped asphyxiation under the knee of a Minneapolis police officer provoked outrage, was arrested after spending a counterfeit $20 bill. Eric Garner, the Staten Island man who famously cried "I can't breathe" while being murdered by an NYPD officer in broad daylight, stood accused of the heinous crime of selling "loosie" individual cigarettes.

None of these alleged offenses are the kind of cops-and-robbers scenario we watch on TV or the exciting manhunt for a dangerous criminal that makes kids (boys, mostly) want to join the police. The trivial nature of these life-ending offenses makes them typical. A typical interaction between the police and a citizen who pays his salary is a traffic stop.³⁴⁶ A traffic stop is an attempt by the cop to bring money to municipal coffers: a smog inspection sticker is out of date, a headlight isn't working, the victim made an improper turn or is driving too fast.

Enforcement measures based on revenue enhancement are inevitably abused. Police issue tickets to innocent people. They exaggerate the gravity of offenses. They can also easily escalate minor rule-breaking into violent confrontations because poor people can't afford exorbitant fines. A broken headlight isn't cause to shake someone down for money; the driver usually doesn't even know it's broken. Pull the driver over and let them know they need to get it fixed. If you are trying to get people to stop speeding, write them tickets with a point system but no fines; if they get too many, they lose their driving privileges. There's no reason to renew automobile registrations other than to tax drivers, so just stop requiring it.

In cities and towns, pull police from squad cars and make them foot-patrol beat cops to naturally engage the community. Stop recruiting from the ranks of traumatized former military veterans trained to adopt a warrior mentality.

Policing is largely a waste of public funds. Spending on local and state law enforcement has soared even while funding for the raison d'être of policing, stopping or deterring crime, has dropped.

You could, and cops and police unions do, argue that these are public safety issues. If the authorities really wanted to disincentivize behavior that threatens pedestrians, bicyclists and fellow motorists, however, a fine would not be the solution. Rich people, after all, don't mind paying tickets. Failure to keep one's car properly maintained or repeatedly exceeding the speed limit—which do imperil the public—could be sanctioned by non-financial inducements such as suspending the offender's license.

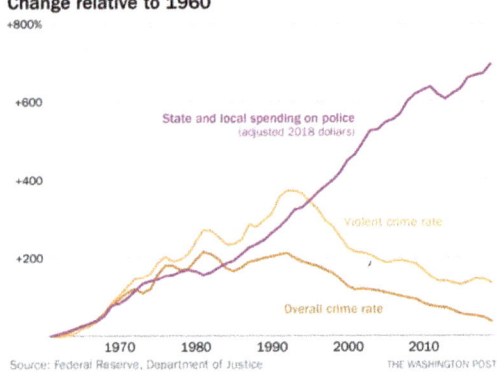

Despite gradually declining crime rates, spending on the police is soaring.

Or, if there's a fine, the money should go somewhere other than the police department or the city. A charity of the offender's choice, say. As things stand, cops care about making cash, not keeping you safe. They are literally highway robbers.

Cops Shouldn't Be Shakedown Artists

If city officials need cash, let them raise taxes. Because to do it differently is to guarantee a conflict of interest, policing should be detached from revenue enhancement.

Whether the police resort to physical force ought to be directly connected to the level of violence of the suspected crime. Depriving New York City of tax revenue and merchants of tobacco sales was the most nonviolent crime imaginable. Had Eric Garner walked away after the confrontation, New Yorkers' safety wouldn't have suffered.

The same was true about George Floyd's counterfeit currency and Sandra Bland's supposed failure to signal a lane change, as well as Walter Scott's broken taillight.[347] Scott, worried about a warrant for overdue child support, was shot to death by a South Carolina cop as he ran away. If these master criminals choose to flee, who cares?

The purpose of the police should be to protect the public from dangerous people and things, period. The only time they should pull out a Taser, a nightstick or a gun should be when they, their partner or another civilian faces imminent danger of serious bodily harm.

The police have become increasingly militarized, from command structures that copy the army down to calling their cops "troops" to accepting decommissioned military hardware from the Afghanistan and Iraq wars and recruiting one-fifth of their members from the ranks of ex-soldiers.[348]

The blurred line between units that occupy war zones overseas and those that patrol our neighborhoods should be restored and sharpened.

I would go further. Throw away the armored personnel carriers and bulletproof vests, yes, but police culture is so toxic that it's reasonable to believe that few if any police currently serving in uniform ought to be retained.

Fire any cop who has been the subject of a civilian complaint about excessive use of force, whether or not their department's fig-leaf "internal affairs" division cleared them, and start from scratch.

Police departments actively discriminate against applicants for being too smart, rejecting those whose IQs are "too high."[349] This is insane. Recruit some liberal arts majors and intellectuals instead of limiting recruitment to those whom police officials believe will unquestioningly follow orders.

At many police academies rookies are taught that their number-one job is to come home alive to their families at the end of each shift. That "warrior" mentality breeds cynicism, insularity and the willingness to resort to violence even when it's counterproductive.

A good cop cares most about getting *you* home safe and sound. They have a "guardian" mentality.

Law and Order, Left-Style

It may come as a surprise, especially to conservatives, that the Left believes in law and order at all. Of course we do. Without it, you can't have much else.

In November 2001, I traveled to Afghanistan as a reporter. It felt like the 14th century if the late Middle Ages took place in an Islamist dystopia and everyone carried an AK-47. To call Afghanistan a failed state would have been too kind; there were no governmental functions of any sort. "What state?" was more like it. There were no paved roads, no operational schools, no reliable form of currency in circulation, not even names for the streets, which was just as well since there weren't any signs either. Most people didn't know their surnames or birthdates. They had never seen their own reflections; there were no mirrors.

When I returned to the United States, interviewers asked me what the people of Afghanistan needed and wanted most. Westerners like Bill O'Reilly when he interviewed me on Fox—none of whom had ever been there or anywhere like it yet didn't hesitate a moment when explaining what ought to be done—offered suggestions: elections, a free press, democracy. From the West, Afghans actually wanted roads and electricity; they could figure out the rest themselves.

People who knew my Leftist politics were surprised when I also suggested what Afghans described as one of their top priorities: law and order. There's no point building a road if bandits rob everyone who tries to travel on it. You can't hold elections if candidates can easily be assassinated. You can't build or maintain an economy if new businesses are constantly at risk of getting robbed or shaken down for cash. Law and order are the foundations of civilization. Left versus right comes later.

Leftists object to bourgeois and capitalist systems of policing, not inherently (with the exception of Leftist anarchists), but because bourgeois cops rely on violence to prop up a specific type of system that we consider to be lawless in a broad, immoral sense and that we therefore seek to tear down.

Under a Leftist government, we must expect counter-revolutionary, reactionary, and corporatist forces to react. They'll try to undermine our efforts to create a more just and equal world in every way they can. This includes terrorizing citizens and new institutions by fostering an atmosphere of lawlessness.

Socialists don't want their banks robbed or their stores fleeced by shoplifters. A Leftist approach to law and order must, however, not merely recreate capitalism's inherent brutality but must reflect the values of dignity and respect that characterize the inspiration for our struggle. More importantly, the criminal and civil justice systems should act as both a counterexample to the Right and as an affirmation of our belief that all humans are capable of redemption, with society morally obligated to do all it can to support them in that process. It almost seems ridiculous to put it into words, but it must be said because it's rarely followed: the purpose of policing is to keep people safe.

Responsive policing is the apex of this mission. When you call 911, a uniformed officer should arrive quickly, thoughtfully assess the situation and act with the bare minimum of physical force necessary, if any, to resolve it—unlike what occurred on July 15, 2017, when a 40-year-old Australian-American woman, Justine Damond, called Minneapolis police to report her fear that a woman was being assaulted behind her home. When the cops arrived, Damond went outside to talk to them. The jittery and high-strung cops were startled, so they shot her.

This kind of thing doesn't occur in the United Kingdom because the police there are trained to guard citizens, not hunt lawbreakers, and they don't carry guns, and they're not jumpy and scared. Police on routine patrol duty should not carry guns. They don't need them. In a situation where firearms might be required, such as a hostage situation involving armed gunmen, a specially-trained tactical team can be dispatched to the scene.

There's also a desperate need for deterrent law enforcement, in which police officers are placed in visible locations to deter criminals and to serve as a point of contact for law-abiding people who need directions or other forms of assistance. You'll find this in Tokyo and other Japanese cities, where police substations are placed at transit stations and major intersections in order to assist the public.

What cops should never be doing is what they mainly do now, roaming neighborhoods with lots of poverty and a majority population of ethnic minorities, occasionally stopping to harass the locals or worse, and writing tickets for parking and moving violations. Police should be trained to understand that disadvantaged populations need their help *more* than privileged groups and that, no matter how sketchy an area looks, 99% of the people who live there are just like them, trying to survive without hurting anyone else.

If government is truly interested in improving public safety, it will abolish regressive monetary fines for mistakes that are not crimes: parking in the wrong place at the wrong time, driving too fast, making an illegal turn, forgetting to obtain a smog test (a vestige of cars without catalytic converters) or renew an automobile registration. Society has a strong interest in promoting orderly parking, encouraging drivers to stay under the speed limit, follow traffic rules, keep their vehicles in good condition, and, of course, preventing anyone from driving under the influence of alcohol. Even in extreme cases where a jail term is warranted, fines are inappropriate; they're too much of a corrupting influence.

End Civil Asset Forfeiture

One of the most corrupt practices in policing is "civil asset forfeiture," in which police can confiscate valuable property like cash, jewelry, cars and even homes if they say they suspect that the goodies may have been acquired or are otherwise vaguely associated with criminal activity. Even if you are charged with a crime and then acquitted, they don't give it back. Even if they never charge you with any wrongdoing, they don't give it back. Up to 80% of civil forfeitures are never associated with a criminal conviction; few, if any, involve Really Bad People like international drug cartels.[350]

They keep it and, in the case of stuff like cars, they use it until you sue to force the police to return it. Which doesn't always work. Because suing a deep-pocketed government agency with laws written to protect it is expensive, many victims decide to let the cops keep the goods they stole.

"No criminal charges are necessary for such seizures, and under federal and state laws, authorities may keep most or all seized assets even in the absence of formal charges. Countless innocent Americans have been victimized by what critics call legalized government theft," according to *The Wall Street Journal*.[351] "Police have made cash seizures worth almost $2.5 billion from motorists and others without search warrants or indictments since the terrorist attacks of September 11, 2001," added *The Washington Post* in 2015. Now it's nearly $2 billion a year.[352] "Police spent the seizure proceeds with little oversight, in some cases buying luxury cars, high-powered weapons and military-grade gear such as armored cars."[353]

Most of the seizures target drivers. But police officers also hang out at FedEx shipping centers, X-raying packages to see if there's cash inside. If so, they steal it; anyone who does business in large cash transactions, they argue, must be breaking some law.[354] They don't have to state which one.

Police have been so pleased with the money and other goodies they nab through asset forfeiture programs that they send officers to seminars that teach them how to maximize their take.[355] Some victims have complained, and successfully proved in court, that they were targeted and entrapped by police whose motivation to detain and arrest them was solely to steal their possessions.

Among the money-making schemes cooked up by greedy cops was a 2009 plan by the DEA to "work closely" with officials of the [Bureau of Alcohol, Tobacco, Firearms and Explosives] "in attacking the guns going to [redacted by government censors] and the gun shows, to include programs/operation with LPRs [license plate readers] at the gun shows."

The DEA and ATF weren't worried about gun violence. "One internal email acknowledged that the tracking program's primary purpose is civil asset forfeiture," the *Journal* reported. They planned to set up checkpoints around gun shows, search attendees' cars using the pretext of a traffic stop, and arrest drivers on whatever charge they could come up with—some legit, others ginned up, in some cases no indictment at all —as an excuse to seize their money and their cars. Which, even if the accused beat the rap, the cops get to keep.

The UK *Guardian* reported: "According to DEA documents, the primary goal of the program was to seize cars, cash and other assets belonging to criminals. However, the [license plate reader] database's expansion 'throughout the United States,' as one email put it, also widened law enforcers' capacity for asset forfeiture."

Bourgeois police officers are deeply imbued with a "gotcha" culture. They receive praise and promotions for catching people doing bad things (and violating minor technicalities) and nailing them for it. Instead, we must train the police to prevent bad things from happening in the first place.

Coming out of a bar late at night in a small Ohio town not long ago, I was immediately pulled over by a cop who had been lurking outside the tavern and hoped to catch patrons driving home drunk. I had only had one beer and everything about my driver's license and my car was kosher, so after a lengthy check of my driving record (which was clean) he let me go with a distinct air of disappointment. Wouldn't it have been better for that town, and my opinion of the police, if instead he'd hung out in front of the bar and offered to drive someone who had had one too many drinks back home?

Talking Points:

Police killings like Daunte Wright's expose a violent, systemic cop culture needing radical change.

Cops prioritize revenue over safety, escalating trivial stops into deadly shakedowns for cash.

Militarized police recruit aggressive ex-soldiers, trained to value their lives over civilians'.

Leftist reform demands guardian cops, not warriors, with no guns on patrol.

End civil asset forfeiture, a corrupt practice letting cops steal without charges.

12

REDEFINE CRIME; RETHINK PUNISHMENT

"Jails and prisons are designed to break human beings, to convert the population into specimens in a zoo—obedient to our keepers, but dangerous to each other."
—Angela Davis

Prisoners are the ultimate wards of the state, which exerts complete control over every facet of their lives.[356] We know what prisoners are expected to do: do what they're told, repent for their sins or pretend to, work for slave wages, don't try to escape. Ignore all those movies that make you root for escaping prisoners! Who ever talks about what society owes prisoners?

Prison terms are way too long and far too harsh. The prison-industrial complex, much of it for-profit or de facto for-profit, extracts money and labor from prisoners. And those who administer prisoners are themselves guilty of countless crimes.

The government has responsibilities to its most vulnerable charges. These include providing inmates with adequate nutrition, housing, security, and medical care. The latter duty has been codified by two landmark Supreme Court rulings. In the first of these decisions, *Estelle v. Gamble* (1972), the Court held that prison authorities who deliberately refuse to address the medical needs of a prisoner inflict cruel and unusual punishment under the Constitution. The Court said "deliberate indifference to serious medical needs of prisoners constitutes the 'unnecessary and wanton infliction of pain'...proscribed by the Eighth Amendment."[357]

The death of LaShawn Thompson fits this description to a T.[358]

While awaiting trial on a misdemeanor case of battery, Thompson, 35, was remanded to Fulton County jail in Atlanta, in the psychiatric wing, because he was behaving erratically. "Three months later Mr. Thompson was found dead in a filthy jail cell after being eaten alive by insects and bed bugs," according to family attorney Michael Harper, who posted nauseating photos of Thompson's squalid cell

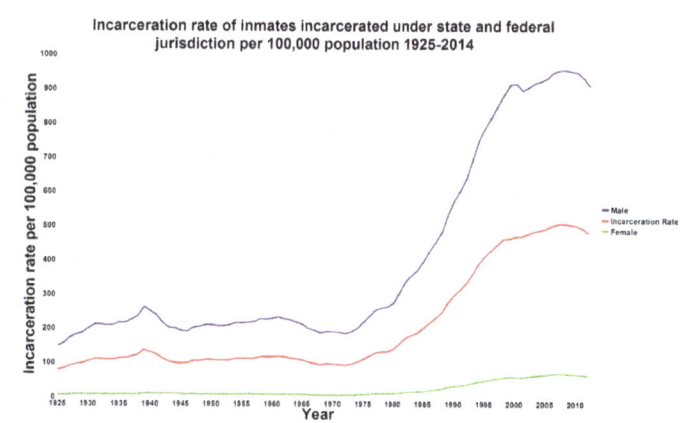

115

on social media.³⁵⁹ "Jail records obtained via Georgia's Open Records Requests establish that the detention officers and medical staff at the jail noticed that Mr. Thompson was deteriorating, but did nothing to administer aid to him or to help him."

Thompson's face and torso were seen covered in parasitic insects.

Michael Potter, an entomologist at the University of Kentucky who specializes in bed bugs, said he'd never seen anything "quite to this level" but confirmed that prolonged exposure to a large number of bed bugs can cause fatal anemia if untreated. "Bed bugs feed on blood and very large numbers of bed bugs feed on very large amounts of blood," Potter said.³⁶⁰

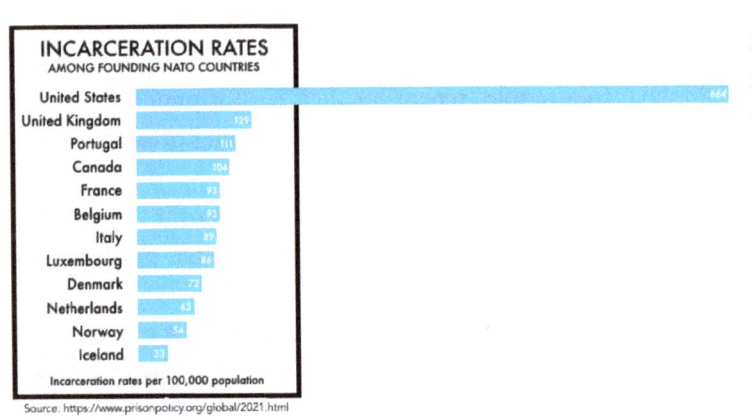

"It's no secret that the dilapidated and rapidly eroding conditions of the current facility make it incredibly difficult to meet the goal of providing a clean, well-maintained and healthy environment for all inmates and staff," the Fulton County Sheriff's Office, which runs the jail, said in a statement.³⁶¹ Appalling jail conditions have been an ongoing, unaddressed problem for years—and not just in Atlanta. In state jails and prisons, more than 20% of prisoners with a chronic medical condition receive no treatment. That jumps to more than 68% in local jails. Since prisoners are more likely to suffer from chronic health conditions like heart disease and diabetes, hundreds of American prisoners die annually due to medical neglect.³⁶²

Joshua Lemore, a 29-year-old Indiana man who struggled with schizophrenia, was arrested for pulling a nurse's hair at the hospital where he'd been taken for a wellness check in 2021.³⁶³ He was locked in solitary confinement—a barbaric practice that Americans take for granted but is mostly banned in Europe—without human contact or medical care.³⁶⁴ Lemore didn't eat, no one checked on him and he starved to death twenty days later. The total lack of psychological help for a detainee in mental health crisis wasn't unusual: "The [Jackson County] jail was cited in 2019, 2020 and June 2021 by the Indiana Department of Corrections for being out of compliance with a state law requiring it to arrange for 24-hour emergency psychological care," according to *USA Today*.

Also in 2021, Larry Price Jr. joined the long list of mentally ill prisoners arrested for minor offenses who have died of neglect and abuse in American jails and prisons.³⁶⁵ A homeless schizophrenic, the 51-year-old Arkansas man had walked into a police station where he rambled threats against cops and made his hand into

the shape of a gun: "terroristic threatening in the first degree," according to the district attorney. This, for Price, turned out to be a crime that called for the death penalty. Price "was found by guards lying in a pool of his own urine and contaminated water, unresponsive in August 2021 after having been detained for more than a year," ABC News reported, "his once 6-foot-2-inch, 185-pound frame emaciated down to 121 pounds, according to the Arkansas state crime lab." The lab determined Price had died of hunger and thirst.

The Bill of Rights and a pair of Supreme Court rulings are supposed to prevent these outrages—but those are obviously not enough. Of the tens of thousands of Americans who perish behind bars each year, many had credibly alleged having been denied medical care or adequate food.[366] Prisons that outsource inmate healthcare to for-profit outside contractors have even higher death rates among their inmates.[367]

Each year of incarceration in a U.S. jail or prison takes two years off average life expectancy.[368]

Since the government refuses or cannot afford to provide for the basic needs of people accused or convicted of a crime, access to healthcare and sanitary conditions included, it should not be in the imprisonment business. We need a federal law that gives a prisoner suffering inhumane conditions, and their family members and lawyers, the right to file an emergency *ex parte* petition for immediate release.

If the conditions are determined to be systemic and facility-wide, the entire detention operation should be shut down at once. That's the case where I live in New York, regarding the city jail on Rikers Island. After "years of mismanagement and neglect"—the Department of Corrections' own spokesman's words[369]—a 2021 *New York Post* exposé revealed "as many as 26 men stuffed body to body in single cells where they were forced to relieve themselves inside plastic bags and take turns sleeping on the fetid floors."[370] Despite an annual $1.2 billion budget, "Dozens of men crammed together for days in temporary holding cells amid a pandemic. Filthy floors sullied with rotten food, maggots, urine, feces and blood. Plastic sheets for blankets, cardboard boxes for beds and bags that substituted for toilets." Nothing has improved since.[371]

Lest you worry that American streets would suddenly be filled with released murderers and rapists, relax. One out of four prisoners is there for the terrifying crime of violating parole.[372] Another one out of five is awaiting trial or serving time for a misdemeanor or civil infraction.[373] Overall, an estimated 40% of the U.S. prison population is behind bars with no compelling public safety reason.[374] They should be released.

What of the rest, the prisoners who might reoffend violently if they were released? They're a legitimate concern. Over 50% of prisoners reoffend within three years of their release.[375]

Rehabilitation, Not Retribution

For inspiration, we should turn to Scandinavia, which is famous for its low criminal recidivism rate. Norway, for instance, has a 20% recidivism rate. "The Norwegian penal philosophy is that traditional, repressive prisons do not work, and that treating prisoners humanely improves their chances of reintegrating in society," according to a white paper issued by Salve Regina University in Rhode Island.

"This is achieved by a 'guiding principle of normality,' meaning that with the exception of freedom of movement, prisoners retain all other rights and life in the prison should resemble life on the outside to the greatest extent possible. Within the walls of Halden, one of the newest maximum-security prisons in Norway, are cells with flat-screen televisions and mini-fridges, long windows to let in more sunlight, and shared living rooms and kitchens 'to create a sense of family,' according to Hans Henrik Hoilund, one of the prison's architects. Prisoners are not left to their own devices upon release, either. There is a safety net. The government guarantees it will do everything possible to ensure that released prisoners have housing, employment, education, as well as health care and addiction treatment, if needed."[376]

Shorter sentences, humane conditions, socialization, support following release—this isn't wimpy liberalism. It's common sense: traumatized ex-prisoners subjected to dehumanizing conditions will be alienated rather than connected to society.

It should go without saying that the Left should also fight to eliminate every vestige of the prison-industrial complex whose defining feature is that the state extracts profits from prisoners and their families while making their lives as difficult as possible. It's cruel, unethical and generates contempt for the system rather than what we want, ex-prisoners who are determined to obey the law and reintegrate into society.

We must not only take care to prevent and end outrages like Pennsylvania's "Kids for Cash" scandal, where a juvenile court judge slammed innocent teens with guilty verdicts and hit guilty ones with exorbitant sentences in order to feed children into a pair of for-profit private prison facilities for young people, which paid him kickback bribes. (President Biden pardoned him.)[377]

Forty states charge people convicted for a crime a nightly fee for their jail terms. Florida's "pay to stay" law, for example, allows the state to charge inmates $50 a day for their prison sentence months, even years after their release date.[378]

Considering that prisoners who hold jobs behind bars earn an average of less than one dollar a day—under the law, they are not subject to minimum wage—and that the median annual income of a prisoner in their first year after release is $11,000, it's hard to see how they can pay up.[379] Many cannot, in no small part because of laws that require them to inform prospective employers that they have been convicted of a crime. So the states re-arrest those who default, and yes, you guessed it: states keep billing them for the additional days in custody.[380]

Many prisons do not provide enough food to survive.³⁸¹ So prisoners rely on the commissary, a major profit center for government agencies that brings in an estimated $1.6 billion per year, mostly subsidized by families that are devastated and impoverished by the incarceration of a loved one.³⁸²

Another $1.4 billion a year comes in from phone calls by prisoners to their families, which are billed at sky-high rates.³⁸³

All these cash grabs should come to an end.

And, obviously, the government should start providing adequate medical care to the people it's in charge of. For example, prison dentists do not fill cavities. All they will do is pull your tooth.³⁸⁴

Although the government doesn't directly profit, another counterproductive and vicious practice is the system's total disregard for society's interest in maintaining former criminals' connections to their families.

Two out of three prisoners are incarcerated at least 100 miles away from their family homes—often much further.³⁸⁵ It goes without saying that destroying families of prisoners not only reduces their chances of successfully integrating into society but harms the people around them. Yet people in the federal system are often kept on the other side of the country.

It should be easy, not hard, for a prisoner to keep in touch with his or her family. Video calls should be free. Visiting should be as frictionless as possible, starting with locating prisoners as close as possible to their families.

We're not a poor country.

Assuming we still want to continue to incarcerate more of our citizens than any other country but China, cities, states and the federal government can surely find the money to create a prison-industrial complex that doesn't feed American citizens to swarms of biting insects and yank healthy teeth.³⁸⁶

The United States being what it is, of course, the prison problem is not limited to the 50 states and territories.

Close Guantánamo Concentration Camp

Two decades ago the U.S. government transformed its naval base at Guantánamo Bay into a legal, moral and foreign-policy disaster. Parents teach their children: you make a mess, you clean it up. It's time for the United States to fulfill its repeated promises to close America's gulag.[387]

Twenty-six prisoners remain at Gitmo. The Pentagon cleared most of them for release; they've never been charged with a crime. Yet they will stay captive until the U.S. finds a country willing to accept them. That country must also offer assurances that they'll be surveilled to ensure they don't threaten U.S. interests or allies.[388] When possible, former detainees are sent home. Others are either denied the right of return by their home countries or would face torture or execution for domestic political reasons.

Most Guantánamo victims were abducted, tortured and isolated without friend or family visits. The U.S. government—the same one that kidnapped them and still holds them prisoner—says they were innocent of anti-American activities. (Not that hating America is, or should be, a crime).[389] Though cleared for release, they endure a Kafkaesque nightmare. They've convinced their interrogators that they shouldn't be there yet remain behind bars at a cost to taxpayers of $1.3 million a year each.[390]

The grand fallacy at the heart of this pseudo-legal purgatory is the assumption that ex-Gitmo detainees must go somewhere, anywhere, other than the United States. Why, if like Thomas Wolfe they can't go home again, shouldn't they be resettled in the country that took and held them captive?

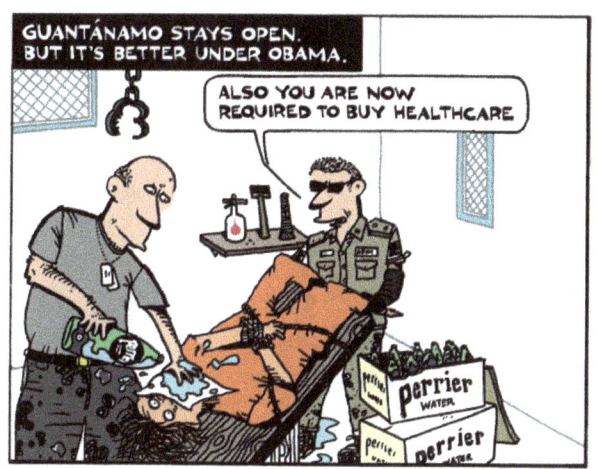

The detainees are part of a mess that we created. Providing them with a home and whatever else they need to lead productive lives in the U.S.—education, job training, psychological treatment—is the least we can do to make amends for the cruelty and injustice they've endured.

Gitmo prisoners were never indicted, much less convicted, of anything, yet they've languished under miserable conditions for years. The Defense Department has determined that they don't present any threat. These men should be treated the same as a U.S. citizen wrongly convicted for a crime they didn't commit; they should receive financial compensation for their years of false imprisonment and ample resources to help them settle wherever they want to go.

Might a former Gitmo prisoner, radicalized and shattered by his experience, commit a violent crime or an act of terrorism on U.S. soil after being released?[391] It's possible. A dozen former detainees returned to Afghanistan and fought against U.S. occupation forces.

Yet, if we have integrity, that's a chance we have to take. On the mainland, we release ex-prisoners despite the possibility that years of incarceration have hardened them, exposed them to fellow criminals and may have left them with hatred and resentment toward the society that wrongfully convicted them.

The Bush Administration saw Guantánamo as a netherworld under U.S. control but free from U.S. legal protections—like the right to a speedy trial or an attorney. They chose this imperialist relic from the Spanish-American War to warehouse and torture hundreds of Muslim men. Their involvement in jihad varied widely: from Khalid Sheikh Mohammed planning 9/11, to Osama bin Laden's chauffeur, to regional opponents of Yemen's regime, to no involvement at all. In 2008, however, the Supreme Court ruled[392] in *Boumediene v. Bush*[393] that Guantánamo inmates were in fact entitled to constitutional protections including the right to file a writ of *habeas corpus* in American courts. Legally, therefore, all Gitmo detainees are already in the United States.

Congress passed a law preventing the use of taxpayer money to transfer Guantánamo detainees to the United States.[394] But the Supreme Court said that they're already here. Guantánamo is, much like a U.S. embassy on foreign soil, in the U.S., so there's no "transfer." Besides, Congress' action was an unconstitutional violation of the president's prerogative as commander-in-chief. But why wait for a lengthy court challenge? We're talking about just over two dozen men. Financing the airfare from Cuba to the lower forty-eight states could be taken care of by a GoFundMe. Count me in.

Notice, I did say over two dozen. That's because *all* Guantánamo victims are legally innocent under American law, including Khalid Sheikh Mohammed. None has ever faced trial in an actual civilian courtroom and never will because their testimony was extracted under duress. KSM, for example, was infamously waterboarded 182 times. If the rule of law and due process still mean anything, all the prisoners—not just those who have been cleared to leave—should not be transferred to maximum-security prisons on the American mainland, as liberals generally suggest. They should all be released in the United States and given every possible resource to live out their lives peacefully and successfully.

The second Trump Administration's plan to indefinitely warehouse thousands of undocumented migrants at Guantánamo signals that the facility is entering a new more expansive era of human-rights abuses. When the Left achieves power, this episode should serve as a reminder that the United States should never create or maintain a prison camp meant to deprive people of their constitutional rights.

Nor should we outsource such a facility. Trump's mass deportation machine, a snarling beast that promises to scoop up millions of migrants and chuck them over the border without so much as a nod to due process, is an assault on the Constitution and common decency. Trump's contract with an El Salvador private prison—a shadowy $300 million scheme via a U.S.-backed contractor—is Gitmo 2.0, a hellhole where migrants get warehoused like cattle before the final shove, no lawyers, no hearings, just a one-way ticket to who-knows-where.

Talking Points:

Prisoners endure harsh, inhumane conditions, neglected by a profit-driven system violating their constitutional rights to medical care and dignity.

The U.S. prison-industrial complex exploits inmates, while Scandinavia's humane model proves rehabilitation reduces recidivism effectively.

13

MAKE LEGAL IMMIGRATION EASY

> *"Life is now a war zone, and as such, the number of people considered disposable has grown exponentially, and this includes low-income whites, poor minorities, immigrants, the unemployed, the homeless and a range of people who are viewed as a liability to capital and its endless predatory quest for power and profits."*
> —Henry Giroux, American-Canadian Cultural Critic

I didn't question the incoming Biden Administration's rollback of the Trump-era stricter border controls in 2021. There's nothing unusual about reversing a previous president's approach to a policy, especially when he belongs to the other party and the policy in question is roundly criticized. You didn't have to be a proponent of "open borders" to feel some seriously icky discomfort about Trump's zero-tolerance stance toward both economic migrants and political asylum applicants, which led to kids in cages,[395] his draconian family separation[396] policy, which caused nearly a thousand children to get disappeared into the system and who were never reunited[397] with their parents, or his "remain in Mexico"[398] scheme, which subjected immigration applicants to gang and cartel violence. By the time he left office, Trump's handling of undocumented people who attempted to cross the U.S.-Mexico border was viewed as inhumane and had become highly unpopular.[399]

As we see so often in American politics, we then swung quickly from one extreme to the other, from xenophobia gone wild to anarchy. President Biden swung past the status quo ante toward immigration policies more liberal than anyone alive today can remember.

To understand the immigration issue, it is important to distinguish between illegal immigrants and legal migrants, two categories nativist activists intentionally conflate. Illegal immigrants sneak across the border. Legal migrants follow whatever procedures happen to be in place at a given time. And, to make things even more confusing, there are also legal immigrants, like workers who are sponsored by their employers for a work visa and foreigners who marry American citizens. Slightly fewer than two million people illegally crossed the U.S.-Mexico border during Trump's four years in office.[400] Under Biden, well over six million crossed. That changed when he returned to Trump's approach, shortly before dropping out of his reelection campaign.[401] Of these six million, Biden deported more than half.[402]

Where the two administrations' policies *really* differed was their handling of applicants who present themselves to border patrol agents and followed the federal government's legal application process for asylum. Fewer than 200,000 asylum seekers were paroled, i.e. admitted into the U.S. pending the resolution of their claim, under Trump. Biden paroled nearly 500,000, with big spikes over his second and third years in office.[403] Biden let in people under special refugee programs for those fleeing conflict zones like Ukraine, Afghanistan and Venezuela. Combined with others, more than a million of them remained in the U.S. as of early 2025.[404]

Biden's policies were unpopular and contributed to Kamala Harris's defeat. More than two-thirds of voters disapproved of the president on immigration (68%) and border security (69%), according to an AP-NORC poll conducted in March 2024.[405] It was a major issue. After the economy, healthcare, crime and guns, immigration was tied for fifth with abortion among the issues voters cared about most in the 2024 race.

Like other leftists, I assumed that Biden's "open border" approach was driven by a pair of well-intentioned albeit shortsighted liberal impulses: opposing all things Trump *just because* and opening America's doors to the poor and oppressed masses desperate for the chance to build new lives, à la Emma Lazarus in homage to our history as a Nation of Immigrants.

I have come to believe that there is another explanation.

The Hidden Fertility Crisis

Democrats read polls. They know their border policies don't play well with the swing voters they need to win elections. Trump's fearmongering landed punches.[406] So why did the Biden Administration stay the course so long? Why did they just stand by and watch as cities including New York and Chicago reeled under the financial stress of hundreds of thousands of new arrivals that they couldn't handle?

A Unified Theory of What Ails America

As Bill Clinton's strategist James Carville famously observed in 1992, it's the economy, stupid. It's *always* the economy, especially in an election year. And you can't hit the ideal GDP growth rate of two or three percent a year if your population—your consumer base and your labor pool—is shrinking.[407]

Democrats knew the Biden migration surge might cost them the White House in 2024. But they were looking beyond November.

The developed world is facing a fertility crisis. For the population to remain stable, the average woman needs to have 2.1 children.[408] (The fraction over two accounts for disease, accidents and mortality in general.) A study published in *The Lancet* finds that the fertility rate for Western Europe, which was at a 1.53 rate in 2021, is expected to drop further to 1.37 by 2100. A major population drop-off could cause a crisis as a smaller workforce is unable to support an older, larger cohort of retirees. Demand for homes and other transgenerational products could collapse, dragging down consumer goods and leading to a deflationary doom loop.

Fortunately for the West—and the East, since the problem is even more pronounced in China—study co-author Natalia V. Bhattacharjee suggests that there's a solution: liberalized immigration from places like the Global South.[409] These are the nations to the south of more industrialized nations that have a relatively low level of economic and industrial development and where birthrates remain high.

"Once nearly every country's population is shrinking, reliance on open immigration will become necessary to sustain economic growth." She told Al Jazeera that "sub-Saharan African countries have a vital resource that aging societies are losing—a youthful population."

Here in the U.S., our fertility rate has dropped from 3.65 in 1960 to 2.08 in 1990 to 1.66 in 2021.[410] At the same time, population has risen from 181 million in 1960 to 250 million to 333 million in 2021. Immigration, legal and illegal, has filled the void created by our failure to make enough babies.

Top government officials hide behind locked, soundproof doors in the White House and other power centers. They stare at demographic charts showing the population growth rate leveling off. They sweat over a fact: the current economic model relies on consistent growth, but a fertility crisis—rarely discussed by them or the media—threatens it. Republicans see an uncontrolled flow of people from Central America and elsewhere pouring across the border with Mexico as threats to American jobholders, possible criminals and perhaps cultural harbingers of a nefarious demographic war against whites called the Great Replacement theory. Democratic economists view them, as does Bhattacharjee, as a convenient solution to the intractable demographic issues of Americans getting married later and in fewer numbers and thus having fewer children than required to keep growing the economy.[411]

The real solution, any Leftist can plainly see, is to replace an economic model that calls for endless expansion regardless of whether there is a market to absorb additional goods and services with one that meets people's needs, no more and no less. That can't happen before a Revolution. Pending the Revolution, making many of the changes suggested in this book would encourage more Americans to have children and to have them at a younger age. Higher wages, better working conditions, affordable healthcare and childcare programs would ease child-rearing burdens.

We can support the case for a justified revolt by advocating for a radical overhaul of the current power and economic systems—changes that could address issues like the fertility crisis if not for those systems' deep-seated corruption and internal contradictions.

There are ways to encourage the United States citizens who already live in the United States to have more kids. Having and raising kids is expensive and difficult. Let's make it cheaper and easier. One city in Japan, whose economy has struggled against a fertility crisis since the 1990s, has succeeded in growing family sizes by investing in free medical care for children, free diapers and, most effectively, free daycare.[412] Other places have achieved similar results. There is a direct correlation between low birth rates and expensive childcare.[413] Sadly, there's no sign that either major party in Washington cares about the issue or is inclined to act.

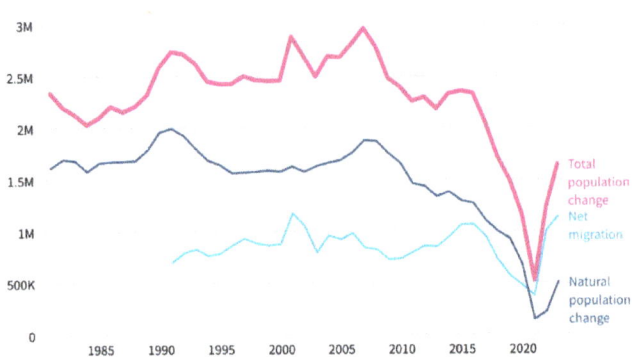

That leaves immigration. Given the stakes and the undeniable capitalistic logic that necessitates throwing open the floodgates, an honest political leader might want to take a shot at something the ones we've had in recent years seem to hate: explaining the facts to the public.

I fantasize about a government that really, if it is not quite by the people, at least tries to act like it is for the people and thus internalizes the principle that the people deserve to be treated like mature adults, not fools.

Nothing about what the media calls the "migrant crisis" withstands the slightest scrutiny. This begins with something that right-wing conservatives and other nativists point out to such great effect that it was largely responsible for launching Trump and his Make America Great Again movement, and their hostile takeover of the Republican Party: (a) no other country allows people to cross its borders without consequence and (b) if the United States wanted to keep people from crossing its border with Mexico, it could. Point (a) has the benefit of mostly being true; while we have witnessed mass refugee flows from, say, Afghanistan to Pakistan, these incidents occur sporadically, under specific circumstances like armed conflicts and revolutions and usually involve failed or weak nations in the developing world. Point (b) is, of course, completely true; poorer countries have managed to secure their frontiers even when they were longer and more hostile, as seen in China and the former Soviet Union. When the U.S. government alters its policies at the border, crossings drop.[414]

America's border with Mexico has, for the most part, been porous since at least the 1970s.[415] In 1986 President Ronald Reagan signed a blanket amnesty granting legal status to three million undocumented workers who could demonstrate they had been in the country since 1982.[416] To obtain passage through Congress, however, the bill was stripped of its original sanctions against employers who knowingly hired foreigners who were not authorized to work. Companies got the message: there is no downside risk to hiring undocumented workers. Since 1990, roughly 750,000 people a year have illegally crossed into the U.S., been apprehended by the Border Patrol and expelled either to Mexico or to another country.[417] Many of these people tried again and again until they successfully found somewhere safe to live, work and, in many cases, raise a family.

Biden's decision to liberalize border entries from 2021 to mid-2024 proved controversial for a variety of reasons: racism and nativism to be sure, but also the sense, following the misery of the Covid pandemic lockdown and its economic misery, that native-born American citizens who had trouble getting help from their government were being passed over in favor of new arrivals given free housing at hotels and preloaded debit cards, as well as smartphones. It came as little surprise that Trump and the Republicans exploited these resentments by promising "the largest deportation in the history of our country."[418]

But THEY were white.

"Open borders," as Republicans call them, is a misnomer. Economic migrants, political refugee applicants and others who seek irregular entry via land across the Southern border are forced to sneak across all or most of Mexico and endure numerous physical hardships.

The asylum-application system during most of the Biden years was akin to Ellis Island, the iconic immigration processing center through which more than twelve million new Americans were admitted from major nations of origin like Ireland, Germany, Italy and France. These immigrants, who are the ancestors of most white Americans living in the U.S. today, boarded ships without holding an entry visa, hoping for the best. Upon arrival, they were quickly processed through medical checks and questionnaires and released into New York City, where many initially gravitated toward such communities as the Lower East Side of Manhattan. Similarly in our time, Biden-era migrants appeared at border entry points like Eagle Pass, Texas, made appointments with U.S. Customs and Border Protection using a smartphone app, presented themselves when told to do so and were processed and released into the U.S.

As was the case a hundred years ago, this latest rapid influx of millions of people has caused consternation that might be alleviated if the federal government were to create a more efficient system that managed migrant flows more intelligently, addressed Americans' concerns, prioritized Americans' needs and, most of all, explained the rationale for a liberal immigration policy.

U.S. immigration has long been characterized by a series of fits and starts, in which long periods of relatively low immigration are suddenly interrupted by massive admissions, which prompt backlashes that result in yet another set of restrictions. Flows should be managed holistically and consistently, with a set number of people permitted to apply both at land crossings and at U.S. embassies and consulates overseas each year.

Clusters of immigrants shouldn't pile up in communities that can't always handle them. Take Springfield, Ohio—a city of 40,000 that took in 20,000 Haitian migrants in two years, now infamous for wild tales of pet dogs and cats being eaten. Instead, the U.S. government should mimic countries with bureaucracies that manage where new arrivals go.

Complaints that recent immigrants receive generous government resources have been overblown. A much-criticized pilot program in which New York City issued gift cards for food purchases amounted to $35 per day for a family of four, hardly enough to eat well to say the least. Americans with longstanding citizenship ought not to have to make do with paltry FEMA grants after losing their homes in a natural disaster.[419] Nor should they become homeless, or see their unemployment benefits run out, or be denied job retraining.

We Need an Explainer-in-Chief

Most people would understand if the president or another top government official were to explain, as Franklin D. Roosevelt did during his "fireside chats" in the 1930s, how immigration not only benefits the economy but is absolutely necessary to sustain our current economic model in the light of our national fertility crisis.[420] Until American families start having bigger families and giving birth to more babies, we are going to have to import them from abroad.

And from a Left perspective, taking in a generous number of people who seek to enter the United States enables the fundamental human right of movement, which is a basic freedom for a species that wandered across great distances for most of our existence, as well as a move toward the world we desire, one in which we are equal and free to live where we please unhindered by the arbitrary political borders of randomly-evolved nation-states.

Porous borders have historically contributed to the destabilization and failure of nation-states by enabling uncontrolled flows of people, goods, and threats that undermine governance. This vulnerability can exacerbate internal weaknesses, leading to collapse.

In Somalia, a quintessential failed state since the 1991 overthrow of Siad Barre, porous borders with Kenya and Ethiopia hastened its descent into chaos. By the early 2000s, weak coastal and land boundaries allowed arms smuggling and pirate activity to flourish, funding warlords and militias like al-Shabaab. Refugees and displaced populations crossed freely, straining resources and complicating governance. The lack of border control prevented any central authority from regaining a monopoly on force, cementing Somalia's status as a failed state with no functioning government for decades.

Yemen's collapse during the 2015 civil war is another example. Its porous border with Saudi Arabia facilitated the influx of weapons and fighters, intensifying the Houthi insurgency. Smuggling networks thrived, undermining the economy and state legitimacy as the government lost control over vast territories. Foreign intervention, enabled by unsecured borders, escalated the conflict, displacing millions and leaving Yemen a humanitarian disaster with no effective central authority by the late 2010s.

Syria's porous borders with Iraq and Turkey accelerated its failure during the 2011 Arab Spring uprising. As the Assad regime weakened, jihadist groups like ISIS exploited open frontiers to move fighters and resources, capturing swathes of territory by 2014. Refugee outflows and arms inflows overwhelmed the state's capacity to respond, while foreign powers exploited the chaos, further eroding sovereignty. Syria became a patchwork of warring factions, its government a shell of its former self.

Porous borders amplify internal fragility—corruption, economic decline, conflict—by inviting external pressures that states cannot contain, hastening their collapse.

A country is not a real nation-state unless it controls its borders. The authorities must determine who enters and departs. It might shock those used to liberal Democrats pushing loosely controlled borders or claiming they shouldn't exist, but the real Left cannot support this globalist perspective for practical, organizational reasons. Under a one-world government or a system in which many current frontiers are abolished, the task of building socialism would be even more daunting than it is now. We cannot abolish the nation-state system until after we have achieved a Leftist government in the United States and as many other countries as possible. As things stand now, no one should come into the United States without permission or without being vetted and approved.

That said, what is done is done. Trump's deportation dragnet scoops up alleged gang members—some innocent—and college students alike, all without due process, ruining lives for his border-warrior cosplay. The 238 supposed Tren de Aragua gang members shipped to El Salvador's notorious CECOT prison on March 15, 2025, for example, were treated shamefully. ICE admits "many" had no U.S. criminal records, yet they're now rotting in a 40,000-capacity hellhole notorious for torture, with no hearings, no evidence, just because Trump wants them there. Kilmar Armando Abrego Garcia was a Salvadoran father deported the same day to the same facility despite an immigration judge's prior ruling that he could stay—ICE later called it an "administrative error" but left him stranded and argued there was nothing they could do for him. Meanwhile, green-card holders like Jose Franco Caraballo Tiapa, a 26-year-old Venezuelan asylum seeker, got nabbed at a routine ICE check-in and shipped to El Salvador for protesting Israel's war in Gaza. These deportations are a weird new normal—people living here, working and studying. They deserve respect and to live free of government harassment, not a one-way ticket to a foreign cage, and if they've broken laws, let them face U.S. courts.

Talking Points:

Biden rolled back Trump's strict border policies, paroling nearly 500,000 asylum seekers, sparking a shift criticized by voters in 2024.

Over six million illegally crossed under Biden, with half deported, straining cities amid his liberal immigration stance.

U.S. fertility fell to 1.66 children per woman, risking economic stagnation, which Democrats countered with immigration despite political backlash.

Trump's harsh tactics, like family separations, contrasted with Biden's approach, both extremes ignoring a balanced border policy.

Leftists advocate controlled borders and economic overhaul, balancing human movement with practical steps toward socialism.

14

PUNISH CORPORATIONS LIKE HUMANS

"A criminal is a person with predatory instincts without sufficient capital to form a corporation."
—Howard Scott, Engineer & I.W.W. Research Director

In 2010, the Supreme Court issued a shocking ruling whose consequences continue to reverberate through electoral politics. Corporations, the majority opinion ruled, would henceforth enjoy many of the same rights and protections as an individual citizen. Not only may an abstract legal entity created by individuals or shareholders with the purpose of operating for profit claim the right of freedom of religion to, for example, refuse to cover birth control under employee insurance, but the landmark case of *Citizens United v. Federal Election Commission* further determined that the First Amendment grants it the right of free speech.[421]

As every child knows and Spider-Man preaches, privileges come with responsibilities.[422] In contrast, the corporation is established by businesspeople to accumulate privileges while avoiding accountability for its actions. It is, thus, antisocial nearly to the point of being psychotic. It exists primarily to protect its hidden puppet masters (its CEO, board of directors and other decision makers) from being held legally or criminally responsible if something it does or a product it makes causes harm. Sometimes, of course, a corporation hurts so many people that it gets nailed anyway. But no worries. If and when the victims of a corporation succeed at securing a substantial verdict or judgment in the courts, often after overcoming daunting legal hurdles, the corporation can and often does declare bankruptcy, leaving its principals free to slither off to their next endeavor without ever being held accountable.

After a Left-led revolution, there would likely not be any place for the corporate structure, at least not one designed specifically for the purpose of avoiding responsibility. Until then, however, we are left with the problem of the corporation and how it should be modified in order to make it, if it must be considered a citizen under American law, a corporate "person" that (who?) doesn't murder, poison and steal with impunity.

The Left should ask a logical question. If corporations enjoy personhood under the law, ought they not face analogous consequences when they do something wrong?

When a corporation commits a serious crime—what you or I would call a felony—it should face consequences like an individual's. These could include prison time, high fines, or even life imprisonment or capital punishment for the corporation. The pain a criminal corporation faces, in other words, ought to be commensurate with what a convicted American individual would have to deal with if they were convicted of a legal offense.

Beginning in 2012 and for the next ten years, Bank of America created fake credit-card accounts in their customers' names without obtaining consent, charging them millions of dollars in fraudulent fees and hurting their credit ratings. They charged customers double bounce fees—one for insufficient balance and another for returning the check—which is also illegal. This, by the way, was their second offense; federal regulators caught them doing the same thing in 2014 and fined them $727 million.

Clearly, those fines were like a cheap speeding ticket—too little to deter repeat corruption. So what did the Consumer Financial Protection Bureau, the Bernie Sanders-Elizabeth Warren brainchild that was supposed to protect us from the worst excesses of scumbag capitalism, do the second time around? They fined them a third as much as the first time, $250 million.[423]

To put the penalty into context, Bank of America's market capitalization is more than $325 billion and it has $3.2 trillion in assets. For acting like total degenerate maniacs year after year, leaving a trail of hundreds of thousands of mugging victims (customers) in their wake, B of A was dinged less than one-thousandth of its net worth.

Let's say that your net worth, including your savings, 401(k) and house equity, is the national average: $1 million. A thousandth of $1 million is $1,000. A $1,000 fine sucks, to be sure. But you can afford it and quickly put it behind you. Basically, it's an unexpected car repair, and not a particularly big one.

What sentence would *you* get from even the softest, most liberal, kindest judge around, if you stole tens of millions of dollars from tens of thousands of people? Whether you held them up at gunpoint or hacked it out of their bank accounts like B of A, you'd be lucky to get out of prison before twenty years. You'd be ordered to make your victims whole and pay some hefty, life-altering fines. And you'd come out with a prison record that would guarantee that you would never find a good job—certainly not a finance job—again.

To punish B of A as a "corporate person," then, you'd need to impose sanctions that looked something like this:

Not allowed to do any business for at least twenty years.

Fines amounting to at least half of its market capitalization, in this case about $162 billion.

Stripped of its banking license.

Effectively, B of A would be put out of business.

But, I hear you saying, under this system of ours, as those of us who lived through the 2008-09 subprime mortgage meltdown recall, giant banks like Bank of America are "too big to fail." They are essential to the economy. If one goes under, it takes many of us with them.

Perhaps. If that's true, there's a solution that doesn't destroy the economy by killing a vital national institution yet does not allow rogue institutions to escape responsibility for their crimes: nationalization. The corporation lives. But it becomes government property.

The government owns it, runs it, appoints its CEO and Board of Directors and sets its policies. The bank officials who broke the law are kicked out. And the government collects the profits.

Nationalization is economic blasphemy in the United States. But governments can and do run banks in other capitalist countries while managing to overcome the challenges of government interference and possible inefficiency. Norway's three largest banks, Mexico's full banking system, all Finnish savings banks, four Israeli banks, all Icelandic banks and several British banks have been nationalized by their governments. By most accounts, these takeovers were a significant improvement over private ownership.

In the U.S., government nationalization of private businesses has been rare and typically tied to crises, reflecting a pragmatic approach. While the U.S. championed laissez-faire capitalism, it intervened when private entities failed to meet national needs, particularly during wartime or economic upheaval.

In the 1800s, nationalization was often indirect. During the Civil War, the federal government seized control of Southern railroads and telegraph lines in order to support the Union war effort, though this was more confiscation than formal nationalization. These assets were returned to private hands post-war. The Spanish-American War of 1898 prompted temporary control of telegraph companies to ensure military communication.

World War I drove broader nationalization. In December 1917, President Woodrow Wilson nationalized the railroad industry under the Federal Control Act, as private companies struggled to coordinate wartime logistics. The U.S. Railroad Administration ran the system until 1920, when it was returned to private ownership. Similarly, the government seized telegraph and telephone lines in 1918, placing them under the Post Office Department to secure wartime communications.

In 1918, the government briefly took over Smith & Wesson to ensure firearm production for World War I. During World War II, the government seized several industries to support the war effort. In 1942, it nationalized coal mines amid labor strikes, with the Army briefly running operations until disputes were resolved. That year, Montgomery Ward, a mail-order corporation, was taken over after refusing to comply with labor agreements.

After 1945, nationalizations dwindled. In 1971, during a financial crisis, Congress established Amtrak by nationalizing passenger rail services from struggling private companies—a model that persists today. Conrail, a consolidated freight rail system under government control since 1976, was privatized in 1987. During the Savings and Loan Crisis of the 1980s and 1990s, the Resolution Trust Corporation took over failed thrifts, managing assets before selling them off.

In recent history, there have been de facto nationalizations, as when the Federal Deposit Insurance Corporation took over three-quarters of GMAC and the flailing insurance company AIG and a third of Citigroup. There's no rule stating that the FDIC cannot or should not take control of an institution like Bank of America—or any other corporation—if it exploits its corporate personhood to engage in criminal activity.

Talking Points:

Corporations evade responsibility for crimes, facing fines too small to deter repeat offenses.

If corporations are "persons" under law, they should face severe penalties—fines, business bans—akin to individual felony punishments.

Nationalizing criminal corporations could preserve economic stability while ensuring accountability and public ownership.

15

MAKE INCOME TAXES FULLY PROGRESSIVE

"We don't pay taxes. Only the little people pay taxes."
—*Leona Helmsley, Businesswoman & Tax Cheat*

When a Republican wins a presidential election, the progressive individual income tax—in which the more you earn, the higher a percentage of your earnings become subject to taxation—becomes a target for dilution or elimination. We have long heard about schemes like the "flat tax," in which tax brackets are abolished in favor of a universal percentage rate. In the final days of his second campaign, Donald Trump pushed further, urging total elimination of the income tax. "When we were a smart country, in the 1890s...this is when the country was relatively the richest it ever was. It had all tariffs. It didn't have an income tax," Trump said. "Now we have income taxes, and we have people that are dying. They're paying tax, and they don't have the money to pay the tax."[424]

We should start by noting that Trump's claim is historical fiction. The individual income tax currently brings in half of federal tax revenues, which is a lot of money.[425] "It's an absurd idea for many reasons, the biggest being that it is mathematically impossible to replace the income tax with tariffs," Erica York, senior economist at the conservative Tax Foundation, told CNN.[426] "Imports are a much smaller tax base than taxable income, and there's no way to squeeze enough revenue from taxing imports to fully replace taxing income." Tariffs currently bring in about 2% of federal revenue.

As for when we were "a smart country," as Trump says about the 1890s, that era wasn't too bad...for a few years. Mark Twain called it the Gilded Age, but it wasn't a compliment. The gleam wore off with the Panic of 1893, which triggered a severe depression, sky-high unemployment and massive social unrest.[427] The

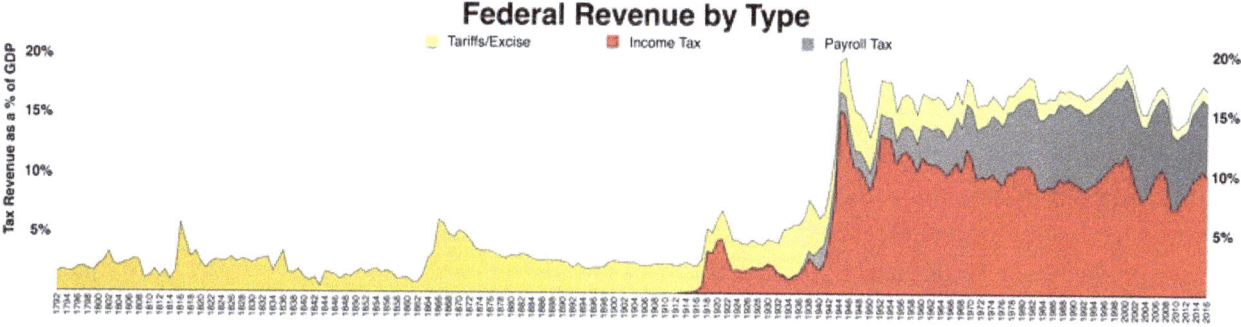

resulting decline in tax collections forced the imposition of—wait for it—an income tax that was overturned about a year later by the Supreme Court. In fact, income taxes came and went throughout the 19th century.

As for the U.S. being "relatively the richest it ever was," that's debatable, but also a ridiculously low bar. The miserable economy of the first century and a half of American history was punctuated by bank failures, stock market crashes, widespread unemployment and depressions so severe that money stopped circulating at times and people had to make do with barter.[428] Between the Panic of 1819, the Panic of 1837, the Panic of 1873 (which led to the Long Depression) and the Depression of 1882-1885, Americans were either losing everything or accumulating wealth that was about to be lost. We were a "shithole country," as Trump so colorfully and sensitively referred to the nation-states of the developing world.

Here we go again, maybe. Trump's tariffs, rolled out in early 2025, slapped a 25% levy on imports from Canada and Mexico, a 20% tax on Chinese goods (up from 10%), and a 10% baseline on nearly everything else, attempting to bully trading partners into submission and drag manufacturing jobs back to U.S. soil. The financial markets freaked out, with the S&P 500 cratering nearly 5% on April 3, 2025—the worst single-day drop since the 2020 pandemic panic. China's retaliatory 34% tariff on U.S. goods sparked a global sell-off, tanking the Nasdaq into bear territory and wiping out $5 trillion in stock value worldwide by April 4. Analysts like J.P. Morgan jacked up recession odds to 60%, warning that Trump's tariffs could kill growth and increase inflation.

The modern income tax as we know it came to be with the ratification of the 16th Amendment in 1913, which clarified Congressional fiscal prerogatives. It is hard to imagine, without this massive new source of income into the federal treasury, that the United States would have successfully fought in World War I, much less developed into the global superpower that it is today. While the boom-and-bust cycle of American capitalism has devastated countless lives and businesses, in the 20th century the federal government collected sufficient funds to create a rudimentary social safety net, something people of the 19th century could only have dreamed of. That was almost entirely due to the income tax.

Progressive income taxes are fair and practical. The richer you are, the more you can afford to pay. A person who earns $200,000 a year and pays 50% of that in taxes still keeps more money in the end than someone who earns $100,000 a year and pays 40% in taxes. The government taxes rich people because, as the bank robber Willie Sutton was falsely said to have said, that's where the money is.[429]

If we want to draw lessons from history about the relationship between taxation and economic prosperity, it would be more relevant to consider the point at which the U.S. tax code achieved peak progressiveness.

In theory, this was the early 1960s, when the highest-income individual taxpayers in the top one hundredth of one percent (0.01%) paid a top marginal rate of 91%. There has been a general downward trend against progressivism since then. Currently, taxpayers who earn more than $609,000 a year are subject to a 37% marginal rate. But taxes are complicated. As the economists Thomas Piketty and Emmanuel Saez wrote

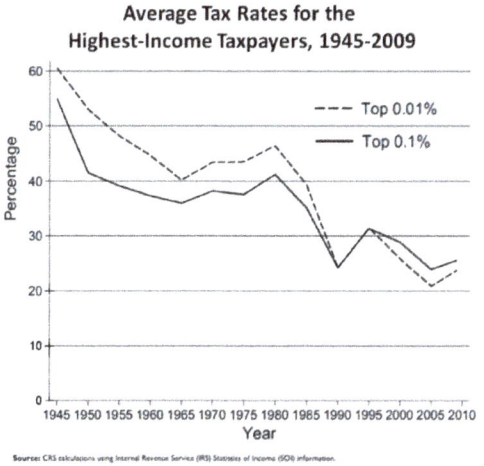

Average Tax Rates for the Highest-Income Taxpayers, 1945-2009

in 2007, "the numerous deductions and exemptions mean that the tax rates listed in the tax tables might be a poor measure of the actual tax burden faced by each income group. In addition, some forms of income, such as capital gains, have traditionally faced lower tax rates, which disproportionately benefits high-income taxpayers."[430]

The effective tax rate—the percentage of your income that you actually end up paying—is what we need to look at when considering whether the current tax system is sufficiently progressive. That data is clear: while the effective tax rate for the average earner has remained at about 14% since World War II, the top marginal rate has fallen from about 50% to about 25% today.[431] Rich people are, more than ever before, where the money is—income disparity is at a record high—but the federal government is taxing them half as much as it used to.[432]

A word about the flat tax, which will likely come up for discussion as even right-wing Republicans in Congress come to realize that the idea is a nonstarter: the only thing to recommend it is its simplicity. No more complicated deductions, no more saving your receipts. It's simple. It's also insane: someone who earns $20,000 a year can't afford to pay taxes at all and shouldn't be asked to do so.

Another idea that conservatives often propose is to replace some or all of the income tax with sales and use taxes. The most recent coherent structure along these lines was a 2023 Republican bill, the Fair Tax Act, that would have eliminated income taxes in favor of a 30% federal sales and use tax on all goods and services sold. It would not, strictly speaking, be a flat-rate sales tax; the Fair Tax Act included a "family consumption allowance" that would have given taxpayers a "prebate," for those who earned less than a percentage of the federal poverty level, designed to offset sales taxes on a baseline level of a defined list of necessities, like groceries.[433] In reality, swapping income tax for sales tax would need a consumer economy-crushing 50% to 60% rate. Republicans no doubt planned to close the gap by slashing social welfare programs. The biggest problem is that sales taxes are highly regressive because everyone, regardless of income

level, pays the same fixed amount which means that lower-income people pay a greater proportion of their income than higher-income people do.

A better idea would be a European-style wealth tax, which targets the super-rich and captures funds from citizens who might not have substantial income but may have inherited wealth (like European aristocrats).

There's nothing wrong with trying to simplify a tax code complicated enough that Americans pay billions of dollars a year to experts to calculate, prepare and file their taxes.[434] Many of the complexities, moreover, are hidden regressive taxes that benefit the rich at the expense of the poor, like the home mortgage interest deduction (rich people own, poor people rent) and the long-term capital gains and qualified dividends deductions (rich people invest, poor people live hand to mouth). But there's nothing complicated about slapping the biggest burden on the wealthiest Americans who, after all, enjoy the best of everything that America has to offer. If you get to sit in the box seats at the arena and eat the best food and hobnob with the top players, you should pay the highest price. Whatever the details, we need a highly progressive tax system. Rich people should pay the most at the highest marginal and effective rates, the middle class should pay less, and the poor should pay nothing at all.

Talking Points:

Trump's plan to replace income tax with tariffs echoes a flawed 1890s model, ignoring modern revenue needs and economic stability.

The 16th Amendment's progressive income tax fueled U.S. growth, funding wars and a safety net absent in the unstable 19th century.

Effective tax rates for the rich dropped from 50% to 25% since the 1960s, despite rising income disparity.

Flat taxes and sales taxes, like the 30% Fair Tax Act, unfairly burden the poor though simplifying a complex system.

A progressive wealth tax targeting the rich, not regressive deductions, would fairly fund society's needs.

16

PROTECT POLITICAL EXPRESSION

"Free speech is the whole thing, the whole ball game. Free speech is life itself."
— *Salman Rushdie*

Your boss can't fire you because of the color of your skin. He can't get rid of you because he doesn't like your religion. Federal law protects you against employment discrimination based on your sex, race, pregnancy status, sexual orientation, gender identity, national origin, disability, genetic information or (if you are over 40) age.[435]

Should your boss be able to deprive you of your ability to pay your rent because you're a Democrat? Or to let your family starve because you're a Republican? Of course not—yet he can.

It's time to add a new protected class to Title VII of the Civil Rights Act of 1964: political expression.

Every year, especially during election years, American employers fire, demote and/or retaliate against loyal workers because they disagree with their constitutionally-guaranteed right to hold a contrary political opinion. While a company may well have a reasonable interest in keeping politics out of the workplace—the owner of a restaurant might not want a waiter to engage in a political debate with a customer, for example—many employees are let go despite never having expressed a political opinion on the job. In most states, they can't sue.

Going after a person because you don't like their politics is unfair. But it's a much bigger problem than a violation of common decency. Because threatening a person's livelihood over their opinions has a chilling effect on the expression of other workers as well, allowing employers to quash one employee's opinions stifles those of dozens of others. Free speech is necessary for a vibrant political system. Allowing companies to fire their workers for expressing their opinion is profoundly undemocratic.

"Most important," a 2022 *New York Times* editorial opined, "freedom of speech is the bedrock of democratic self-government."[436] The paper continued: "If people feel free to express their views in their communities, the democratic process can respond to and resolve competing ideas. Ideas that go unchallenged by opposing views risk becoming weak and brittle rather than being strengthened by tough scrutiny." Fine words, especially for a media organization that doesn't employ any Leftists—or if it does, none free to express their opinions on its opinion pages. But it's a joke. Most Americans do not really feel that they live in a Land of the Free. Only a third of voters said they felt free to express their political views freely, according to a contemporaneous poll.[437]

Nowhere is speech circumscribed more than at work—unless you're a government employee, where you're protected by the First Amendment, or you live in one of the handful of states that protect private-sector workers who express political opinions. Private employers are authoritarian dictatorships where it's best to keep your views to yourself. Your boss's harsh governance should end at the end of your work shift.

Yet it does not.

Employment discrimination in response to political expression is not limited to victims with fringe political views, like the pizza shop[438] and hot dog joint workers[439] who got fired after online sleuths discovered that they had attended a far-right white-nationalist rally in Charlottesville in 2017, or the white-collar workers canned for their presence at the January 6th Capitol riot.[440] To be clear, there was no evidence that the doxxed-and-dumped employees in these situations had expressed their views while on the job. They should not have been let go.

Citizens with vanilla affiliations within the duopoly are targeted as well.

An Alabama woman was famously fired from her job at an insulation company in 2004 for being a Democrat, and more specifically for the Kerry-Edwards bumper sticker on her car, which she parked in the employee parking lot.[441] (Her boss, a Bush supporter, had passed out GOP flyers to his workers.) She had no right to sue.

In 2022 a woman who co-founded a nonprofit that provides financial stipends for Congressional interns was fired by her own board of directors after it learned she was a conservative Republican.[442] She filed a long-shot federal lawsuit, which is pending. More recently, antiwar activists who opposed Israel's war against Gaza found themselves the victims of retaliation.[443] People were fired[444] for personal[445] social-media posts[446] supporting the Palestinians. Pro-Palestine college students were doxxed,[447] expelled[448] and blacklisted[449] by prospective employers.

Google fired fifty employees for staging a protest against the company's contracts with Israeli tech firms; the company said they lost their jobs for causing a disruption rather than because of their opinions.[450] A baker's dozen of federal judges went so far as to declare that they wouldn't hire *any* student who graduated from Columbia University—my alma mater and ground zero for a wave of campus encampment protests—regardless of their views, or lack thereof, about the Israel-Hamas War.[451]

Corporations routinely discriminate based on politics. A 2019 study in the *Journal of Applied Psychology* found that employers are less likely to hire a job applicant when they become aware that they favor different parties.[452] Workers are not stupid. They are well aware that they face political discrimination. A 2020 Cato Institute/YouGov poll found that 32% of workers "personally are worried about missing out on career opportunities or losing their job if their political opinions became known."[453]

Only 32%?

As with the federal minimum wage law, which has failed to keep up with market realities and has been supplanted by state and local regulations with higher minimum wages, the federal government's failure to make political expression a protected class has been supplemented by state and local statutes that do so. Colorado, Louisiana, Minnesota, Missouri, Nebraska, Nevada, South Carolina, Utah and West Virginia are among the states that ban firing for "political activity" including speech. Washington D.C., Iowa, Puerto Rico and the Virgin Islands protect workers from being canned for belonging to a political party.[454] There is no evidence that any of these places have suffered economic hardship as a result of these protections.

The vexing case of Mahmoud Khalil reminds us that the urge to stifle free expression is not limited to the workplace. Khalil, a graduate student at Columbia University's School of International and Public Affairs, was a high-profile protester at a campus encampment protesting Israel's saturation bombing campaign in Gaza during spring 2024. Shortly after taking office, the second Trump Administration, closely allied with

Israel, ordered ICE agents to arrest and try to deport Khalil to his native Syria despite his status as a legal permanent resident with a green card. He was married to an American citizen, who was eight months pregnant when they were accosted by government thugs on a Manhattan street. According to the government itself, Khalil was not suspected of committing any crime. He was, according to President Trump himself, targeted in retaliation for supporting the Palestinian cause in a public space.

This incident followed a series of repressive actions on the Columbia campus, all intended to force students and faculty who support Palestine to shut up. Campus organizations favoring Palestinian rights were banned, public demonstrations were prohibited, public streets across campus were illegally closed to the public, professors were fired and students were expelled.

No one should be punished for peacefully voicing their views, however offensive they seem to some. Retaliation and suppression of speech in any forum, including educational institutions, should be illegal and punishable by civil and criminal penalties.

We have a choice. We can build a politically permissive society where a wide range of views and opinions may be freely voiced (with exceptions for defamation or calling for specific violence) without fear of being discriminated against, understanding that we will often dislike what is being said. Or we can continue to push politics underground, keeping our views so secret that some "shy" voters won't even admit their party affiliation to pollsters.[455] We may feel more comfortable in a seemingly politics-free zone but, as the *Times* editorial above argued, censorship and self-censorship will encourage the spreading of outlandish, stupid and demonstrably wrong ideas that occasionally become the law of the land.

Talking Points:

Federal law bans workplace discrimination on traits like race or sex, but political expression remains unprotected, risking job loss.

States like Colorado protect political speech, proving broader safeguards could work without economic harm.

17

GUARANTEE THE RIGHT TO BODILY AUTONOMY

> *"Bodily autonomy means a person has control over who or what uses their body, for what, and for how long. It's why you can't be forced to donate blood, tissue, or organs. Even if you are dead. Even if you'd save or improve twenty lives. It's why someone can't touch you, have sex with you, or use your body in any way without your continuous consent."*
> —*Hannah Goff*

Much of this book concerns abstract issues like free expression and diplomacy. Your body is no less important than your mind. You have the right to control your body. No one should be able to hit you, inject you, infect you, operate on you or otherwise impact your physical being without your consent.

No. Physical. Assaults. Ever.

The idea of bodily autonomy as a human right clawed its way into history through centuries of rebellion against kings, priests and physicians who treated people like pawns or property. It flickered in the 17th century with John Locke, who argued that life and liberty hinged on controlling your own flesh, though he conveniently ignored women and the enslaved. By the 19th century, suffragettes and abolitionists built upon it, protesting that forced labor and denied votes were thefts of self. The 20th century saw it harden into law with the 1948 Universal Declaration of Human Rights, where Article 3's "right to life, liberty, and security of person" became a vessel for autonomy claims. Mid-century fights over forced sterilization—like the 1927 *Buck v. Bell* case where the U.S. Supreme Court validated eugenics—rolled back rights, but it was *Roe v. Wade* in 1973 that etched bodily autonomy into American political culture, tying it to privacy and choice. Globally, the 1994 Cairo Conference on Population and Development cemented it further, with 179 nations agreeing to reproductive self-rule.

This may seem painfully obvious, like one of the most basic of all basic human rights, but recent history features many examples of the state or other authorities violating this precept. Eugenicists persuaded local and state officials to forcibly sterilize Black women as late as the 1970s.[456] Prison doctors in California did it to female inmates into the 2000s.[457] Immigrants, poor people, unmarried mothers, the disabled, the mentally ill—tens of thousands of victims were denied their right to reproduce in federally funded eugenics programs in 32 states throughout the 20th century.[458] Corporal punishment against children attending public schools is still legal in 17 states and practiced in 14.[459]

When Americans think of the right to make decisions about one's own body and life without fear of coercion or violence, they tend to reference abortion rights. And, though there has been much effort to confuse the issue by both sides, there is nothing complicated about it from the standpoint of the Left. The Left should accept scientific consensus, which is that life begins at conception with the fertilization of the egg and that rejects the facile sophistry of reclassifying whether something is really alive or not based on subjective and constantly evolving definitions of "fetal viability" and the like. Abortion kills unborn babies.

For the Left, however, the right to life of the unborn (or preborn) child inside a woman's womb yields to an even higher societal need, the right of every woman to control her own destiny and what takes place inside her body. Women must have the right to kill their unborn children.

At this writing, biology and science necessitate this stance. If humans were like fish, we could preserve fertilized eggs outside a woman's body and figure out how to care for them after they hatched. If it were medically possible to easily extract an embryo and bring it to term outside a woman's body, we might have to reassess the balance between the right of a new life to come into the world and the right of its mother to choose not to become a mother. But we are not there and, at least for the time being, assume that we never will be. The right to terminate pregnancy is essential for the simple reason that no woman should be forced to bear a child unless she wants to.

Bodily autonomy also extends to your right not to be subjected to forced medical treatments and medicines, including vaccinations. During the Covid pandemic, many Americans were coerced into being injected by the then-new mRNA vaccines developed under emergency authorization protocols rushed through by the Trump Administration. To be clear: I was elated by the quick development of those shots because I suffer from chronic respiratory problems, nearly died from Covid in late 2019 and was terrified that

additional infections by the disease might finish me off. I was thrilled to manage an extra booster shot during a time when government approval was delayed, and pharmacies were discarding millions of unused, expiring doses.

But getting vaccinated against Covid was my personal decision to make, as well as my risk to take—issues that I considered carefully. Doctors, nurses and other healthcare workers were ordered to be vaccinated or lose their jobs, even though it became clear that the vaccines did not prevent or reduce transmission. Teachers, school administrators and students were similarly required to show proof of vaccination in order to participate in the education system. What began as a common-sense attempt to safeguard the population rapidly degenerated into control for control's sake.

Both before and after the recent pandemic, public schools and numerous other institutions required and continue to require proof of vaccinations for childhood and other diseases in order to attend, in accordance with a 1922 Supreme Court case that established the right of school authorities to mandate vaccinations for attending students. This is in clear contravention of the constitutional right to a public education.

And, in the military, which considers soldiers' bodies to be government property, the history of mandatory vaccinations dates back to the Revolutionary War, when General George Washington ordered his troops inoculated against smallpox. Violating soldiers' bodily autonomy has often been cloaked under the guise of national security or operational necessity, with soldiers treated more like equipment than individuals with rights. During the 1950s and 1960s, the Army conducted secret chemical and biological weapons tests, exposing unwitting troops to agents like LSD and VX nerve gas—experiments only unearthed through Freedom of Information Act lawsuits years later. In the late 1990s, the mandatory Anthrax Vaccine Immunization Program forced troops to take an experimental shot linked to severe side effects, injuring over 100,000 service members and prompting Congress to curb such mandates.

The U.S. military has a dark history of violating soldiers' bodily autonomy, exposing them to nuclear tests, Agent Orange, and burn pits while dismissing the fallout. From the 1940s to 1960s, 400,000 "atomic veterans" faced over 200 nuclear blasts with minimal protection, later battling cancers the VA long denied. Vietnam's Agent Orange doused two million troops with dioxin from 1961-1971, causing nerve damage and birth defects, with the government resisting claims until the 1991 Agent Orange Act. Post-9/11 burn pits at bases like Balad burned toxic waste daily, sickening troops with lung diseases and rare cancers, yet the VA rejected most claims until the 2022 PACT Act forced change. It's a grim cycle: expose soldiers, deny harm, and delay justice while they suffer.

As of 2020, before the Covid lockdown, U.S. soldiers stationed in North America were required to be vaccinated for hepatitis B, MMR (measles, mumps, and rubella), Tdap (tetanus, diphtheria, and pertussis), polio, meningococcal disease, and influenza.[460] From Cold War guinea pigs to modern-day vaccine battles, the military's habit of steamrolling consent reveals a grim pattern: when the brass demands compliance, soldiers' bodies become fair game, rights be damned.

Vaccine mandates are justified as necessary to protect public health. *The New England Journal of Medicine* has noted a pattern. Multiple studies show a higher local risk of vaccine-preventable diseases where people refusing vaccination cluster geographically. Outbreaks often start among those who refuse vaccines. They spread quickly within unvaccinated groups and then to other subpopulations."[461]

As compelling as these concerns are, the right to bodily autonomy must take priority even over public health. No one should have to submit to vaccinations against their will in order to keep a job or their place in school. When public-health authorities determine that mass vaccinations are necessary, they should convince citizens, not bully them by threatening their jobs and education.

Talking Points:

You have the right to bodily autonomy, free from assault, forced sterilization, or medical procedures without consent.

Historically, states violated this right, sterilizing Black women and inmates, while 14 states still allow school corporal punishment.

Abortion, though ending a life, is a woman's right to control her body, prioritizing her autonomy over the unborn.

Bodily autonomy trumps public health; persuasion, not coercion, should drive vaccination efforts.

WHAT'S LEFT?

18

PRIORITIZE THE ENVIRONMENT

"Water and air, the two essential fluids on which all life depends, have become global garbage cans."
—Jacques Cousteau

We face so many challenges that the task of choosing which ones to emphasize and which can be edited out for the sake of brevity is nearly impossible. Humanity faces so many injustices that deciding which ones to prioritize for action and resolution is an impossible task. Yet we must and we shall. This process is called "politics."

One matter, however, is so self-evidently far ahead of the rest that calling it an "issue" doesn't come close to doing it justice: the environment. Without a clean, healthy planet to live on, nothing else matters. Human extinction or, failing that, the collapse of civilization that has been predicted by 2050, renders all debate on all other issues and policies moot.[462]

Without a planet that sustains life, college affordability is irrelevant. If you are starving and there isn't enough food, access to free healthcare cannot save you. A nuclear war would not be as devastating or as final as environmental collapse. Without a viable environment to sustain your species, nothing matters.

Ecocide's vast scale feels overwhelming. Splitting it into parts—global warming, climate change, pollution, drought, extinctions, food scarcity—makes it feel manageable. There's nothing wrong with that—we need our best and brightest experts working on every facet of threats to the environment. If ever there has been a phenomenon that requires holistic analysis by society as a whole, however, it's ecocide.[463] You can't separate drought from rising temperatures. These problems are so intricately and inexorably intertwined and intimately interdependent that it's nonsensical to discuss them discretely on a political level, lest we get lost in the dying weeds. There is one issue, the biggest issue ever: humanity is killing its habitat and so is imperiling our survival as a species.

Healthy soil, a basic necessity for life on Earth, including agriculture, is composed of at least three to six percent organic matter. But forty percent of the earth's dirt has so few nutrients that it is completely degraded.[464] By 2050, an additional area the size of South America will be depleted.[465] And that will be with a global population of ten billion.[466] Even if we abolish rapacious capitalism on a near-global scale to favor feeding the hungry over profits—an essential move toward saving ourselves—there won't be enough decent soil to grow enough food to feed us all.

Thirty percent of the world's commercially-fished waters are overfished.[467] Not only does this mean less to eat, fish-free waters are under-oxygenated and have become dead zones for other life. Oceans absorb a third of carbon dioxide emissions—or they did, before ocean acidification and seas of plastics destroyed it.[468]

This is not new. We were warned. "We believe that the damage done to the ocean in the last 20 years is somewhere between 30% and 50%, which is a frightening figure. And this damage carries on at very high speed—to the Indian Ocean, to the Red Sea, to the Mediterranean, to the Atlantic...Everywhere around the world the coral reefs are disappearing at a very great rate, to such an extent we are not sure we will see anything like what we know now," Jacques Cousteau wrote in 1971, for a *New York Times* op-ed titled "Our Oceans Are Dying."[469] Coral reefs host diverse marine life and shield coasts from storms and erosion. They also hold potential for new drugs. They are more than half gone and will be completely dead by 2050.[470]

Ninety-six percent of all ocean life, fish big and small and everything that swims, will vanish too.[471] There's nothing we can do to save them.

The cause is obvious and well known: rapid and extreme global warming caused by humans, pollution and overhunting. We don't have to look far to see that the ocean is boiling: at this writing, water temperatures off the Florida Keys have reached 101°F.[472] Caribbean waters are/were normally an average high of 82°F all year round.[473] The shock isn't that 96% of ocean life is doomed. It's that 4% may *survive*.

A 2023 study found that there is a 95% chance that the Atlantic Meridional Overturning Circulation, a system of ocean currents including the Gulf Stream that carry warm water from the tropics into the North Atlantic, will collapse between now and 2095—it could happen at any time. This happens because it's blocked by cold water from melting glaciers and ice caps flooding the northern ocean.[474] Without the AMOC, as soon as two years from now and no later than seventy, Europe will be buried under sheets of ice, like in the disaster movie *The Day After Tomorrow*.

Several years ago, flying west from Istanbul to New York, my plane's pilot announced that he and his colleagues could see that the Gulf Stream was breaking down—and had been for some time. As a result, we'd arrive earlier than scheduled. He explained why and how this was scary. He urged us to write our congressmen. I wonder if anyone on the plane did. I didn't. What would have been the point? Congress doesn't care or help or act.

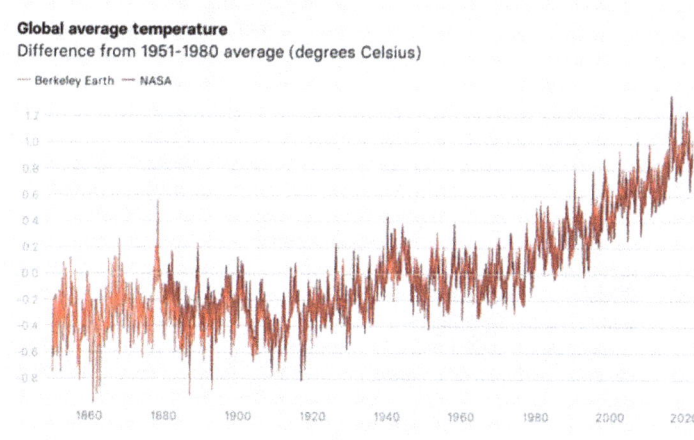

In an apocalyptic film like *2012* or *Armageddon*, politicians and CEOs drop everything to meet a grave threat to humanity. I fantasize that climate change would be taken as seriously. World leaders gather in a blue-lit situation room chock full of computer screens displaying cool infographics, some in business attire, others in exotic garb, all wearing somber holy-crap expressions as the camera pans around. Someone, either the United Nations Secretary General or the U.S. president (these are *American* movies), calls on nations to drop everything, set aside their differences and dedicate all their resources and attention to the existential crisis of climate change, the worst threat—by far—that humanity has ever faced.

Because this is a film, where politicians are sometimes evil but never total idiots, everyone nods in agreement, rolls up their sleeves and gets to work to save humanity.

In the European version of this film, we all die in the end after waging a valiant and noble struggle.

Actual American politics, however, are not as logical or commonsensical as movies.

So it goes, on and on and on. Air pollution kills millions of people a year. Ninety percent of humans breathe air containing sky-high levels of toxic particulate. Within five years, the world will be down to ten percent of its forests; they'll all be gone by 2100. Populations of mammals, fish, birds, reptiles and amphibians plunged an average of 68% between 1970 and 2016.[475] Plenty were lost before and since. Oceans are boiling, hurricanes are more powerful than ever, sea levels are rising, hundreds of thousands of species of animals and plants are going extinct. Even among scientists, few are aware of what we've lost since industrialization.

"It's a common misconception that the human impact on climate began with the large-scale burning of coal and oil in the industrial era," says Julia Pongratz of the Carnegie Institution's Department of Global Ecology.[476] "Actually, humans started to influence the environment thousands of years ago by changing the vegetation cover of the Earth's landscapes when we cleared forests for agriculture." Pongratz was referring to her work on the 13th century Mongol invasion of Central Asia and Eastern Europe. Millions of Genghis Khan's horses chomped their way east, with a massive impact on what are now grassland steppes. Native Americans subjected North America to mass deforestation.[477] Likewise, ancient Romans cut down so many trees that they contributed to global warming.

Rising ocean levels caused by melting glaciers and ice caps and the expansion of water from heat threaten a billion people in Bangladesh, China, India and the Netherlands.478 Low-lying island Pacific nations like the Maldives, Kiribati, Tuvalu and the Marshall Islands are at immediate risk of becoming uninhabitable due to the contamination of arable land by salt-water flooding before they disappear under the waves.479 Droughts, wildfires, more extreme storms and other weather events are becoming bigger, more frequent and deadlier year after year.

Climate change begets so many unforeseen consequences that the ecosystem feels like it's in a doom loop.

In California, where ferocious wildfires devastated Los Angeles early in 2025, a pernicious side effect was the smoke's effect on air quality, which erased the public-health gains from a drop in air pollution from automobiles and factories. Because they release carbon dioxide and other greenhouse gases, wildfires contribute to climate change; wildfires in Canada in 2023 produced more greenhouse gases than the burning of fossil fuels in all but three countries.480

Melting Arctic permafrost releases sediment that contains highly toxic mercury that had been frozen for millennia, threatening five million Arctic residents.481 The release of methane from thawing permafrost causes more global warming, thaws more permafrost and releases more methane.482 Ancient diseases we don't think about, like bubonic plague, could make a comeback. A 12-year-old boy died and dozens of people fell ill due to an outbreak of anthrax in Siberia in 2016. It was released by the thawing of permafrost covering a reindeer carcass. Microbes over 400,000 years old have been found in permafrost.483 So were a pair of prehistoric roundworms from 46,000 years ago—they came back to life after being unfrozen.484

A recent survey of successful prognosticators found that the average forecaster believes there is a six percent chance that humanity will go extinct by 2100 and a ten percent chance that a catastrophic environmental event or series of events could kill ten percent of global population.485 (World War II killed under four percent.) Considering that we've been around for hundreds of thousands of years, those are high odds.

Many climate experts believe that the climate crisis poses a relatively low risk of human extinction.486 Others disagree. Calling the existential threat to *Homo sapiens* "dangerously unexplored," a 2022 statement487 in the *Proceedings of the National Academy of Sciences* warned: "Facing a future of accelerating climate change while [staying] blind to worst-case scenarios is naive risk management at best and fatally foolish at worst."[488]

Dr. Luke Kemp at the University of Cambridge's Centre for the Study of Existential Risk, who led the analysis, explained: "Paths to disaster are not limited to the direct impacts of high temperatures, such as extreme weather events. Knock-on effects such as financial crises, conflict and new disease outbreaks could trigger other calamities." A cyclone might destroy infrastructure needed to cool people during a heatwave. Crops could fail. Countries might go to war over geoengineering.

A relatively low risk of catastrophe should be weighted more heavily than a higher risk of problems with lower consequences. If there were a six percent probability that an asteroid impact might wipe out the human race, no sane astrophysicist would advise us not to worry about it. Logic suggests that stopping that asteroid would become the world's top priority, with massive resources directed toward averting the catastrophe as lesser threats were put on hold. Six percent is too high to cross your fingers and hope for the best. It follows logically that we should do the same now when it comes to the environment.

To the contrary, we are actively making things worse. We are buying bigger cars, drilling more oil, and prioritizing short-term economic growth over slightly-less-short-term human and natural survival. Our politicians act as though global warming/climate change was not settled science. And the media dutifully amplifies that disinformation.

The Trump administration has unleashed a relentless assault on environmental protections, weak as they were previously, slashing over 100 rules that partially safeguarded air, water, and wildlife, all to increase fossil fuel profits. They yanked the U.S. out of the Paris Climate Agreement, gutted the Clean Power Plan and torched vehicle emissions standards, which will pump an extra billion tons of carbon dioxide into the atmosphere by 2030, according to the EPA. Rules on methane leaks, mercury emissions and coal ash were eliminated or watered down, with the administration shrugging off studies predicting thousands of premature deaths—80,000 per decade, per Harvard estimates. The Interior Department opened up pristine lands like the Arctic National Wildlife Refuge to drilling, shredding habitat protections, while the EPA's budget got chopped by 31% to cripple enforcement. Environmental justice and climate research took a backseat as Trump's picks—ex-coal lobbyist Andrew Wheeler and oil-friendly Scott Pruitt—steered the agency into a tailspin, ignoring their own scientists. Courts are striking down some rollbacks but the damage is already done.

WHAT'S LEFT?

The U.S. and other nations—but we're Americans, so let's us do us and hope other countries join us after we set an example—should adopt a prime directive into our constitutions that puts the planet first. It should read something like this:

In any situation where a conflict arises between a policy or law or regulation that would benefit the environment and a competing concern, including but not limited to the economy, nature should come first.

Talking Points:

Environmental collapse trumps all issues, threatening human survival by 2050 with no viable planet left.

Soil degradation and overfished oceans signal food scarcity, worsened by climate change and pollution.

Ocean warming and AMOC collapse could freeze Europe, while coral reefs may vanish by 2050.

Wildfires, thawing permafrost, and ancient diseases amplify a doom loop of ecological disasters.

A six percent extinction risk demands prioritizing the environment over economy in policy.

WHAT'S LEFT?

19

A PEOPLE'S GOVERNMENT IS TRANSPARENT

"Nothing so diminishes democracy as secrecy."
—*Ramsey Clark, Attorney General Under LBJ 1967-1969*

A government by the people and for the people isn't what we have, obviously. Still, it's a good idea.

Whatever the structure of the government that ultimately comes to power under the Left—and please don't ask me what that will be because determining such things is not my job nor something I'd be good at nor would it be appropriate for me to try even if I were. It's inappropriate for one person to decide; it's a collective responsibility. Still, no government can claim accountability to its people unless they know what's happening.

That's certainly not the case here in the United States. Throughout his four years in office, for example, President Joe Biden hardly ever reported what he was doing to we, the people. There were very few speeches from the Oval Office or press conferences where he answered questions from reporters in an unscripted fashion. Biden was the latest in a line of presidents since Richard Nixon who have consistently reduced their interactions with the American people or with journalists. Very few members of Congress or the United States Senate spend much time talking to their constituents either in person, by phone or otherwise. In fact, it's almost impossible to get through to a member of Congress via email, much less to get an answer, personal or otherwise.

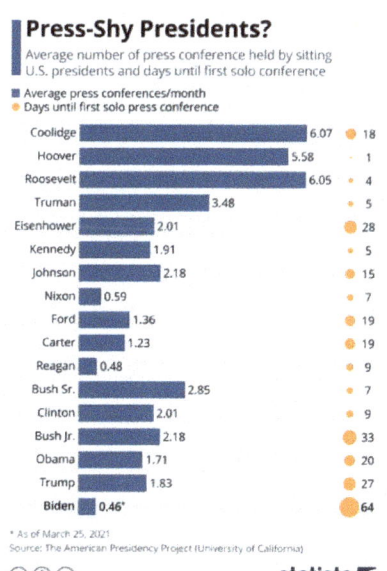

When political scientists and sociologists search for explanations for voters' diminishing trust in government and other institutions throughout the United States and Western Europe, experts don't often mention the most evident explanation: political leaders and governments don't seem to feel any pressure whatsoever to talk to the people whom they claim to serve. They announce, they proclaim, yet they never explain. And so they don't get any buy-in.

In a Left government, there would be very few secrets. Every meeting in every department and agency, including at the highest levels, would be livestreamed and video archived. Private meetings, for example between lobbyists and government representatives, would be illegal. Diplomatic meetings between heads of state would be live-cast. Every document would be a public record searchable on the Internet. Only the most highly classified material concerning grave and present security threats could be considered for secret treatment, and even then, those should be made public as soon as practicable.

Heads of state and cabinet and agency heads would be required to meet with the press and members of the public frequently, at least weekly but daily doesn't seem unreasonable, to answer questions and to report on their activities.

Hey, government!

You work for us.

It's not the other way around.

Talking Points:

U.S. government lacks accountability, with leaders like Biden rarely engaging directly with the public. Congress and senators avoid constituents, dodging emails and personal interaction, eroding trust.

A Left government would mandate transparency, live-streaming all meetings and banning private lobbyist talks.

Diplomatic talks and documents would be public, with minimal secrets only for urgent security threats.

Leaders would face weekly or daily press and public Q&A sessions to ensure openness.

20

WHAT IS TO BE DONE NOW?

What, you may be asking (maybe you have long been asking), can or should I do?

I understand that there isn't a Leftist political party or militant organization I can join, not yet anyway. I get that individual action can't change society. But what am I supposed to do, just sit around and hope that things will eventually improve?

Talk about politics whenever you can. Whenever you have the opportunity to engage your friends, partners, coworkers, neighbors and total strangers, argue for ambitious rather than moderate solutions to the problems you are discussing.

Organize at the local level. In Manhattan, where I live, it's easy to join local community boards. In your community, you might have better luck on the school board.

Spread radical ideas online. Post comments to news media message boards and social media. Much politicking takes place in the digital town square. It's also where you have an opportunity to change hearts and minds.

Fight off moderation and centrism and corporatism everywhere.

Though frustrating, a big part of being a revolutionist involves waiting.

Wait and watch.

When spasms of radical political activity occur, try to identify whether the actions and the people undertaking them are authentic and revolutionary or are, as is more often the case, opportunistic and incrementalist—i.e., performative. A recent example of the latter was the People's Party, formerly called the Movement for a People's Party, founded in 2017 by some former 2016 Bernie Sanders staffers. The closest this progressive-leaning entity came to participating in electoral politics was the nine days in June 2023 during which Cornel West was its presidential candidate. It has never held an in-person event or rally and appears to have died, the victim of internal squabbling. For the 400,000 people who "attended" its virtual convention during the 2020 pandemic lockdown, this is yet another disappointment. The top-down organizational structure of the PP ought to have alerted Leftists to the fact that it was yet another waste of time destined to fail. Another red flag was its emphasis on celebrity bold-face Democrats.

"Hands Off" rallies erupted across the U.S. on April 5, 2025, with over 1,300 events in all 50 states, drawing tens of thousands to protest Trump's tariffs, deportations and agency gutting, painting it as a billionaire power grab. So far, so good.

But these weren't scrappy grassroots uprisings but slick operations orchestrated by Democratic front groups like MoveOn, Indivisible and Women's March, flexing their muscle with a coalition of unions, NGOs, and center-left outfits. Rallygoers waved signs like "Hands Off Our Democracy" and "Protect Our Constitution," chanting against Trump and Elon Musk, while speakers like Democratic Congressman Jamie Raskin—who supports Israel and votes for huge defense bills—fired up crowds with warnings of dictatorship. Bizarrely, these groups included "Hands Off NATO" among their demands, despite its decades of bombing innocent civilians from Libya to Afghanistan. The rallies, fueled by justifiable panic over Social Security and civil rights, were a tool of a Democratic machine that is the ultimate enemy of the Left.

Develop and support radical action for radical problems.

You might cite the issues and solutions suggested here in *What's Left*. Or you may hate them and come up with an entirely different set of problems you care about more and/or prefer to fix in entirely different ways. There will be issues and solutions you learn about elsewhere. Or they may be *your ideas*. Do not dismiss your own ideas simply because they're yours!

Where and how radical solutions originate does not matter. Push them, write about them, talk about them, think about them, spread them around however you can.

How will you know when a movement is real and truly Left?

You will just *know*.

In the meantime, before that movement materializes, it's about ideas. Ideas for a better world, a better country, a better way for us to be with one another.

There's no skipping ahead. Start with ideas.

CITATIONS

Chapter 1: What Is "The Left"?

[1] Pew Research Center. 2011. "The American-Western European Values Gap." Pew Research Center. November 17, 2011, https://www.pewresearch.org/global/2011/11/17/the-american-western-european-values-gap.

[2] Saad, Lydia. 2023. "Democrats' Identification as Liberal Now 54%, a New High." Gallup, January 12, 2023. https://news.gallup.com/poll/467888/democrats-identification-liberal-new-high.aspx.

[3] Melcher, Cody R. 2022. "What Do Socialists Actually Believe?" *Jacobin*, May 25, 2022. https://jacobin.com/2022/05/survey-socialists-data-liberals-poll-racial-resentment.

[4] Nadeem, Reem. 2022. "Modest Declines in Positive Views of 'Socialism' and 'Capitalism' in U.S." Pew Research Center, September 19, 2022. https://www.pewresearch.org/politics/2022/09/19/modest-declines-in-positive-views-of-socialism-and-capitalism-in-u-s.

[5] Melcher, Cody R. 2022. "What Do Socialists Actually Believe?" *Jacobin*, May 25, 2022. https://jacobin.com/2022/05/survey-socialists-data-liberals-poll-racial-resentment.

[6] Gallup, Inc. 2021. "Socialism, Capitalism Ratings in U.S. Unchanged." Gallup, December 6, 2021. https://news.gallup.com/poll/357755/socialism-capitalism-ratings-unchanged.aspx.

[7] Gallup, Inc. 2021. "Deconstructing Americans' Views of Socialism, Capitalism." Gallup, December 17, 2021. https://news.gallup.com/opinion/polling-matters/358178/deconstructing-americans-views-socialism-capitalism.aspx.

[8] Wikipedia Contributors. 2020. "2016 Democratic Party Presidential Primaries." Wikipedia, July 24, 2020. https://en.wikipedia.org/wiki/2016_Democratic_Party_presidential_primaries.

[9] Wikipedia Contributors. 2022. "Results of the 2020 Democratic Party Presidential Primaries." Wikipedia, December 3, 2022. https://en.wikipedia.org/wiki/Results_of_the_2020_Democratic_Party_presidential_primaries.

[10] Budowsky, Brent. 2017. "The DNC Owes Bernie Sanders and All Dems an Apology." *The Hill*, November 2, 2017. https://thehill.com/opinion/campaign/358389-the-dnc-owes-bernie-sanders-and-all-dems-an-apology.

[11] Wikipedia Contributors. 2024. "List of Democratic Socialists of America Public Officeholders." Wikipedia, August 4, 2024. https://en.wikipedia.org/wiki/List_of_Democratic_Socialists_of_America_public_officeholders.

[12] Wikipedia Contributors. 2019. "Anti-Communism." Wikipedia, March 7, 2019. https://en.wikipedia.org/wiki/Anti-communism.

[13] Wikipedia Contributors. 2019. "Eugene v. Debs." Wikipedia, October 27, 2019. https://en.wikipedia.org/wiki/Eugene_V._Debs.

[14] Reuters Staff. 2020. "True Claim: Poll Shows 76 Percent of Democrats Say They Would Vote for a Socialist for President." Reuters, March 11, 2020. https://www.reuters.com/article/world/true-claimpoll-shows-76-percent-of-democrats-say-they-would-vote-for-a-sociali-iduskbn20x35h/.

[15] Robbins, Christopher. 2011. https://gothamist.com/staff/christopher-robbins. 2025. "Justice Dept: Homeland Security Advised Raids on Occupy Wall Street Camps." *Gothamist*, November 16, 2011. https://gothamist.com/news/justice-dept-homeland-security-advised-raids-on-occupy-wall-street-camps.

[16] Wikipedia Contributors. 2024. "List of Left and Far-Left Parties in Europe." Wikipedia., October 29, 2024.

[17] Green Party. "Ballot Access." www.gp.org. n.d. https://www.gp.org/ballot_access.

[18] Memory Alpha. 2018. "Who are the Borg." "Borg." Memory Alpha, 2018. https://memory-alpha.fandom.com/wiki/Borg.

[19] Gill, Dee. 2020. "Voters Often Opt for Candidate They Expect to Win." *UCLA Anderson Review*, December 9, 2020. https://anderson-review.ucla.edu/voters-often-opt-for-candidate-they-expect-to-win

[20] Morton, Rebecca B. and Ou, Kai. 2015. "What motivates bandwagon voting behavior: Altruism or a desire to win?" *Science Direct*, 2015. https://www.sciencedirect.com/science/article/abs/pii/S0176268015000488

[21] Cooper, Michael. 2012. "Conservatives Sowed Idea of Health Care Mandate, Only to Spurn It Later." *The New York Times*, February 14, 2012, sec. Health. https://www.nytimes.com/2012/02/15/health/policy/health-care-mandate-was-first-backed-by-conservatives.html.

[22] Song, Zirui. 2021. "Making the Affordable Care Act Marketplace More Affordable." *JAMA Health Forum* 2, no. 5 (May): e210276. https://doi.org/10.1001/jamahealthforum.2021.0276.

[23] Pearl, Robert. 2023. "U.S. Healthcare: A Conglomerate of Monopolies." *Forbes*, January 16, 2023. https://www.forbes.com/sites/robertpearl/2023/01/16/us-healthcare-a-conglomerate-of-monopolies.

[24] KFF. 2022. Network Adequacy Standards and Enforcement." KFF, February 3, 2022. https://www.kff.org/affordable-care-act/issue-brief/network-adequacy-standards-and-enforcement.

[25] Norman, Jane. "Obama Shying Away from Public Option—or Not?" Commonwealth Fund, August 17, 2019. https://www.commonwealthfund.org/publications/newsletter-article/obama-shying-away-public-option-or-not.

[26] McGreal, Chris. 2009. "Why Joe Lieberman Is Holding Barack Obama to Ransom over Healthcare." *The Guardian*, December 16, 2009. https://www.theguardian.com/world/2009/dec/16/joe-lieberman-barack-obama-us-healthcare.

[27] Wilson, Scott. 2009. "Obama Rejects Criticism on Health Legislation." NBC News, December 22, 2009. https://www.nbcnews.com/id/wbna34533255.

[28] Thomson-DeVeaux, Amelia. 2019. "Americans Want the Health Care System to Change. Just Not Their Own Health Care." FiveThirtyEight, December 19, 2019. https://fivethirtyeight.com/features/americans-want-the-health-care-system-to-change-just-not-their-own-health-care.

[29] Sanchez, Gabriel R. 2024. "Health Care Costs Are a Top Concern for Voters in the 2024 Election." Brookings, July 3, 2024. https://www.brookings.edu/articles/health-care-costs-are-a-top-concern-for-voters-in-the-2024-election.

[30] Radnofsky, Louise. 2016. "President Obama Pushes for 'Public Option' in Affordable Care Act." Professional Group Plans, July 12, 2016. https://www.pgpbenefits.com/president-obama-pushes-public-option-affordable-care-act.

[31] Rall, Ted. *The Anti-American Manifesto*. Seven Stories Press, 2011.

[32] Ewing, Jack. 2020. "United States Is the Richest Country in the World, and It Has the Biggest Wealth Gap." *The New York Times*, September 23, 2020, sec. Business. https://www.nytimes.com/2020/09/23/business/united-states-is-the-richest-country-in-the-world-and-it-has-the-biggest-wealth-gap.html.

Chapter 2: Identity Politics Must Die

[33] Ence, Clara. 2024. "Meet the Top 50 Campaign Donors Pumping Millions into the 2024 Election." *The Washington Post*, August 26, 2024. https://www.washingtonpost.com/elections/interactive/2024/biggest-campaign-donors-election-2024.

[34] Svitek, Patrick. 2024. "On Differences with Biden, Harris Says 'Not a Thing That Comes to Mind.'" *The Washington Post*, October 8, 2024. https://www.washingtonpost.com/politics/2024/10/08/harris-biden-differences-view-howard-stern.

35 Data for Progress. 2025. "Democrats and Democratic-Leaning Independents Want the DNC to Align with Working People, Not Corporate Interests." *Data for Progress*, January 8, 2025. https://www.dataforprogress.org/blog/2025/1/8/democrats-and-democratic-leaning-independents-want-the-dnc-to-align-with-working-people-not-corporate-interests

36 Flores, Andrew R., Stotzer, Rebecca L., Meyer, Ilan H. and Langton, Lynn L. 2022. "Hate Crimes against LGBT People: National Crime Victimization Survey, 2017-2019." Edited by Syed Ghulam Sarwar Shah. *Plos One* 17, no. 12 (December): e0279363. https://doi.org/10.1371/journal.pone.0279363.

37 Nietzel, Michael T. 2024. "Women Continue to Outpace Men in College Enrollment and Graduation." *Forbes*, August 7, 2024. https://www.forbes.com/sites/michaeltnietzel/2024/08/07/women-continue-to-outpace-men-in-college-enrollment-and-graduation.

38 Modi, Monica N., Sheallah Palmer and Alicia Armstrong. 2014. "The Role of Violence against Women Act in Addressing Intimate Partner Violence: A Public Health Issue." *Journal of Women's Health* 23, no. 3 (March): 253–59. https://doi.org/10.1089/jwh.2013.4387.

39 Statista. 2022. "Median Household Income by Race and Ethnicity U.S. 2022." *Statista*, 2022. https://www.statista.com/statistics/233324/median-household-income-in-the-united-states-by-race-or-ethnic-group.

40 Kang, Jay Caspian. 2019. "Where Does Affirmative Action Leave Asian-Americans?" *The New York Times*, August 28, 2019, sec. Magazine. https://www.nytimes.com/2019/08/28/magazine/where-does-affirmative-action-leave-asian-americans.html.

41 Alesina, Alberto and Stantcheva, Stefanie. "Mobility: Real and Perceived." *Harvard City Journal*, accessed January 13, 2025. https://scholar.harvard.edu/files/stantcheva/files/city_journal_alesina_stantcheva.pdf.

42 Johnson, Sharon. 2016. "Wages, Guns, Student Debt: See How Sanders and Clinton Stack up." *Women's ENews*, May 24, 2016. https://womensenews.org/2016/05/wages-guns-student-debt-see-how-sanders-and-clinton-stack-up.

43 Lynch, Colum. 2020. "Bernie Sanders May Become the First U.S. President in Decades to Declare Israel's Settlements Illegal." *Foreign Policy*, February 25, 2020. https://foreignpolicy.com/2020/02/25/bernie-sanders-presidential-election-jewish-israel-middle-east.

44 Voice of America. 2009. "African Americans React with Tears, Pride to Obama Victory." Voice of America, November 1, 2009. https://www.voanews.com/a/a-13-2008-11-05-voa77/404685.html.

45 Cohen, Sharon and Hajela, Deepti. 2021. "Obama Racial Legacy: Pride, Promise, Regret _ and Deep Rift." AP News, April 28, 2021. https://apnews.com/article/jackie-robinson-barack-obama-chicago-politics-il-state-wire-29b24a7985a442d8b890261da99cad86.

46 Gallup, Inc. 2016. "Presidential Approval Ratings--Barack Obama." Gallup, April 21, 2016. https://news.gallup.com/poll/116479/barack-obama-presidential-job-approval.aspx.

47 Owusu, Tony. 2017. "Barack Obama Is Now among 10 Highest-Paid Public Speakers." *The Street*, September 25, 2017. https://www.thestreet.com/investing/highest-paid-public-speakers-14315669.

48 Lerer, Lisa, King, Maya and Epstein, Reid J. 2024. "Kamala Harris Created a Wave of Energy. How Long Can Democrats Ride It?" *The New York Times*, July 31, 2024. https://www.nytimes.com/2024/07/31/us/politics/kamala-harris-democrats-campaign.html.

49 Epstein, Reid J. 2024. "Why the Kamala Harris of Four Years Ago Could Haunt Her in 2024." *The New York Times*, July 29, 2024, sec. U.S. https://www.nytimes.com/2024/07/29/us/politics/kamala-harris-2020-positions.html.

[50] Amazon.com. 2025. "I'm with Her Kamala Vote for 2024 President Kamala-Harris T-Shirt : Clothing, Shoes & Jewelry." Amazon.com, 2025. https://www.amazon.com/Her-Kamala-Vote-President-Kamala-Harris/dp/B0D9VXB8Z5.

[51] BBC News. 2014. "Obama Plays down Marijuana Dangers." BBC News, January 20, 2014, sec. US & Canada. https://www.bbc.com/news/world-us-canada-25805206.

[52] Reuters Staff. 2009. "Obama Says Abortion Rights Law Not a Top Priority." Reuters, April 30, 2009. https://www.reuters.com/article/markets/us/obama-says-abortion-rights-law-not-a-top-priority-idUSN29466420.

[53] Lowrey, Annie. 2009. "CIA Officers Granted Immunity, Obama to Release Torture Memos." *Foreign Policy*, April 16, 2009. https://foreignpolicy.com/2009/04/16/cia-officers-granted-immunity-obama-to-release-torture-memos.

[54] U.S. Central Command. 2009. "President Calls for 30,000 More U.S. Troops in Afghanistan." U.S. Central Command, December 2, 2009. https://www.centcom.mil/media/news-articles/News-Article-View/Article/883960/president-calls-for-30000-more-us-troops-in-afghanistan.

[55] Collinson, Stephen. 2014. "Obama Sends 1,500 Troops to Iraq." CNN, November 7, 2014. https://www.cnn.com/2014/11/07/politics/obama-sends-troops-to-iraq/index.html.

[56] Purkiss, Jessica and Serle, Jack. 2017. "Obama's Covert Drone War in Numbers: Ten Times More Strikes than Bush." *The Bureau of Investigative Journalism*, January 17, 2017. https://www.thebureauinvestigates.com/stories/2017-01-17/obamas-covert-drone-war-in-numbers-ten-times-more-strikes-than-bush.

[57] Johnston, Jake. 2017. "How Pentagon Officials May Have Encouraged a 2009 Coup in Honduras." *The Intercept*, August 29, 2017. https://theintercept.com/2017/08/29/honduras-coup-us-defense-departmetnt-center-hemispheric-defense-studies-chds.

[58] Greenwald, Glenn. 2013. "The Untouchables: How the Obama Administration Protected Wall Street from Prosecutions." *The Guardian*, January 23, 2013. https://www.theguardian.com/commentisfree/2013/jan/23/untouchables-wall-street-prosecutions-obama.

[59] Volle, Adam. 2022. "Occupy Wall Street." *Encyclopedia Britannica*, November 9, 2022. https://www.britannica.com/topic/Occupy-Wall-Street.

[60] Johnston, Jake. 2017. "How Pentagon Officials May Have Encouraged a 2009 Coup in Honduras." *The Intercept*, August 29, 2017. https://theintercept.com/2017/08/29/honduras-coup-us-defense-departmetnt-center-hemispheric-defense-studies-chds.

[61] Saad, Lydia. 2023. "Democrats' Identification as Liberal Now 54%, a New High." Gallup, January 12, 2023. https://news.gallup.com/poll/467888/democrats-identification-liberal-new-high.aspx.

[62] Gaffney, Adam. 2024. "What Happens to American Healthcare after November?" *The Nation*, July 31, 2024. https://www.thenation.com/article/society/healthcare-trump-harris/.

[63] Wikipedia Contributors. 2019. "Trust." Wikipedia, October 25, 2019. https://en.wikipedia.org/wiki/Trust.

[64] Illing, Sean. 2018. "What Is Fascism? A Yale Philosopher Explains How It Works." Vox, September 19, 2018. https://www.vox.com/2018/9/19/17847110/how-fascism-works-donald-trump-jason-stanley.

[65] Morlin-Yron, Sophie. 2016. "Why Nearly Half of Africans Don't Trust Elections." CNN, September 26, 2016. https://www.cnn.com/2016/09/25/africa/africa-view-election-distrust/index.html.

Chapter 3: Where To Start? Defend the Pentagon

[66] Wolff, Jonathan. 2017. "Karl Marx." Edited by Edward N. Zalta. *Stanford Encyclopedia of Philosophy*. Metaphysics Research Lab, Stanford University, 2017. https://plato.stanford.edu/entries/marx.

[67] Marx, Karl. 1867. "Economic Manuscripts: Capital Vol. I - Chapter Twenty-Five." Marxists.org, 1867. https://www.marxists.org/archive/marx/works/1867-c1/ch25.htm.

[68] Sherman, Erik. 2015. "America Is the Richest, and Most Unequal, Country." *Fortune*, September 30, 2015. https://fortune.com/2015/09/30/america-wealth-inequality.

[69] Rall, Ted. 2024. "What's Left." Rall.com, January 30, 2024. https://rall.com/2024/01/30/whats-left-socialism-marxism.

[70] U.S. Treasury Department. 2023. "Your Guide to America's Finances." Treasury.gov, 2023. https://fiscaldata.treasury.gov/americas-finance-guide.

[71] U.S. Federal Reserve Bank. 2024. "National Totals of State and Local Tax Revenue: Total Taxes for the United States." Stlouisfed.org, 2024. https://fred.stlouisfed.org/series/qtaxtotalqtaxcat1usno.

[72] HowStuffWorks. 2000. "If All the Money in the U.S. Only Totals $6 Trillion How Can the New York Stock Exchange Have Stocks Valued at $15 Trillion?" HowStuffWorks, April 1, 2000. https://money.howstuffworks.com/question241.htm.

[73] Fram, Alan and Lemire, Jonathan. 2018. "Trump: Why Allow Immigrants from 'Shithole Countries'?" AP News, January 12, 2018. https://apnews.com/article/immigration-north-america-donald-trump-ap-top-news-international-news-fdda2ff0b877416c8ae1c1a77a3cc425.

[74] Haynie, Devon. 2020. "Report: American Quality of Life Declines over Past Decade." *U.S. News & World Report*, 2020. https://www.usnews.com/news/best-countries/articles/2020-09-11/a-global-anomaly-the-us-declines-in-annual-quality-of-life-report.

[75] Cernadas, Gisela. 2023. "Actual U.S. Military Spending Reached $1.537 Trillion in 2022—More than Twice Acknowledged Level: New." *Monthly Review*, November 2023. https://monthlyreview.org/2023/11/01/actual-u-s-military-spending-reached-1-53-trillion-in-2022-more-than-twice-acknowledged-level-new-estimates-based-on-u-s-national-accounts.

[76] Mallinder, Lorraine. 2023. "'Elephant in the room': The US military's devastating carbon footprint." *Al Jazeera*, December 12, 2023. https://www.aljazeera.com/news/2023/12/12/elephant-in-the-room-the-us-militarys-devastating-carbon-footprint

[77] U.S. Department of Veterans Affairs. "PFAS - Perfluoroalkyl and polyfluoroalkyl substances." *Public Health*. n.d. https://www.publichealth.va.gov/exposures/pfas.asp

[78] Johnson, Chalmers. "The Sorrows of Empire: Militarism, Secrecy, and the End of the Republic." Amazon.com. 2025. https://www.amazon.com/Sorrows-Empire-Militarism-Republic-American/dp/0805077979.

[79] Kruse, Michael. 2015. "Where in the World Is the U.S. Military?" *Politico*, July/August 2015. https://www.politico.com/magazine/story/2015/06/us-military-bases-around-the-world-119321.

[80] U.S. Defense Department. 2025. "ContentKeeper Content Filtering." Defense.gov, 2025. https://www.defense.gov/News/News-Stories/Article/Article/3659809/3-us-service-members-killed-others-injured-in-jordan-following-drone-attack.

[81] Statista. 2023. "Military Expenditure in Brazil 2023." *Statista*, 2023. https://www.statista.com/statistics/794473/military-spending-value-brazil.

82 Rev.com. 2024. "Alexandria Ocasio-Cortez (AOC) Calls to Cut Pentagon Budget Speech Transcript." Rev.com, 2024. https://www.rev.com/blog/transcripts/alexandria-ocasio-cortez-aoc-calls-to-cut-pentagon-budget-speech-transcript.

83 Johnson, Jake. 2023. "Just 11 Senators Voted for a 10 Percent Cut to Military Spending." *Truthout*, July 28, 2023. https://truthout.org/articles/just-11-senators-voted-for-a-10-percent-cut-to-military-spending.

84 Rao, Pallavi. 2023. "Which Countries Are the Most Polarized?" *Visual Capitalist*, January 19, 2023. https://www.visualcapitalist.com/polarization-across-28-countries.

85 DeSilver, Drew. 2022. "The Polarization in Today's Congress Has Roots That Go Back Decades." Pew Research Center, March 10, 2022. https://www.pewresearch.org/short-reads/2022/03/10/the-polarization-in-todays-congress-has-roots-that-go-back-decades.

86 Warburton, Moira. 2024. "Why Congress Is Becoming Less Productive." Reuters, March 12, 2024. https://www.reuters.com/graphics/usa-congress/productivity/egpbabmkwvq.

87 O'Brien, Connor. 2024. "House Republicans Narrowly Pass Defense Bill Loaded with Culture War Issues." *Politico*, June 14, 2024. https://www.politico.com/news/2024/06/14/house-republicans-narrowly-pass-defense-bill-loaded-with-culture-war-issues-00163453.

88 Donnelly, John M. 2023. "Members Want $26 Billion for Programs the Pentagon Didn't Seek." *Roll Call*, December 2023. https://rollcall.com/2023/12/01/members-want-26-billion-for-programs-the-pentagon-didnt-seek.

89 San Diego Union-Tribune. 2009. "How Obama Voted on War Funding Bills in Congress." *San Diego Union-Tribune*, April 9, 2009. https://www.sandiegouniontribune.com/2009/04/09/how-obama-voted-on-war-funding-bills-in-congress.

90 Vote Smart. 2024. "Vote Smart." 2024. https://justfacts.votesmart.org/candidate/key-votes/27110/bernie-sanders/22/defense.

91 U.S. Army Corps of Engineers. 2012. "The Geopolitics of the United States, Part 1: The Inevitable Empire." 2012. https://www.mvd.usace.army.mil/Portals/52/docs/stratfor%20article.pdf.

92 U.S. Army Corps of Engineers. 2012. "The Geopolitics of the United States, Part 1: The Inevitable Empire." 2012. https://www.mvd.usace.army.mil/Portals/52/docs/stratfor%20article.pdf.

93 U.S. National Park Service. "Japanese Occupation Site National Historic Landmark." nps.gov. n.d. https://www.nps.gov/places/japanese-occupation-site.htm.

94 World Population Review. 2022. "How Many Countries Has the Us Invaded 2022." *World Population Review*. n.d. https://worldpopulationreview.com/country-rankings/how-many-countries-has-the-us-invaded.

95 Kelly, Christopher and Laycock, Stuart. 2015. "America Invades." Book Pub Network.

96 The Heritage Foundation. 2019. "The Growing Threat of Cyberattacks." The Heritage Foundation, 2019. https://www.heritage.org/cybersecurity/heritage-explains/the-growing-threat-cyberattacks.

97 Jawad, Ashar. 2023. "5 Countries That Have No Army, Navy or Air Force." *Insider Monkey*, November 18, 2023. https://www.insidermonkey.com/blog/5-countries-that-have-no-army-navy-or-air-force-12242721.

98 Duff-Brown, Beth. 2022. "Californians Living with Handgun Owners More than Twice as Likely to Die by Homicide, Study Finds." Stanford University, April 4, 2022. https://med.stanford.edu/news/all-news/2022/04/handguns-homicide-risk.html.

Chapter 4: We Waste $3.8 Trillion. Let's Spend It on People

[99] Bowman, Alisa. 2024. "What's behind the decline in American life expectancy?" Mayo Clinic, August 16, 2024. https://mcpress.mayoclinic.org/healthy-aging/whats-behind-the-decline-in-american-life-expectancy/

[100] Rall, Ted. 2024. "What's Left 2: We're a Rich Country. Let's Act like It." Ted Rall's Rallblog, February 5, 2024. https://rall.com/2024/02/05/whats-left-2-were-a-rich-country-lets-act-like-it.

[101] Shirazi, Elina. 2023. "Rand Paul Unveils 'Festivus' List of $900B in Wasteful Government Spending." NewsNation, December 26, 2023. https://www.newsnationnow.com/politics/rand-paul-festivus-report-wasteful-government-spending.

[102] Luhby, Tami. 2023. "Interest Payments on the Nation's Debt Are Soaring. It's Only Going to Get Worse." CNN, November 16, 2023. https://www.cnn.com/2023/11/16/politics/interest-payments-federal-government-debt/index.html.

[103] Pressley, Ayanna. 2022. "Pressley Calls for Better Tools to Combat Inflation, Protect Workers and Families." Ayanna Pressley, June 23, 2022. https://pressley.house.gov/2022/06/23/pressley-calls-for-better-tools-to-combat-inflation-protect-workers-and-families.

[104] Statista. 2022. "U.S. Banker Opinion on Rising Interest Rates 2022." Statista, 2022. https://www.statista.com/statistics/1121091/us-banker-perspective-fed-interest-rates.

[105] Vernengo, Matías. 2023. "Inflation Paranoia and the Return of the New Consensus in Macroeconomics ." ProMarket, July 12, 2023. https://www.promarket.org/2023/07/12/inflation-paranoia-and-the-return-of-the-new-consensus-in-macroeconomics.

[106] Smith, Noah. 2021. "Much of What You've Heard about Carter and Reagan Is Wrong." Noahpinion.blog, November 3, 2021. https://www.noahpinion.blog/p/much-of-what-youve-heard-about-carter.

[107] Herbst, Julia. 2023. "Is the Age of the Empowered Employee Over?" *Fast Company,* February 27, 2023. https://www.fastcompany.com/90855904/is-the-age-of-the-empowered-employee-over.

[108] Sløk, Torsten. 2024. "Number of Months from Last Fed Hike to Start of Recession." Apollo Academy, July 6, 2024. https://www.apolloacademy.com/number-of-months-from-last-fed-hike-to-start-of-recession.

[109] Davidson, Paul. 2024. "Should the Fed Relax Its 2% Inflation Goal and Cut Interest Rates? Yes, Some Experts Say." *USA Today,* May 20, 2024. https://www.usatoday.com/story/money/2024/05/20/fed-inflation-goal-too-rigid/73718450007.

[110] U.S. Federal Reserve Bank. 2020. "Why Does the Federal Reserve Aim for 2 Percent Inflation over Time?" Board of Governors of the Federal Reserve System, August 27, 2020. https://www.federalreserve.gov/faqs/economy_14400.htm.

[111] Troutman, Elizabeth. 2023. "Federal Government Wastes Enough Money to Buy Half a Million Houses Every Month: Report." Fox Business, June 14, 2023. https://www.foxbusiness.com/economy/federal-government-wastes-enough-money-half-million-houses-every-month-report.

[112] Lee, Juhohn. 2023. "The Federal Government Wastes at Least $247 Billion in Taxpayer Money Each Year. Here's How." CNBC, April 18, 2023. https://www.cnbc.com/2023/04/18/heres-how-the-federal-government-wastes-tax-money.html.

[113] Picchi, Aimee. 2023. "Americans Failed to Pay Record $688 Billion in Taxes in 2021, IRS Says. Look for More Audits." CBS News, October 13, 2023. https://www.cbsnews.com/news/tax-irs-says-unpaid-tax-gap-at-record-688-billion.

[114] Haines, Julia. 2024. "Countries That Receive the Most Foreign Aid from the U.S." *U.S. News & World Report*, January 18, 2024. https://www.usnews.com/news/best-countries/articles/countries-that-receive-the-most-foreign-aid-from-the-u-s.

[115] Shirazi, Elina. 2023. "Rand Paul Unveils 'Festivus' List of $900B in Wasteful Government Spending." NewsNation, December 26, 2023. https://www.newsnationnow.com/politics/rand-paul-festivus-report-wasteful-government-spending.

[116] Forgey, Pat. 2015. "How a 'Bridge to Nowhere' Became a Road from Nowhere to Nowhere." *Anchorage Daily News*, November 17, 2015. https://www.adn.com/alaska-news/article/how-bridge-nowhere-became-road-nowhere/2015/11/17.

[117] Invisible People. 2021. "59% of Americans Are Just One Paycheck Away from Homelessness." Invisible People, June 14, 2021. https://invisiblepeople.tv/59-of-americans-are-just-one-paycheck-away-from-homelessness.

[118] New York Focus. 2025. https://nysfocus.com/2024/11/27/new-york-water-leaks-drought.

[119] Peter G. Peterson Foundation. 2023. "Should We Eliminate the Social Security Tax Cap? Here Are the Pros and Cons." www.pgpf.org, December 13, 2023. https://www.pgpf.org/blog/2023/12/should-we-eliminate-the-social-security-tax-cap-here-are-the-pros-and-cons.

[120] Blazina, Carrie. 2023. "Top Tax Frustrations for Americans: The Feeling That Some Corporations, Wealthy People Don't Pay Fair Share." Pew Research Center, April 7, 2023. https://www.pewresearch.org/short-reads/2023/04/07/top-tax-frustrations-for-americans-the-feeling-that-some-corporations-wealthy-people-dont-pay-fair-share.

[121] Tax Policy Center. 2017. "How Do US Corporate Income Tax Rates and Revenues Compare with Other Countries'?" Tax Policy Center, 2017. https://taxpolicycenter.org/briefing-book/how-do-us-corporate-income-tax-rates-and-revenues-compare-other-countries.

[122] Peter G. Peterson Foundation. 2023. "Five Different Ways of Raising Taxes on the Wealthiest Americans." 2023. www.pgpf.org, April 6, 2023. https://www.pgpf.org/blog/2023/04/five-different-ways-of-raising-taxes-on-the-wealthiest-americans.

[123] Bunn, Daniel. 2022. "What the U.S. Can Learn from the Adoption (and Repeal) of Wealth Taxes in the OECD." Tax Foundation, January 18, 2022. https://taxfoundation.org/blog/wealth-taxes-in-the-oecd.

[124] Adamczyk, Alicia. 2024. "Only 2.5% of Workers Would Benefit from No Taxes on Tips—and in the Long Term, It Could Hurt Them." *Fortune*, August 15, 2024. https://fortune.com/2024/08/15/only-2-5-of-workers-would-benefit-from-no-taxes-on-tips-and-in-the-longterm-it-could-hurt-them.

[125] U.S. Government Accountability Office. 2022. "Earned Income Tax Credit Eligibility and Participation." gao.gov, 2022. https://www.gao.gov/products/gao-02-290r.

[126] Solá, Ana Teresa. 2024. "'Starter Home' Tax Breaks, Aid for First-Time Buyers: What to Know about Harris' Affordable Housing Proposals." CNBC, August 20, 2024. https://www.cnbc.com/2024/08/20/what-to-know-about-harris-affordable-housing-economic-proposals.html.

[127] Huggel, Christian, Bouwer, Laurens M., Juhola, Sirkku, Mechler, Reinhard, Muccione, Veruska, Orlove, Ben and Wallimann-Helmer, Ivo. 2022. "The Existential Risk Space of Climate Change." *Climatic Change* 174, no. 1-2 (September). https://doi.org/10.1007/s10584-022-03430-y.

[128] Salter, Jim and Izaguirre, Anthony. 2024. "A Pro-Israel Super PAC Helped Defeat One Squad Member. Now It's Going after Another, Cori Bush." AP News, August 2024. https://apnews.com/article/cori-bush-aipac-house-race-missouri-568c1a84974b8ba176a8d27a8375de42.

[129] Jimenez, Omar, Morales, Mark and Cummings, Julian. 2024. "3 Columbia Deans Resign after Being Removed Earlier This Summer for 'Very Troubling' Antisemitic Text Messages." CNN, August 9, 2024. https://www.cnn.com/2024/08/08/us/columbia-deans-resign-antisemitic-texts/index.html.

[130] Louise, Nickie. 2020. "These 6 Corporations Control 90% of the Media Outlets in America. The Illusion of Choice and Objectivity." *Tech Startups News*, September 18, 2020. https://techstartups.com/2020/09/18/6-corporations-control-90-media-america-illusion-choice-objectivity-2020.

[131] Montanaro, Domenico. 2024. "NPR Poll: Democrats Fear Fascism, and Republicans Worry about a Lack of Values." NPR, May 1, 2024. https://www.npr.org/2024/05/01/1248249250/election-poll-trump-biden-voters.

[132] Blazina, Carrie. 2020. "Key Findings about Voter Engagement in the 2020 Election." Pew Research Center, December 14, 2020. https://www.pewresearch.org/short-reads/2020/12/14/key-findings-about-voter-engagement-in-the-2020-election.

[133] Shueh, Jason. 2020. "Civic Engagement: Where Does America Rank?" Accela, June 2, 2020. https://www.accela.com/blog/civic-engagement-where-does-america-rank.

[134] Williams, Rhiannon. 2023. "The Download: CRISPR Crops, and Busting Renewables Myths." *MIT Technology Review*, February 2023. https://doi.org/1085094/10-breakthrough-technologies-2024.

Chapter 5: Octuple the Minimum Wage

[135] Gallup, Inc. 2019. "Most Important Problem." Gallup, January 16, 2019. https://news.gallup.com/poll/1675/most-important-problem.aspx.

[136] Allianz Life. 2023. "Majority of Americans Are More Concerned about Paying Bills Right Now than Financial Future." Allianz Life, 2023. https://www.allianzlife.com/about/newsroom/2023-Press-Releases/Majority-of-Americans-are-More-Concerned-About-Paying-Bills-Right-Now-Than-Financial-Future.

[137] Economic Policy Institute. 2019. "Decades of Rising Economic Inequality in the U.S.: Testimony before the U.S. House of Representatives Ways and Means Committee." Economic Policy Institute, 2019. https://www.epi.org/publication/decades-of-rising-economic-inequality-in-the-u-s-testimony-before-the-u-s-house-of-representatives-ways-and-means-committee.

[138] Potts, Monica. 2016. "The American Social Safety Net Does Not Exist." *The Nation*, October 13, 2016. https://www.thenation.com/article/archive/the-american-social-safety-net-does-not-exist.

[139] Brand, David. 2022. "The Rent Is Still Too Damn High: Catching up with Jimmy McMillan." *City Limits*, October 18, 2022. https://citylimits.org/2022/10/18/the-rent-is-still-too-damn-high-catching-up-with-jimmy-mcmillan.

[140] Zaveri, Mihir. 2022. "Is Homeownership Slipping Even Further out of Reach for New Yorkers?" *The New York Times*, November 24, 2022, sec. New York. https://www.nytimes.com/2022/11/24/nyregion/home-ownership-new-york-city.html.

[141] Morabito, Charlotte. 2023. "Here's Why Even Americans Making More than $100,000 Live Paycheck to Paycheck." CNBC, December 11, 2023. https://www.cnbc.com/2023/12/11/why-even-americans-making-more-than-100000-live-paycheck-to-paycheck.html.

[142] Findlaw. "At-Will Employment and Wrongful Termination." Findlaw, n.d. https://www.findlaw.com/employment/losing-a-job/at-will-employment-and-wrongful-termination.html.

[143] Rosenfeld, Jake. 2024. "1 in 10 U.S. Workers Belong to Unions—a Share That's Stabilized after a Steep Decline." *Fast Company*. January 24, 2024. https://www.fastcompany.com/91016225/1-in-10-u-s-workers-belong-to-unions-a-share-thats-stabilized-after-a-steep-decline.

[144] U.S. Occupational Safety and Health Administration. 2023. "Workplace Stress - Overview." www.osha.gov, 2023. https://www.osha.gov/workplace-stress.

[145] Cramer, Katherine J. and Cohen, Jonathan D. 2024. "Many Americans Believe the Economy Is Rigged." *The New York Times*, February 21, 2024. https://www.nytimes.com/2024/02/21/opinion/economy-research-greed-profit.html.

[146] Capuano, Michael. 2023. "New Labor Stats Show Foreign Workers Gaining Jobs While Native-Born Workers See Decline." Federation for American Immigration Reform, September 7, 2023. https://www.fairus.org/legislation/biden-immigration-border-policy/illegal-legal-immigration-and-economy/new-labor-stats.

[147] U.S. Office of Disease Prevention and Health Promotion. 2020. "Crime and Violence - Healthy People 2030." Health.gov. 2020. https://health.gov/healthypeople/priority-areas/social-determinants-health/literature-summaries/crime-and-violence.

[148] Hayes, Adam. 2019. "Maximum Wage." Investopedia, 2019. https://www.investopedia.com/terms/m/maximum-wage.asp.

[149] Center for American Progress. 2021. "Americans Want the Federal Government to Help People in Need." Center for American Progress, March 10, 2021. https://www.americanprogress.org/article/americans-want-federal-government-help-people-need.

[150] Burke, Katie. 2023. "Stream of Major Companies Cut Back on Remote Work with Renewed Return-To-Office Mandates." CoStar, 2023. https://www.costar.com/article/1449349796/stream-of-major-companies-cut-back-on-remote-work-with-renewed-return-to-office-mandates.

[151] Bonitatibus, Steve. 2024. "The Minimum Wage Is a Poverty Wage." Center for American Progress, July 24, 2024. https://www.americanprogress.org/article/the-minimum-wage-is-a-poverty-wage.

[152] World Population Review. 2023. "Least Expensive States 2023." Worldpopulationreview.com, 2023. https://worldpopulationreview.com/state-rankings/least-expensive-states.

[153] Harris, Ben and Kearney, Melissa S. 2014. "The 'Ripple Effect' of a Minimum Wage Increase on American Workers." Brookings, January 10, 2014. https://www.brookings.edu/articles/the-ripple-effect-of-a-minimum-wage-increase-on-american-workers.

[154] Hayes, Adam. 2022. "Does Raising the Minimum Wage Increase Inflation?" Investopedia. June 10, 2022. https://www.investopedia.com/ask/answers/052815/does-raising-minimum-wage-increase-inflation.asp.

[155] Carinci, Justin. 2000. "Does Increasing the Minimum Wage Lead to Higher Prices?" W.E. Upjohn Institute, 2000. https://www.upjohn.org/research-highlights/does-increasing-minimum-wage-lead-higher-prices.

[156] Easterly, Carson. 2023. "Study: Increasing Minimum Wage Has Positive Effects on Employment." School of Social Policy & Practice, October 5, 2023. https://sp2.upenn.edu/study-increasing-minimum-wage-has-positive-effects-on-employment-in-fast-food-sector-and-other-highly-concentrated-labor-markets.

[157] Baker, Dean. 2020. "This Is What Minimum Wage Would Be If It Kept Pace with Productivity." CEPR, January 21, 2020. https://cepr.net/publications/correction-this-is-what-minimum-wage-would-be-if-it-kept-pace-with-productivity.

[158] CUNY. "Principles of Macroeconomics 2e, Economic Growth, Labor Productivity and Economic Growth." CUNY, n.d. https://opened.cuny.edu/courseware/lesson/518/student/?section=4.

[159] Baily, Martin and Montalbano, Nicholas. 2016. Brookings Institute. Accessed January 13, 2025. https://www.brookings.edu/wp-content/uploads/2016/09/wp22_baily-montalbano_updated1.pdf.

[160] Konish, Lorie. 2024. "The Federal Minimum Wage Has Been $7.25 for 15 Years. How the Election May Change That." CNBC, August 16, 2024. https://www.cnbc.com/2024/08/16/federal-minimum-wage-has-been-7point25-for-15-years-how-that-may-change.html.

[161] Senator Bernie Sanders. 2021. "Sanders Announces $15 Minimum Wage Amendment to Reconciliation Bill, Calls for Senate Democrats to Ignore Parliamentarian." Senator Bernie Sanders, March 2021. https://www.sanders.senate.gov/press-releases/news-sanders-announces-15-minimum-wage-amendment-to-reconciliation-bill-calls-for-senate-democrats-to-ignore-parliamentarian.

[162] Carville, James. 2025. "I Was Wrong about the 2024 Election. Here's Why." *The New York Times*, January 2, 2025. https://www.nytimes.com/2025/01/02/opinion/democrats-donald-trump-economy.html.

[163] Hochwald, Lambeth. 2018. "5 Ways to Get around That Pesky 40X-The-Rent Requirement." Apartment Therapy, September 17, 2018. https://www.apartmenttherapy.com/40x-rent-rule-nyc-262581.

[164] ABC7 New York. 2024. "A Family of 4 Needs to Make at Least $318k/Year to Live Comfortably in NYC, Study Finds." ABC7 New York, April 2024. https://abc7ny.com/cost-of-living-nyc-new-yorkers-need-to-make-a-higher-salary-than-people-in-other-us-cities-live-comfortably-study-finds/14603757.

[165] University of Michigan. 2023. "U.S. Cities Factsheet." Center for Sustainable Systems, 2023. https://css.umich.edu/publications/factsheets/built-environment/us-cities-factsheet.

[166] Shierholz, Heidi, Cooper, David, Wolfe, Julia and Zipperer, Ben. 2017. "Employers Would Pocket $5.8 Billion of Workers' Tips under Trump Administration's Proposed 'Tip Stealing' Rule." Economic Policy Institute, 2017. https://www.epi.org/publication/employers-would-pocket-workers-tips-under-trump-administrations-proposed-tip-stealing-rule.

[167] U.S. Department of Labor. "Fair Labor Standards Act Advisor." webapps.dol.gov, n.d. https://webapps.dol.gov/elaws/whd/flsa/screen75.asp.

[168] Polychroniou, C. J. "'Be Realistic, Demand the Impossible!'" Al Jazeera, n.d. https://www.aljazeera.com/opinions/2018/5/21/be-realistic-demand-the-impossible.

Chapter 6: Pay Everyone

[169] Iacurci, Greg. 2021. "U.S. Is Worst among Developed Nations for Worker Benefits." CNBC, February 4, 2021. https://www.cnbc.com/2021/02/04/us-is-worst-among-rich-nations-for-worker-benefits.html.

[170] Hall, Mike. "U.S. Rated Alarmingly High in Global Survey of Worst Places for Workers' Rights." AFL-CIO, n.d. https://aflcio.org/2014/5/22/us-rated-alarmingly-high-global-survey-worst-places-workers-rights.

[171] McHugh, David. 2020. "Pandemic Shows Contrasts between US, European Safety Nets." PBS NewsHour, May 10, 2020. https://www.pbs.org/newshour/world/pandemic-shows-contrasts-between-us-european-safety-nets.

[172] Rosenfeld, Jake. 2024. "1 in 10 U.S. Workers Belong to Unions—a Share That's Stabilized after a Steep Decline." *Fast Company*, January 24, 2024. https://www.fastcompany.com/91016225/1-in-10-u-s-workers-belong-to-unions-a-share-thats-stabilized-after-a-steep-decline.

[173] Economic Policy Institute. 2023. "Workers Want Unions, but the Latest Data Point to Obstacles in Their Path: Private-Sector Unionization Rose by More than a Quarter Million in 2023, While Unionization in State and Local Governments Fell." Economic Policy Institute, 2023. https://www.epi.org/publication/union-membership-data.

[174] Associated Press. 2015. "Judge Approves Settlement in Apple, Google Wage Case." *Los Angeles Times*, September 3, 2015. https://www.latimes.com/business/technology/la-fi-tn-tech-jobs-settlement-20150903-story.html.

[175] Wilsey, Matt and Lichtig, Scott. 2002. "The Nike Controversy." Stanford, 2002. https://web.stanford.edu/class/e297c/trade_environment/wheeling/hnike.html.

[176] Riggs, Mike. 2019. "American Taxpayers Are Subsidizing Ultra-Cheap Shipping from China." *Reason*, November 11, 2019. https://reason.com/2019/11/11/american-taxpayers-are-subsidizing-ultra-cheap-shipping-from-china.

[177] World Data. 2024. "Average Income around the World." Worlddata.info, 2024. https://www.worlddata.info/average-income.php.

[178] Qatar Company Formation. 2023. "Obtain Citizenship in Qatar - Guide for 2024." Qatar Company Formation, January 27, 2023. https://qatarcompanyformation.com/qatar-citizenship.

[179] Posner, Eric. 2018. "Companies Have Monopoly Power over Workers' Wages. That's Killing the Economy." Vox, April 6, 2018. https://www.vox.com/the-big-idea/2018/4/6/17204808/wages-employers-workers-monopsony-growth-stagnation-inequality.

[180] Findlaw. "At-Will Employee FAQ's." Findlaw, n.d. https://www.findlaw.com/employment/hiring-process/at-will-employee-faq-s.html.

[181] Allyn, Bobby. 2024. "Nearly 25,000 Tech Workers Were Laid off in the First Weeks of 2024. Why Is That?" NPR, January 28, 2024. https://www.npr.org/2024/01/28/1227326215/nearly-25-000-tech-workers-laid-off-in-the-first-weeks-of-2024-whats-going-on.

[182] U.S. National Labor Relations Board. 2023. "Employer/Union Rights and Obligations." www.nlrb.gov, 2023. https://www.nlrb.gov/about-nlrb/rights-we-protect/your-rights/employer-union-rights-and-obligations.

[183] Economic Policy Institute. 2021. "Shortchanged—Weak Anti-Retaliation Provisions in the National Labor Relations Act Cost Workers Billions." Economic Policy Institute, 2021. https://www.epi.org/publication/shortchanged-weak-anti-retaliation-provisions-in-the-national-labor-relations-act-cost-workers-billions.

[184] PBMares. 2022. "What Is a Right-To-Work State?" PBMares, September 17, 2022. https://www.pbmares.com/insights-what-is-a-right-to-work-state.

[185] Wikipedia Contributors. 2019. "Taft–Hartley Act." Wikimedia Foundation, July 25, 2019. https://en.wikipedia.org/wiki/Taft%E2%80%93Hartley_Act.

[186] Cornell Law School. "10 U.S. Code § 976 - Membership in Military Unions, Organizing of Military Unions, and Recognition of Military Unions Prohibited." LII / Legal Information Institute, n.d. https://www.law.cornell.edu/uscode/text/10/976.

[187] U.S. Office of Justice Programs. "Arbitration and the Public Employee - an Alternative to the Right to Strike." www.ojp.gov, n.d. https://www.ojp.gov/ncjrs/virtual-library/abstracts/arbitration-and-public-employee-alternative-right-strike.

[188] Franklin, Ben A. 1978. "U.S. Court Orders Coal Miners Back to Work for 80-Day Period." *The New York Times*, March 10, 1978. https://www.nytimes.com/1978/03/10/archives/us-court-orders-coal-miners-back-to-work-for-80day-period-effective.html

189 Shepardson, David and Bose, Nandita. 2022. "Biden Signs Bill to Block U.S. Railroad Strike." Reuters, December 2, 2022, sec. United States. https://www.reuters.com/world/us/biden-signs-bill-block-us-railroad-strike-2022-12-02.

190 U.S. Federal Register. 2024. "Employee or Independent Contractor Classification Under the Fair Labor Standards Act." *Federal Register*, January 10, 2024. https://www.federalregister.gov/documents/2024/01/10/2024-00067/employee-or-independent-contractor-classification-under-the-fair-labor-standards-act.

191 Pew Research Center. 2015. "Three-In-Ten U.S. Jobs Are Held by the Self-Employed and the Workers They Hire." Pew Research Center, October 22, 2015. https://www.pewresearch.org/social-trends/2015/10/22/three-in-ten-u-s-jobs-are-held-by-the-self-employed-and-the-workers-they-hire.

192 Described and Captioned Media Program. 2015. "Boom and Bust: Who Can Explain the Business Cycle?" Dcmp.org, 2015. https://dcmp.org/media/7335-boom-and-bust-who-can-explain-the-business-cycle.

193 U.S. Bank. 2023. "Consumer Spending." www.usbank.com. September 7, 2023. https://www.usbank.com/investing/financial-perspectives/market-news/consumer-spending.html.

194 Johnson, Arianna. "Which Jobs Will AI Replace? These 4 Industries Will Be Heavily Impacted." *Forbes*, March 30, 2023. https://www.forbes.com/sites/ariannajohnson/2023/03/30/which-jobs-will-ai-replace-these-4-industries-will-be-heavily-impacted.

195 Zahidi, Saadia. 2023. "See How the Future of Jobs Is Changing in the Age of AI." World Economic Forum, May 3, 2023. https://www.weforum.org/agenda/2023/05/future-of-jobs-in-the-age-of-ai-sustainability-and-deglobalization.

196 Thompson, Neil. 2024. "New Research May Calm Some of the AI Job-Loss Clamor-for Now." MIT Initiative on the Digital Economy, January 23, 2024. https://ide.mit.edu/insights/neil-thompson-research-may-calm-some-of-the-ai-job-loss-clamor.

197 Ellingrud, Kweilin, Sanghvi, Saurabh, Dandona, Gurneet Singh, Madgavkar, Anu, Chui, Michael. White, Olivia and Hasebe, Paige. 2023. "Generative AI and the Future of Work in America." McKinsey Global Institute, July 26, 2023. https://www.mckinsey.com/mgi/our-research/generative-ai-and-the-future-of-work-in-america.

198 Kelly, Samantha, Murphy. "Elon Musk says AI will take all our jobs." MSN, 2024. https://www.msn.com/en-us/money/technology/elon-musk-says-ai-will-take-all-our-jobs/ar-BB1mWeMk.

199 TWOWP. 2019. "Disruption in Action: An Historic Perspective." The World of Work Project. July 5, 2019. https://worldofwork.io/2019/07/disruption-in-action.

200 Fitzsimmons, Emma G. 2018. "Why Are Taxi Drivers in New York Killing Themselves?." *The New York Times*, December 2, 2018, sec. New York. https://www.nytimes.com/2018/12/02/nyregion/taxi-drivers-suicide-nyc.html.

201 Wikipedia Contributors. 2019. "Creative Destruction." Wikimedia Foundation, February 22, 2019. https://en.wikipedia.org/wiki/Creative_destruction.

202 Mondo Insights. 2023. "The Future of Work: How to Offset AI Job Automation." Mondo Staffing Agency, March 13, 2023. https://mondo.com/insights/how-to-offset-ai-job-automation.

203 Mondo Insights. 2023. "The Future of Work: How to Offset AI Job Automation." Mondo Staffing Agency, March 13, 2023. https://mondo.com/insights/how-to-offset-ai-job-automation.

Chapter 7: House the Homeless

[204] U.S. Census Bureau. 2024. "Housing Vacancies and Homeownership - Press Release." www.census.gov, January 30, 2024. https://www.census.gov/housing/hvs/current/index.html.

[205] U.S. Census Bureau. 2024. "Housing Vacancies and Homeownership - Press Release." www.census.gov, January 30, 2024. https://www.census.gov/housing/hvs/current/index.html.

[206] Sindewald, Erin. 2023. "Hidden Homelessness in the United States." Chicago Coalition to End Homelessness, March 3, 2023. https://www.chicagohomeless.org/hidden-homelessness-in-the-united-states.

[207] Casey, Michael. 2024. "US Homelessness up 18% as Affordable Housing Remains out of Reach for Many People." ABC7 New York. December 28, 2024. https://abc7ny.com/post/how-many-people-are-homeless-2024/15715340.

[208] Magdoff, Fred. 2004. "Disposable Workers: Today's Reserve Army of Labor." *Monthly Review*, April 2004. https://monthlyreview.org/2004/04/01/disposable-workers-todays-reserve-army-of-labor.

[209] Foster, John Bellamy. 2011. "Monopoly and Competition in Twenty-First Century Capitalism." *Monthly Review*, April 2011. https://monthlyreview.org/2011/04/01/monopoly-and-competition-in-twenty-first-century-capitalism.

[210] Open Secrets. 2024. "Real Estate Summary." OpenSecrets, 2024. https://www.opensecrets.org/industries/indus?ind=F10.

[211] Harvard University. 2024. "New Report Shows Housing Costs Strain Owners and Renters Alike; Millions Priced out of Homeownership." Joint Center for Housing Studies. www.jchs.harvard.edu, June 20, 2024. https://www.jchs.harvard.edu/press-releases/new-report-shows-housing-costs-strain-owners-and-renters-alike-millions-priced-out.

[212] Security.org. 2022. "Homelessness in America 2023: Statistics, Analysis, & Trends." Security.org, n.d. https://www.security.org/resources/homeless-statistics.

[213] Hanson, Devlin, Gillespie, Sarah, Oneto, Alyse D., Jannetta, Jesse, Fallon, Katie, Spinner, Brittney, Melgar, Luis, Marazzi, Michael and Peiffer, Emily. 2022. "Policing Doesn't End Homelessness. Supportive Housing Does." Urban.org, October 25, 2022. https://apps.urban.org/features/ending-homelessness-through-supportive-housing-not-policing.

[214] Independent Budget Office of the City of New York. "Close to Home: Does Proximity to a Homeless Shelter Affect Residential Property Values in Manhattan?" ibo.nyc.ny.us, n.d. https://ibo.nyc.ny.us/iboreports/close-to-home-does-proximity-to-a-homeless-shelter-affect-residential-property-values-in-manhattan-2019.html.

[215] Green Doors. 2008. "The Costs of Homelessness." Greendoors.org, 2008. https://www.greendoors.org/facts/cost.php.

[216] Crime in America. 2022. "The Homeless Are Far More Likely to Commit Crimes and to Be Victims." Crime in America.net, March 30, 2022. https://www.crimeinamerica.net/the-homeless-are-far-more-likely-to-commit-crimes-and-to-be-victims.

[217] HomelessHub. 2023. Mental Health and Homelessness." HomelessHub, 2023. https://homelesshub.ca/collection/homelessness-101/mental-health.

[218] Harrison, Danielle J. 2024. "Schizophrenia and Homelessness: What's the Link?" MentalHealth.com, January 3, 2024. https://www.mentalhealth.com/library/schizophrenia-and-homelessness.

[219] SAMHSA. 2021. "Behavioral Health Services for People Who Are Homeless." https://store.samhsa.gov/sites/default/files/pep20-06-04-003.pdf.
[220] Verdin, Jorge. 2022. "What Is the Cost of Homelessness?" Father Joes Villages, March 8, 2022. https://my.neighbor.org/what-is-the-cost-of-homelessness.
[221] Boesche, Harry. 2024. "Camping Revisited: U.S. Supreme Court Changes the Landscape of Penalizing Public Sleeping." mrsc.org, 2024. https://mrsc.org/stay-informed/mrsc-insight/july-2024/grants-pass-v-johnson.
[222] Mission Harbor Behavioral Health. "What's the Connection between Homelessness and Addiction?" Mission Harbor Behavioral Health, n.d. https://sbtreatment.com/homelessness-addiction.
[223] *Catholic Herald*. 2017. "Pope Francis Gives Interview to Magazine Run by Homeless." *Catholic Herald*, February 28, 2017. https://catholicherald.co.uk/pope-francis-gives-interview-to-magazine-run-by-homeless.
[224] Nematchoua, Modeste, Rakotomalala, Kameni, Sendrahasina, Minoson, Malmedy, Charline, Orosa, Jose A., Simo, Elie and Reiter, Sigrid. 2022. "Analysis of Environmental Impacts and Costs of a Residential Building over Its Entire Life Cycle to Achieve Nearly Zero Energy and Low Emission Objectives." *Journal of Cleaner Production* 373, no. November (November): 133834. https://doi.org/10.1016/j.jclepro.2022.133834.
[225] USAFacts. 2023. "How Many Vacant Homes Are There in the US?" USAFacts, October 13, 2023. https://usafacts.org/articles/how-many-vacant-homes-are-there-in-the-us.
[226] Zelas, Kent. 2016. "Fewer Vacant Homes in U.S., but 3 out of 4 Belong to Investors." *Investor's Business Daily*, September 15, 2016. https://www.investors.com/news/fewer-vacant-homes-in-u-s-but-3-out-of-4-belong-to-investors.
[227] Rosalsky, Greg. 2021. "A Startup Is Turning Houses into Corporations, and the Neighbors Are Fighting Back." NPR, August 24, 2021, sec. Newsletter. https://www.npr.org/sections/money/2021/08/24/1030151330/a-unicorn-startup-is-turning-houses-into-corporations.
[228] Kim, Whizy. 2024. "Is This Algorithm Driving Your Rent Higher?" Vox, September 6, 2024. https://www.vox.com/money/370351/realpage-doj-lawsuit-rent-algorithm-pricing.
[229] Eason, Brian. 2023. "American Dream for Rent: Investors Elbow out Individual Home Buyers." *The Atlanta Journal-Constitution*, 2023. https://www.ajc.com/american-dream/investor-owned-houses-atlanta.
[230] Roberts, Sam. 2011. "More Apartments Are Empty yet Rented or Owned, Census Finds." *The New York Times*, July 7, 2011. https://www.nytimes.com/2011/07/07/nyregion/more-apartments-are-empty-yet-rented-or-owned-census-finds.html.
[231] Zaveri, Mihir. 2024. "New York City's Housing Crunch Is the Worst It Has Been in over 50 Years." *The New York Times*, February 8, 2024. https://www.nytimes.com/2024/02/08/nyregion/apartment-vacancy-rate-housing-crisis.html.
[232] Kimmelman, Michael, Tompkins, Lucy and Lee, Christopher. 2022. "How Houston Moved 25,000 People from the Streets into Homes of Their Own." *The New York Times*, June 14, 2022, sec. Headway. https://www.nytimes.com/2022/06/14/headway/houston-homeless-people.html.
[233] Tars, Eric. 2021. "Housing as a Human Right." https://nlihc.org/sites/default/files/AG-2021/01-06_Housing-Human-Right.pdf.

Chapter 8: Free Healthcare For All

[234] Glaser, James, and Berry, Jeffrey. n.d. "Why Are Democratic Voters More Approving of Compromise than Republicans?" The Conversation, https://theconversation.com/why-are-democratic-voters-more-approving-of-compromise-than-republicans-98828.

[235] Trump White House Archives. 2018. "The Council of Economic Advisers the Profitability of Health Insurance Companies." 2018. https://trumpwhitehouse.archives.gov/wp-content/uploads/2018/03/The-Profitability-of-Health-Insurance-Companies.pdf.

[236] KFF. 2021. "Insurer Participation on the ACA Marketplaces, 2014-2021." KFF, February 23, 2021. https://www.kff.org/private-insurance/issue-brief/insurer-participation-on-the-aca-marketplaces-2014-2021.

[237] Gunja, Munira Z., Gumas, Evan D., and Williams II, Reginald D. 2023. "U.S. Health Care from a Global Perspective, 2022: Accelerating Spending, Worsening Outcomes." The Commonwealth Fund, January 31, 2023. https://www.commonwealthfund.org/publications/issue-briefs/2023/jan/us-health-care-global-perspective-2022.

[238] Reed, Paul. 2024. "Prevention Is Still the Best Medicine." Health.gov, 2024. https://odphp.health.gov/news/202401/prevention-still-best-medicine.

[239] Cuffari, Benedette. 2024. "Proactive Health: The Shift Towards Preventative Healthcare." News-Medical, July 31, 2024. https://www.news-medical.net/health/Proactive-Health-The-Shift-Towards-Preventative-Healthcare.aspx.

[240] Public Citizen. 2019. "Medicare-For-All Prevents Medical Bankruptcies." Public Citizen, April 27, 2019. https://www.citizen.org/article/medicare-for-all-prevents-medical-bankruptcies.

[241] Saad, Lydia. 2023. "Americans Sour on U.S. Healthcare Quality." Gallup, January 19, 2023. https://news.gallup.com/poll/468176/americans-sour-healthcare-quality.aspx.

[242] *Economic Times*. 2024. "Over 90,000 people mock a Facebook post about slain UnitedHealthcare CEO Brian Thompson with laughing emojis; why are Americans treating him like this?" *Economic Times*, December 8, 2024.https://economictimes.indiatimes.com/news/international/us/over-90000-people-mock-a-facebook-post-about-slain-unitedhealthcare-ceo-brian-thompson-with-laughing-emojis-why-are-americans-treating-him-like-this/articleshow/116145053.cms.

[243] MacDonald, Heather. 2024. "Luigi Mangione and America's Broken Moral Compass." *City Journal*, December 24, 2024. https://www.city-journal.org/article/luigi-mangione-unitedhealthcare-ceo-brian-thompson.

[244] Gil, Bruce. 2024. "No One Knows How Often Health Insurers Deny Claims. Here's Why." Yahoo News, December 5, 2024. https://www.yahoo.com/news/no-one-knows-often-health-202056665.html.

[245] Scott, Dylan. 2024. "The Deep Roots of Americans' Hatred of Their Health Care System." Vox, December 6, 2024. https://www.vox.com/future-perfect/390111/united-healthcare-ceo-shot-insurance-hospitals-doctors.

[246] Luhby, Tami, and Duffy, Clare. 2024. "Killing of UnitedHealthcare CEO Prompts Flurry of Stories on Social Media over Denied Insurance Claims." CNN, December 6, 2024. https://www.cnn.com/2024/12/06/business/insurance-claim-denials-unitedhealthcare-ceo/index.html.

[247] Peterson, Lucy. 2024. "Rising Costs, Declining Health: U.S. Health Care System in Dire Straits." BenefitsPro, 2024. https://www.benefitspro.com/2024/10/01/rising-costs-declining-health-u-s-health-care-system-in-dire-straits.

248 Pollitz, Karen, Pestaina, Kaye, Lopes, Lunna, Wallace, Rayna and Lo, Justin. 2023. "Consumer Survey Highlights Problems with Denied Health Insurance Claims." KFF, September 29, 2023. https://www.kff.org/affordable-care-act/issue-brief/consumer-survey-highlights-problems-with-denied-health-insurance-claims.

249 Miller, David, Armstrong, Patrick, and Rucker, Maya. 2023. "UnitedHealthcare Tried to Deny Coverage to a Chronically Ill Patient. He Fought Back, Exposing the Insurer's Inner Workings." ProPublica, February 2, 2023. https://www.propublica.org/article/unitedhealth-healthcare-insurance-denial-ulcerative-colitis.

250 Pollitz, Karen, Pestaina, Kaye, Lopes, Lunna, Wallace, Rayna and Lo, Justin. 2023. "Consumer Survey Highlights Problems with Denied Health Insurance Claims." KFF, September 29, 2023. https://www.kff.org/affordable-care-act/issue-brief/consumer-survey-highlights-problems-with-denied-health-insurance-claims.

251 Fields, Maya and Miller, Robin. 2023. "Health Insurers Have Been Breaking State Laws for Years." ProPublica, November 16, 2023. https://www.propublica.org/article/health-insurance-denials-breaking-state-laws.

252 Rosenthal, Elisabeth. 2023. "Analysis: Health Insurance Claim Denials Are on the Rise, to the Detriment of Patients." PBS NewsHour, May 28, 2023. https://www.pbs.org/newshour/health/analysis-health-insurance-claim-denials-are-on-the-rise-to-the-detriment-of-patients.

253 Gil, Bruce. 2024. "How UnitedHealthcare and Other Insurers Use AI to Deny Claims." Yahoo News, December 6, 2024. https://www.yahoo.com/news/unitedhealthcare-other-insurers-ai-deny-202000141.html.

254 Seitz, Amanda. 2022. "Majority of Americans Unhappy with Health Care System: AP- NORC Poll." PBS NewsHour, September 12, 2022. https://www.pbs.org/newshour/politics/majority-of-americans-unhappy-with-health-care-system-ap-norc-poll.

255 Reddit.com. 2023. "Reddit - Dive into Anything." Reddit.com, 2023. https://www.reddit.com/r/tax/comments/16vn0qv/i_paid_10000_in_out_of_pocket_medical_expenses.

256 Simon, Scott and Benk, Ryan. "Outdated Provider Lists on Health Insurers' Websites May Be Costing You." NPR, January 6, 2024. https://www.npr.org/2024/01/06/1223287102/outdated-provider-lists-on-health-insurers-websites-may-be-costing-you.

257 Santoro, Helen. 2024. "Health Insurance Giants' Directories Are Falsely Listing In-Network Providers." *Jacobin*, January 2024. https://jacobin.com/2024/01/health-insurance-giants-companies-unitedhealthcare-directory-in-network-providers.

258 Butala, Neel M., Jiwani, Kuldeep and Bucholz, Emily M. 2023. "Consistency of Physician Data across Health Insurer Directories." *JAMA* 329, no. 10 (March): 841. https://doi.org/10.1001/jama.2023.0296.

259 ABC27. 2023. "Almost 40% of health insurance directory listings are out of date – Atlas Systems." ABC27, June 7, 2023. https://www.abc27.com/business/press-releases/ein-presswire/638148711/almost-40-of-health-insurance-directory-listings-are-out-of-date-atlas-systems.

260 Kelly, Stephanie and Steenhuysen, Julie. 2024. "Killing of UnitedHealthcare Exec Ignites Patient Anger over Insurance." Reuters, December 9, 2024. https://www.reuters.com/business/healthcare-pharmaceuticals/americans-face-challenges-health-insurance-costs-rise-delays-mount-2024-12-09.

261 Santoro, Helen. 2024. "Health Insurers' Profits Are Reaching New Heights." *Jacobin*, December 11, 2024. https://jacobin.com/2024/12/health-insurance-profits-unitedhealthcare-aca.

262 Keane, Isabel. 2024. "UnitedHealth CEO Says Insurer Will Continue to Prevent 'Unnecessary Care' in Leaked Video as Sick Trolls Warn, 'Dude's Next.'" *New York Post*, December 9, 2024. https://nypost.com/2024/12/09/us-news/unitedhealth-ceo-says-insurer-will-continue-to-prevent-unnecessary-care-in-leaked-video.

263 Wendling, Julia. 2024. "Which Countries Have Universal Health Coverage?" *Visual Capitalist*, June 11, 2024. https://www.visualcapitalist.com/which-countries-have-universal-health-coverage.

264 Moore, David. 2021. "Health Insurance and Pharma Lobbyists Max out to the Dem Party." Sludge, November 29, 2021. https://readsludge.com/2021/11/29/health-insurance-and-pharma-lobbyists-max-out-to-the-dem-party.

265 Hilton, John. 2024. "Insurers, Trade Groups Seek Influence via Donations in Divisive Election." InsuranceNewsNet, September 24, 2024. https://insurancenewsnet.com/innarticle/insurers-trade-groups-seek-influence-via-donations-in-divisive-election.

266 Public Citizen. 2019. "Public Support for Medicare-For-All." Public Citizen, April 27, 2019. https://www.citizen.org/article/public-support-for-medicare-for-all.

267 U.S. Social Security Administration. 1970. "Private Health Insurance in 1970: Population Coverage, Enrollment, and Financial Experience I." U.S. Social Security Administration, n.d. https://www.ssa.gov/policy/docs/ssb/v35n2/v35n2p3.pdf.

268 Luthra, Shefali, and Shefali Luthra. 2020. "Would 'Medicare for All' Cost More than U.S. Budget? Biden Says So. Math Says No." KFF Health News, February 14, 2020. https://kffhealthnews.org/news/does-medicare-for-all-cost-more-than-the-entire-budget-biden-says-so-but-numbers-say-no

269 Blair, Jenny. 2020. "Study: More than 335,000 Lives Could Have Been Saved during Pandemic If U.S. Had Universal Health Care." Yale School of Public Health, June 20, 2022. https://ysph.yale.edu/news-article/yale-study-more-than-335000-lives-could-have-been-saved-during-pandemic-if-us-had-universal-health-care.

270 Merelli, Annalisa. 2023. "U.S. Government Spent More on Health Care in 2022 than Six Countries with Universal Health Care Combined." Stat, December 19, 2023. https://www.statnews.com/2023/12/19/us-healthcare-costs-government-covers-41-percent-of-total.

271 Heavey, Susan. 2009. "Study links 45,000 U.S. deaths to lack of insurance." Reuters, September 18, 2009. https://www.reuters.com/article/business/healthcare-pharmaceuticals/study-links-45000-us-deaths-to-lack-of-insurance-idustre58g6w5.

272 Bird, Beverly. 2023. "How Much Does the Average American Pay in Taxes?" *The Balance*, January 12, 2023. https://www.thebalancemoney.com/what-the-average-american-pays-in-taxes-4768594.

273 Rall, Ted. 2024. "What's Left 3: What If We Had $4.5 Trillion a Year to Spend on Ordinary People?" Ted Rall's Rallblog, February 12, 2024. https://rall.com/2024/02/12/whats-left-3-what-if-we-had-4-5-trillion-a-year-to-spend-on-ordinary-people

274 Galvani, Alison P., Parpia, Alyssa S., Foster, Eric M., Singer, Burton H. and Fitzpatrick, Meagan C. 2020. "Improving the Prognosis of Health Care in the USA." *The Lancet* 395, no. 10223 (February): 524–33. https://doi.org/10.1016/s0140-6736(19)33019-3.

275 Sellers, Frances Stead. 2022. "Much Has Changed since the Start of the Pandemic. But the Nation's Public Health System Remains Fractured." *The Washington Post*, 2022. https://www.washingtonpost.com/health/2022/01/01/covid-what-has-changed.

276 Wikipedia Contributors. 2019. "National Health Service." Wikimedia Foundation, March 5, 2019. https://en.wikipedia.org/wiki/National_Health_Service.

277 MacFarquhar, Neil. 2021. "Murders Spiked in 2020 in Cities across the United States." *The New York Times*, September 27, 2021, sec. U.S. https://www.nytimes.com/2021/09/27/us/fbi-murders-2020-cities.html.

278 New York State Office of Mental Health. "HIPAA Privacy Rules for the Protection of Health and Mental Health Information." Omh.ny.gov, n.d. https://omh.ny.gov/omhweb/hipaa/phi_protection.html

[279] Sipherd, Ray. 2018. "The Third-Leading Cause of Death in US Most Doctors Don't Want You to Know About." CNBC, February 22, 2018. https://www.cnbc.com/2018/02/22/medical-errors-third-leading-cause-of-death-in-america.html.

[280] Mayo Clinic. 2023. "Sexually Transmitted Diseases (STDs) - Symptoms and Causes." Mayo Clinic, September 8, 2023. https://www.mayoclinic.org/diseases-conditions/sexually-transmitted-diseases-stds/symptoms-causes/syc-20351240.

[281] Popkin, Helen A.S. 2012. "You Are Naked on the Internet." Today, March 13, 2012. https://www.today.com/money/you-are-naked-internet-430952

[282] Hanushek, Eric, and Woessmann, Ludger. 2019. "Prepared for the European Commission the Economic Benefits of Improving Educational Achievement in the European Union: An Update and Extension." https://eenee.eu/wp-content/uploads/2021/05/eenee_ar39.pdf.

Chapter 9: Make Higher Education Free

[283] Wikipedia Contributors. 2019. "The Anatomy of Revolution." Wikimedia Foundation, January 2, 2019. https://en.wikipedia.org/wiki/The_Anatomy_of_Revolution.

[284] Kelly, Andrew P. 2014. "Does College Really Improve Social Mobility?" Brookings, February 11, 2014. https://www.brookings.edu/articles/does-college-really-improve-social-mobility.

[285] Cerullo, Megan. 2024. "More than Half of College Graduates Are Working in Jobs That Don't Require Degrees." CBS News, February 23, 2024. https://www.cbsnews.com/news/college-grads-jobs-underemployed.

[286] Lohr, Steve. 2022. "A 4-Year Degree Isn't Quite the Job Requirement It Used to Be." *The New York Times*, April 8, 2022, sec. Business. https://www.nytimes.com/2022/04/08/business/hiring-without-college-degree.html.

[287] Cohen, Rachel M. 2023. "Stop Requiring College Degrees for Jobs That Don't Need Them." Vox, March 19, 2023. https://www.vox.com/policy/23628627/degree-inflation-college-bacheors-stars-labor-worker-paper-ceiling.

[288] Lee, Juhohn. 2023. "Here's Why Some Economists Are Concerned Student Loans May Cause the next Big Bubble." CNBC, August 31, 2023. https://www.cnbc.com/2023/08/31/why-student-loans-may-be-the-next-bubble.html.

[289] Hanson, Melanie. 2021. "Average Student Loan Interest Rate in 2021." EducationData, October 29, 2021. https://educationdata.org/average-student-loan-interest-rate.

[290] Bengali, Leila, Valletta, Robert G. and Zhao, Cindy. 2023. "Falling College Wage Premiums by Race and Ethnicity." San Francisco Fed, August 28, 2023. https://www.frbsf.org/research-and-insights/publications/economic-letter/2023/08/falling-college-wage-premiums-by-race-and-ethnicity

[291] Helhoski, Anna and Lane, Ryan. 2021. "2020 Student Loan Debt Statistics." NerdWallet, August 19, 2021. https://www.nerdwallet.com/article/loans/student-loans/student-loan-debt.

[292] Cooper, Preston. 2019. "America Spends More on College than Virtually Any Other Country." *Forbes*, September 22, 2019. https://www.forbes.com/sites/prestoncooper2/2019/09/22/america-spends-more-on-college-than-virtually-any-other-country.

[293] World Population Review. 2023. "Countries with Free College 2020." Worldpopulationreview.com. 2023. https://worldpopulationreview.com/country-rankings/countries-with-free-college.

[294] Rall, Ted. "What's Left 3: What If We Had $4.5 Trillion a Year to Spend on Ordinary People?" Ted Rall's Rallblog, February 12, 2024. https://rall.com/2024/02/12/whats-left-3-what-if-we-had-4-5-trillion-a-year-to-spend-on-ordinary-people.

[295] Hanson, Melanie. 2022. "National Student Loan Default Rate [2021]: Delinquency Data." EducationData, January 8, 2022. https://educationdata.org/student-loan-default-rate.

[296] Harvard Kennedy School Institute of Politics. 2019. "Student Debt Viewed as Major Problem; Financial Considerations Important Factor for Most Millennials When Considering Whether to Pursue College." The Institute of Politics at Harvard University, 2019. https://iop.harvard.edu/student-debt-viewed-major-problem-financial-considerations-important-factor-most-millennials-when.

[297] Committee for a Responsible Federal Budget. 2020. "Canceling Student Loan Debt Is Poor Economic Stimulus." Committee for a Responsible Federal Budget, November 18, 2020. https://www.crfb.org/blogs/canceling-student-loan-debt-poor-economic-stimulus.

[298] Shaner, Kyle. 2023. "How Student Loan Forgiveness Could Affect the Economy." UC News, March 8, 2023. https://www.uc.edu/news/articles/2023/03/how-student-loan-forgiveness-could-affect-the-economy.html.

[299] Lloyd, Alcynna. 2019. "America's Debt-Burdened Millennials Are Delaying Homeownership by 7 Years." HousingWire, August 9, 2019. https://www.housingwire.com/articles/49819-americas-debt-burdened-millennials-are-delaying-homeownership-by-7-years.

[300] Armstrong, Martin. 2021. "Infographic: The World's Highest and Lowest Tuition Fees." Statista, September 17, 2021. https://www.statista.com/chart/11058/bachelor-tuition-fees-international-comparison.

[301] International Student. 2023. "UK vs. USA Education System | Study Abroad Guide." International Student, 2023. https://www.internationalstudent.com/study-abroad/guide/uk-usa-education-system.

[302] Hanson, Melanie. 2022. "National Student Loan Default Rate [2021]: Delinquency Data." EducationData, January 8, 2022. https://educationdata.org/student-loan-default-rate.

[303] World Population Review. 2023. "Countries with Free College 2020." Worldpopulationreview.com, 2023. https://worldpopulationreview.com/country-rankings/countries-with-free-college.

[304] Delisle, Jason. 2019. "What European Countries Sacrifice for Free College." Yahoo News, August 15, 2019. https://www.yahoo.com/news/european-countries-sacrifice-free-college-183955022.html.

[305] AccreditedSchoolsOnline.org. 2022. "Countries with Free College." AccreditedSchoolsOnline.org, 2022. https://www.accreditedschoolsonline.org/resources/which-countries-offer-free-college.

Chapter 10: Create a Foreign Policy for Peace, Not War

[306] Davenport, Kelsey. 2023. "Nuclear Weapons: Who Has What at a Glance." Arms Control Association, June 2023. https://www.armscontrol.org/factsheets/Nuclearweaponswhohaswhat.

[307] Dodge, Michaela. 2024. "U.S. Nuclear Weapons." The Heritage Foundation, January 24, 2024. https://www.heritage.org/military-strength/assessment-us-military-power/us-nuclear-weapons.

[308] Stratfor. 2025. "U.S.: Naval Dominance and the Importance of Oceans." Stratfor, 2025. https://worldview.stratfor.com/article/us-naval-dominance-and-importance-oceans.

[309] Stilwell, Blake. 2022. "5 Reasons Why Geography Is America's Greatest Weapon against an Invasion." Military.com, March 11, 2022. https://www.military.com/history/5-reasons-why-geography-americas-greatest-weapon-against-invasion.html.

310 Kruse, Michael. 2015. "Where in the World Is the U.S. Military?" *Politico Magazine*, 2015. https://www.politico.com/magazine/story/2015/06/us-military-bases-around-the-world-119321.
311 Hartung, William. 2022. "We're #1: The U.S. Government Is the World's Largest Arms Dealer." *Forbes*, March 18, 2022. https://www.forbes.com/sites/williamhartung/2022/03/18/were-1-the-us-government-is-the-worlds-largest-arms-dealer.
312 China Military. "Why Has the U.S. Been Fighting for 228 of the Last 245 Years?." Eng.chinamil.com.cn, n.d. http://eng.chinamil.com.cn/opinions_209196/Opinions_209197/10115979.html.
313 UCL. 2022. "'English Is Often Considered the de Facto Global Language…" Culture Online, March 22, 2022. https://www.ucl.ac.uk/culture-online/case-studies/2022/mar/english-often-considered-de-facto-global-language.
314 Hunt, Jonathan R. 2022. "The Nuclear Club: How America and the World Policed the Atom from Hiroshima to Vietnam." Stanford University Press, 2022. https://www.sup.org/books/title/?id=33916.
315 U.S. Office of the Director of National Intelligence. 2024. "Members of the IC." Dni.gov, 2024. https://www.dni.gov/index.php/what-we-do/members-of-the-ic.
316 Office of the Historian. 2019. "Milestones: 1977–1980 - Office of the Historian." State.gov, 2019. https://history.state.gov/milestones/1977-1980/human-rights.
317 Encyclopedia.com. "Human Rights Abuses in Shahist Iran." www.encyclopedia.com, n.d. https://www.encyclopedia.com/history/legal-and-political-magazines/human-rights-abuses-shahist-iran.
318 Bakircioglu, Onder. 2009. "The Right to Self-Defence in National and International Law: The Role of the Imminence Requirement." mckinneylaw.iu.edu, 2009. https://mckinneylaw.iu.edu/iiclr/pdf/vol19p1.pdf.
319 NATO. 1949. The North Atlantic Treaty. NATO, April 4, 1949. https://www.nato.int/cps/en/natohq/official_texts_17120.htm
320 Little, Becky. 2022. "How a Regional Conflict Escalated into World War I." A&E Television Networks, February 4, 2022. https://www.history.com/news/regional-conflict-world-war-i-beginning.
321 Mecklin, John. 2022. "The Pathways of Inadvertent Escalation: Is a NATO-Russia War (Now) Possible?" *Bulletin of the Atomic Scientists*, February 24, 2022. https://thebulletin.org/2022/02/the-pathways-of-inadvertent-escalation-is-a-nato-russia-war-now-possible.
322 Rall, Ted. 2024. "What's Left 2: We're a Rich Country. Let's Act like It." Ted Rall's Rallblog, February 5, 2024. https://rall.com/2024/02/05/whats-left-2-were-a-rich-country-lets-act-like-it.
323 Rall, Ted. 2024. "What's Left 2: We're a Rich Country. Let's Act like It." Ted Rall's Rallblog, February 5, 2024. https://rall.com/2024/02/05/whats-left-2-were-a-rich-country-lets-act-like-it.
324 GT Staff Reporters. 2021. "GT Investigates: US Wages Global Color Revolutions to Topple Govts for the Sake of American Control." *Global Times*, December 2021. https://www.globaltimes.cn/page/202112/1240540.shtml.
325 Johnston, Jake. 2017. "How Pentagon Officials May Have Encouraged a 2009 Coup in Honduras." *The Intercept*, August 29, 2017. https://theintercept.com/2017/08/29/honduras-coup-us-defense-departmetnt-center-hemispheric-defense-studies-chds.
326 ABC News. 2018. "US Soldiers Killed in Niger Were Outgunned, 'Left Behind' in Hunt for ISIS Leader." ABC News, May 3, 2018. https://abcnews.go.com/International/us-soldiers-killed-niger-outgunned-left-hunt-isis/story?id=54909240.
327 Matamis, Joaquin. 2024. "What Is the US Doing in a Disputed Triangle on the Jordan/Syria/Iraq Border?" Stimson Center,. February 20, 2024. https://www.stimson.org/2024/tower-22-us-disputed-triangle-jordan-syria-iraq-border.

328 Hadley, Stephen. 2017. "Q&A: The Risks of Isolationism." United States Institute of Peace, January 31, 2017. https://www.usip.org/publications/2012/02/qa-risks-isolationism.

329 Lodal, Jan. 2001. "Pledging 'No First Strike': A Step toward Real WMD Cooperation." www.armscontrol.org, March 2001. https://www.armscontrol.org/act/2001-03/features/pledging-first-strike-step-toward-real-wmd-cooperation.

330 U.N. Office for Disarmament Affairs. "Anti-Personnel Landmines Convention." UNODA, n.d. https://disarmament.unoda.org/anti-personnel-landmines-convention.

331 Mizokami, Kyle. 2024. "The Mysterious Drones in New Jersey May Not Be a Threat—but America's Anti-Drone Weapons Sure Are." *Popular Mechanics*, December 18, 2024. https://www.popularmechanics.com/military/weapons/a63228727/anti-drone-weapons.

332 Pape, Robert A. 1997. "Why Economic Sanctions Do Not Work." *International Security* 22, no. 2: 90–136. https://doi.org/10.2307/2539368.

333 Rachman, Gideon. 2023. "Is There Such a Thing as a Rules-Based International Order?" *Financial Times*, April 20, 2023, sec. Transcript. https://www.ft.com/content/664d7fa5-d575-45da-8129-095647c8abe7.

334 CFR.org Editors. 2022. "What to Know about Sanctions on North Korea." Council on Foreign Relations, July 27, 2022. https://www.cfr.org/backgrounder/north-korea-sanctions-un-nuclear-weapons.

335 Milburn, Thomas W. and Christie, Daniel J. 1989. "Rewarding in International Politics." *Political Psychology* 10, no. 4 (December): 625. https://doi.org/10.2307/3791331.

336 Yerushalmy, Jonathan. 2024. "What Does Taiwan Get from the Foreign Aid Bill and Why Is the US Economy among the Biggest Winners?" *The Guardian*, April 26, 2024, sec. World news. https://www.theguardian.com/world/2024/apr/26/us-foreign-aid-bill-package-details.

337 Kasianenko, Nataliia. 2021. "Statelessness and Governance in the Absence of Recognition: The Case of the 'Donetsk People's Republic.'" www.manchesterhive.com, Manchester University Press. October 12, 2021. https://www.manchesterhive.com/display/9781526156426/9781526156426.00017.xml.l

338 Pew Research Center. 2014. "Despite Concerns about Governance, Ukrainians Want to Remain One Country." Pew Research Center, May 8, 2014. https://www.pewresearch.org/global/2014/05/08/despite-concerns-about-governance-ukrainians-want-to-remain-one-country.

339 Strupczewski, Jan. 2024. "Exclusive: Nine European Countries Protest against IMF Resuming Missions to Russia." Reuters, September 13, 2024. https://www.reuters.com/world/europe/nine-european-countries-protest-against-imf-resuming-missions-russia-2024-09-13.

Chapter 11: Police Can Do Something New: They Can Help People

340 The Associated Press. 2021. "Minnesota Police Shoot, Kill Man after Traffic Stop Incident." *The Denver Post*, April 12, 2021. https://www.denverpost.com/2021/04/11/minnesota-police-shoot-kill-man-brooklyn-center.

341 Ranalli, Michael. 2020. "Above All Else: Why Officer Safety Must Be a Top Agency Priority." Lexipol, July 10, 2020. https://www.lexipol.com/resources/blog/above-all-else-why-officer-safety-must-be-a-top-agency-priority-here

342 Scudieri, Terrence. 2017. "Fleeing While Black: How Massachusetts Reshaped the Contours of the Terry Stop." *American Criminal Law Review*, 2017. https://www.law.georgetown.edu/american-criminal-law-review/aclr-online/volume-54/fleeing-while-black-how-massachusetts-reshaped-the-contours-of-the-terry-stop

[343] Siemaszko, Corky. 2021. "Daunte Wright Was Stopped for Expired Plates, but Driving While Black May Have Been His 'Crime.'" NBC News, April 12, 2021. https://www.nbcnews.com/news/us-news/daunte-wright-was-stopped-expired-plates-driving-while-black-may-n1263878.

[344] Porter, Tom. 2021. "Daunte Wright: Minn. Rearview Mirror Law Said to Target Black Drivers." Business Insider, April 12, 2021. https://www.insider.com/daunte-wright-minnesota-rearview-mirror-law-2021-4.

[345] McCullough, Jolie and Pollock, Cassandra. 2020. "Texas Lawmakers behind Sandra Bland Act Will Advocate for More Police Reforms." *The Texas Tribune*, June 9, 2020. https://www.texastribune.org/2020/06/09/texas-sandra-bland-act-police.

[346] U.S. Bureau of Justice Statistics. "Contacts Between the Public and the Police." Bureau of Justice Statistics, 2018. https://www.bjs.gov/content/pub/pdf/cpp08.pdf.

[347] Schmidt, Michael S., and Matt Apuzzo. 2015. "South Carolina Officer Is Charged with Murder of Walter Scott." *The New York Times*, April 7, 2015, sec. U.S. https://www.nytimes.com/2015/04/08/us/south-carolina-officer-is-charged-with-murder-in-black-mans-death.html.

[348] Brooks, Rosa. 2020. "Stop Training Police Like They're Joining the Military." *The Atlantic*, June 10, 2020. https://www.theatlantic.com/ideas/archive/2020/06/police-academies-paramilitary/612859.

[349] ABC News. 2000. "Court OKs barring High IQs for Cops." ABC News, September 8, 2000. https://abcnews.go.com/US/court-oks-barring-high-iqs-cops/story?id=95836.

[350] Ciaramella, C. J. 2024. "Supreme Court Rules No Due Process Right to Preliminary Hearings in Civil Asset Forfeiture Cases." *Reason*, May 9, 2024. https://reason.com/2024/05/09/supreme-court-rules-no-due-process-right-to-preliminary-hearings-in-civil-asset-forfeiture-cases.

[351] Stillman, Sarah. 2013. "Punishment without Crime." *The New* Yorker, August 12, 2013. http://www.newyorker.com/magazine/2013/08/12/taken.

[352] Congressman Tim Walberg. 2013. "Epoch Times: Civil Forfeiture: How the Government Makes Billions by Taking Americans' Private Property." Walberg.house.gov, August 24, 2023. https://walberg.house.gov/media/in-the-news/epoch-times-civil-forfeiture-how-government-makes-billions-taking-americans.

[353] O'Harrow, Jr., Robert, Horwitz, Sari and Rich, Steven. 2015. "Holder Limits Seized-Asset Sharing Process That Split Billions with Local, State Police." *The Washington Post*, January 16, 2015. http://www.washingtonpost.com/investigations/holder-ends-seized-asset-sharing-process-that-split-billions-with-local-state-police/2015/01/16/0e7ca058-99d4-11e4-bcfb-059ec7a93ddc_story.html.

[354] Santucci, Jeanine. 2024. "Old Legal Quirk Lets Police Take Your Money with Little Reason, Critics Say." *USA Today*, August 18, 2024. https://www.usatoday.com/story/news/nation/2024/08/18/civil-asset-forfeiture-explained/74802279007.

[355] O'Harrow, Jr., Robert, Horwitz, Sari and Rich, Steven. 2015. "Holder Limits Seized-Asset Sharing Process That Split Billions with Local, State Police." *The Washington Post*, January 16, 2015. http://www.washingtonpost.com/investigations/holder-ends-seized-asset-sharing-process-that-split-billions-with-local-state-police/2015/01/16/0e7ca058-99d4-11e4-bcfb-059ec7a93ddc_story.html.

Chapter 12: Redefine Crime; Rethink Punishment

[356] O'Connell, Danielle. "It Starts with Reentry: Examining the Needs of Parolees in Illinois and the Actionable Goals of Prison Abolition." The University of Chicago, April 2021. https://repository.upenn.edu/dissertations/AAI10260949

[357] Justia. 1976. *Estelle v. Gamble,* 429 U.S. 97 (1976). U.S. Supreme Court, 1976. https://supreme.justia.com/cases/federal/us/429/97

[358] Youd, Chris. 2023. "Family Says Deplorable Conditions and Insect Bites in Atlanta Jail Contributed to Inmate's Death." CNN, April 14, 2023. https://www.cnn.com/2023/04/13/us/atlanta-inmate-dies-jail-conditions-family/index.html.

[359] CBS News/WKRC. 2023. "Inmate Dies after Being 'Eaten Alive' by Bed Bugs, Attorney Claims." WHP, 2023. https://local21news.com/news/nation-world/inmate-dies-after-being-eaten-alive-by-bed-bugs-attorney-claims.

[360] BBC News. 2023. "Man 'Eaten Alive' by Bed Bugs in Atlanta Jail - Family," April 14, 2023, sec. US & Canada. https://www.bbc.com/news/world-us-canada-65267971.

[361] BBC News. 2023. "Man 'Eaten Alive' by Bed Bugs in Atlanta Jail - Family," April 14, 2023, sec. US & Canada. https://www.bbc.com/news/world-us-canada-65267971.

[362] McCann, Sam. 2022. "Health Care behind Bars: Missed Appointments, No Standards, and High…." Vera Institute of Justice, June 29, 2022. https://www.vera.org/news/health-care-behind-bars-missed-appointments-no-standards-and-high-costs.

[363] Abdollah, Tami. 2023. "A Man with Mental Illness Died after 20 Days in Solitary Confinement. Did the Jail System Fail Him?" *USA Today*, April 12, 2023. https://www.usatoday.com/story/news/nation/2023/04/12/jail-reform-mentally-ill-man-dies-after-solitary-confinement/11566175002.

[364] Penal Reform International. 2020. "Separation and Solitary Confinement in the Revised 2020 European Prison Rules - First Thoughts." *Penal Reform International*, 2020. September 16, 2020. https://www.penalreform.org/blog/separation-and-solitary-confinement-in-the-revised-2020.

[365] Negussie, Tesfaye. "Arkansas detainee died of starvation and neglect, lawsuit claims." ABC News, January 18, 2023. https://abcnews.go.com/US/arkansas-detainee-died-starvation-neglect-lawsuit-claims

[366] Jaildeathandinjurylaw.com. 2024. https://www.jaildeathandinjurylaw.com/blog/16/jail-medical-neglect-kills.

[367] Szep, Jason, Ned Parker, Linda So, Peter Eisler and Grant Smith. 2020. "As U.S. Jails Outsource Health Care, Inmate Deaths Rise." Reuters, October 26, 2020. https://www.reuters.com/investigates/special-report/usa-jails-privatization.

[368] Prison Policy Initiative. 2021. "New Data: State Prisons Are Increasingly Deadly Places." Prisonpolicy.org, 2021. https://www.prisonpolicy.org/blog/2021/06/08/prison_mortality.

[369] Lurie, Julia. 2022. "New Photos Reveal Squalid, Dangerous Conditions at Rikers Island." *Mother Jones*, October 8, 2022. https://www.motherjones.com/crime-justice/2022/10/rikers-island-dangerous-conditions-photos-squalid.

[370] Fonrouge, Gabrielle. 2021. "Photos inside Rikers Island Expose Hellish, Deadly Conditions." *New York Post*, October 21, 2021. https://nypost.com/2021/10/21/photos-inside-rikers-island-expose-hellish-deadly-conditions.

[371] News 12. 2023. "Lawmakers Make Unannounced Rikers Island Visit amid Bail Reform Conflict, Reports of Unsafe Conditions." News 12, 2023. https://bronx.news12.com/lawmakers-make-unannounced-rikers-island-visit-amid-bail-reform-conflict-reports-of-unsafe-conditions.

[372] National Conference of State Legislatures. 2023. "Limiting Incarceration for Technical Violations of Probation and Parole." www.ncsl.org, n.d. https://www.ncsl.org/civil-and-criminal-justice/limiting-incarceration-for-technical-violations-of-probation-and-parole.

[373] Sawyer, Wendy and Wagner, Peter. 2023. "Mass Incarceration: The Whole Pie 2023." Prison Policy Initiative, March 14, 2023. https://www.prisonpolicy.org/reports/pie2023.html.

[374] Eisen, Lauren-Brooke. 2016. "How Many Americans Are Unnecessarily Incarcerated?" Brennan Center for Justice, December 9, 2016. https://www.brennancenter.org/our-work/research-reports/how-many-americans-are-unnecessarily-incarcerated.

[375] Deady, Carolyn. 2014. "Incarceration and Recidivism: Lessons from Abroad." http://www.antoniocasella.eu/nume/Deady_march2014.pdf.

[376] Deady, Carolyn. 2014. "Incarceration and Recidivism: Lessons from Abroad." http://www.antoniocasella.eu/nume/Deady_march2014.pdf.

[377] Juvenile Law Center. 2014. "Luzerne 'Kids for Cash' Scandal." Juvenile Law Center, 2014. https://jlc.org/luzerne-kids-cash-scandal.

[378] Florida Policy Project. 2024. "Pay to Stay: State Law Charging Inmates for Prison Cells Being Applied Differently from County to County." Florida Policy Project, July 2, 2024. https://floridapolicyproject.com/news-events/pay-to-stay-state-law-charging-inmates-for-prison-cells-being-applied-differently-from-county-to-county.

[379] Looney, Adam. 2018. "5 Facts about Prisoners and Work, before and after Incarceration." Brookings, March 14, 2018. https://www.brookings.edu/articles/5-facts-about-prisoners-and-work-before-and-after-incarceration.

[380] ACLU. 2010. "In for a Penny: the Rise of America's New Debtors' Prisons." ACLU, 2010. https://www.aclu.org/wp-content/uploads/publications/InForAPenny_web.pdf.

[381] Brown, Patricia Leigh. 2021. "The 'Hidden Punishment' of Prison Food." *The New York Times*, March 2, 2021, sec. Opinion. https://www.nytimes.com/2021/03/02/opinion/prison-food-farming-health.html.

[382] Raher, Stephen. 2018. "The Company Store." Prison Policy Initiative, May 2018. https://www.prisonpolicy.org/reports/commissary.html.

[383] Lin, Rosalie Chan, Belle. 2021. "The High Cost of Phone Calls in Prisons Generates $1.4 Billion a Year, Disproportionately Driving Women and People of Color into Debt." Business Insider,. June 30, 2021. https://www.businessinsider.com/high-cost-prison-communications-driving-debt-racial-wealth-gap-2021-6.

[384] Innocence Project. 2024. "Injustice beyond Bars: How Poor Oral Health Care in Prison Continues to Burden Wrongfully Convicted People." Innocence Project, March 28, 2024. https://innocenceproject.org/effects-of-poor-oral-health-on-the-wrongfully-convicted.

[385] Lockwood, Beatrix and Lewis, Nicole. 2019. "This Is What It's like to Visit a Family Member in Prison." The Marshall Project, December 18, 2019. https://www.themarshallproject.org/2019/12/18/the-long-journey-to-visit-a-family-member-in-prison.

[386] Statista. 2021. "Ranking: Most Prisoners per Capita by Country 2021." Statista, 2021. https://www.statista.com/statistics/262962/countries-with-the-most-prisoners-per-100-000-inhabitants.

[387] Kaufman, Ellie. 2021. "Biden Administration Says It Intends to Close Guantanamo Prison." CNN, February 12, 2021. https://www.cnn.com/2021/02/12/politics/biden-guantanamo-bay/index.html.

[388] Kaufman, Ellie. 2022. "5 Guantanamo Detainees Cleared for Release as Prison Marks 20 Years." CNN, January 12, 2022. https://www.cnn.com/2022/01/11/politics/guantanamo-detainees-cleared-for-release/index.html.

[389] Miles, Tom. 2017. "U.N. Expert Says Torture Persists at Guantanamo Bay; U.S. Denies." Reuters, December 13, 2017. https://www.reuters.com/article/us-usa-guantanamo-torture/u-n-expert-says-torture-persists-at-guantanamo-bay-u-s-denies-iduskbn1e71qo.

[390] Szoldra, Paul. 2019. "Guantanamo Bay Remaining Prisoners Cost US over Half-Billion a Year." Business Insider, September 17, 2019. https://www.businessinsider.com/guantanamo-bay-prisoners-cost-us-over-half-billion-a-year-2019-9.

[391] Raphael, Sam, Black, Crofton and Blakeley, Ruth. n.d. "CIA Torture Unredacted." The Bureau of Investigative Journalism, n.d. https://www.therenditionproject.org.uk/documents/rdi/190710-trp-tbij-cia-Torture-Unredacted-Full.pdf.

[392] Wikipedia Contributors. 2024. "Habeas Corpus Petitions of Guantanamo Bay Detainees." Wikipedia, January 7, 2024.

[393] Wikipedia Contributors. 2019. "Boumediene v. Bush." Wikipedia, October 31, 2019. https://en.wikipedia.org/wiki/Boumediene_v._Bush.

[394] Landers, Peter. December 23, 2010. *The Wall Street Journal*, December 23, 2010. https://www.wsj.com/articles/SB10001424052748704774604576036520690885858

Chapter 13: Make Legal Immigration Easy

[395] Miroff, Nick. 2020. "'Kids in Cages': It's True That Obama Built the Cages at the Border. But Trump's 'Zero Tolerance' Immigration Policy Had No Precedent." *Washington Post*, October 23, 2020. https://www.washingtonpost.com/immigration/kids-in-cages-debate-trump-obama/2020/10/23/8ff96f3c-1532-11eb-82af-864652063d61_story.html.

[396] American Oversight. 2023. "A Timeline of the Trump Administration's Family Separation Policy." American Oversight, January 4, 2023. https://www.americanoversight.org/a-timeline-of-the-trump-administrations-family-separation-policy.

[397] Hesson, Ted. 2023. "Close to 1,000 Migrant Children Separated by Trump yet to Be Reunited with Parents." Reuters, February 2, 2023, sec. United States. https://www.reuters.com/world/us/close-1000-migrant-children-separated-by-trump-yet-be-reunited-with-parents-2023-02-02.

[398] Ahmed, Sofia. 2022. "Explainer: What Is the Trump-Era 'Remain in Mexico' Program the Supreme Court Said Biden Can End?" Reuters, June 30, 2022, sec. United States. https://www.reuters.com/world/us/what-is-trump-era-remain-mexico-program-supreme-court-said-biden-can-end-2022-06-30.

[399] PRRI. 2021. "Immigration after Trump: What Would Immigration Policy That Followed American Public Opinion Look Like?" PRRI, January 20, 2021. https://www.prri.org/research/immigration-after-trump-what-would-immigration-policy-that-followed-american-public-opinion-look-like.

[400] Camilo Montoya-Galvez. 2024. "Migrant Crossings along the Southern Border Increase as Officials Prepare for Larger Spike." CBS News, March 5, 2024. https://www.cbsnews.com/news/us-mexico-border-migrant-crossings-increase-texas-spring-spike.

[401] Miroff, Nick, Sacchetti, Maria and Frostenson, Sarah. 2024. "Trump vs. Biden on Immigration: 12 Charts Comparing U.S. Border Security." *The Washington Post*, February 11, 2024. https://www.washingtonpost.com/immigration/2024/02/11/trump-biden-immigration-border-compared.

402 Miroff, Nick, Sacchetti, Maria and Frostenson, Sarah. 2024. "Trump vs. Biden on Immigration: 12 Charts Comparing U.S. Border Security." *The Washington Post*, February 11, 2024. https://www.washingtonpost.com/immigration/2024/02/11/trump-biden-immigration-border-compared.

403 TRAC Reports, 2024. "A Ten-Year Look at Inadmissible Migrants and Paroled Migrants at Ports of Entry." TRAC Reports, January 12, 2024. https://trac.syr.edu/reports/735

404 Montoya-Galvez, Camilo. 2024. "Biden Administration Has Admitted More than 1 Million Migrants into U.S. Under Parole Policy Congress Is Considering Restricting." CBS News, January 22, 2024. https://www.cbsnews.com/news/immigration-parole-biden-administration-1-million-migrants.

405 Blake, Aaron. 2024. "Some Important Numbers on Biden's Border Problem." The Washington Post, April 2024. https://www.washingtonpost.com/politics/2024/04/01/some-important-numbers-bidens-border-problem.

406 Gold, Michael, and Anjali Huynh. 2024. "Trump Again Invokes 'Blood Bath' and Dehumanizes Migrants in Border Remarks." *The New York Times*, April 2, 2024, sec. U.S. https://www.nytimes.com/2024/04/02/us/politics/trump-border-blood-bath.html.

407 Amadeo, Kimberly. 2023. "What Is the Ideal GDP Growth Rate?" The Balance, January 26, 2023. https://www.thebalancemoney.com/what-is-the-ideal-gdp-growth-rate-3306017.

408 The Economist. 2023. "Global Fertility Has Collapsed, with Profound Economic Consequences." *The Economist*, June 1, 2023. https://www.economist.com/leaders/2023/06/01/global-fertility-has-collapsed-with-profound-economic-consequences.

409 Soussi, Alasdair. 2024. "Why Will Low Birthrate in Europe Trigger 'Staggering Social Change'?" Al Jazeera, April 3, 2024. https://www.aljazeera.com/economy/2024/4/3/staggering-social-change-from-low-birth-rate-in-west-scientists-warn.

410 Datacommons.org. "United States - Place Explorer." Datacommons.org, n.d. https://datacommons.org/place/country/USA.

411 Minkin, Rachel, Horowitz, Juliana Menasce and Aragao, Carolina. 2024. "The Experiences of U.S. Adults Who Don't Have Children." Pew Research Center, July 25, 2024. https://www.pewresearch.org/social-trends/2024/07/25/the-experiences-of-u-s-adults-who-dont-have-children

412 Kuhn, Anthony. 2023. "Japan's Plan to Boost Its Birthrate Raises Doubt. But One City Has Reason for Hope." NPR, June 24, 2023. https://www.npr.org/2023/06/24/1182457365/japan-low-birthrate-akashi-success-story.

413 World Economic Forum. 2023. "These Countries Have the Highest Childcare Costs in the World." World Economic Forum, July 19, 2023. https://www.weforum.org/agenda/2023/07/highest-childcare-costs-by-country.

414 *The Economist*. 2024. "Fewer Migrants Are Crossing America's Southern Border." *The Economist*, May 23, 2024. https://www.economist.com/united-states/2024/05/23/fewer-migrants-are-crossing-americas-southern-border

415 Orozco, Fernando. 2023. "'You Are in America': A Trek across the Border in the 1970s." LAist, March 3, 2023. https://laist.com/news/essays/you-are-in-america-a-trek-across-the-border-in-the-1970s.

416 NPR. 2010. "A Reagan Legacy: Amnesty for Illegal Immigrants." NPR, July 4, 2010. https://www.npr.org/2010/07/04/128303672/a-reagan-legacy-amnesty-for-illegal-immigrants.

417 Statista. 2023. "Border Crossing Encounters U.S. 1990-2023." Statista, 2023. https://www.statista.com/statistics/329256/alien-apprehensions-registered-by-the-us-border-patrol.

[418] Alvarez, Alayna. 2024. "Trump Pledges 'Largest Deportation' in U.S. History, Starting in Ohio and Colorado." Axios. September 13, 2024. https://www.axios.com/2024/09/13/trump-deportation-immigrants-springfield-ohio-aurora-colorado.

[419] McCarthy, Craig. 2024. "NYC to Hand out Prepaid Credit Cards to Migrant Families for Food." *New York Post*, February 2, 2024. https://nypost.com/2024/02/02/metro/nyc-to-hand-out-prepaid-credit-cards-to-migrant-families-for-food.

[420] Goodkind, Nicole. 2024. "The Fertility Crisis Is Here and It Will Permanently Alter the Economy." CNN, June 25, 2024. https://www.cnn.com/2024/06/25/investing/premarket-stocks-trading/index.html.

Chapter 14: Punish Corporations Like Humans

[421] Totenberg, Nina. 2014. "When Did Companies Become People? Excavating the Legal Evolution." NPR, July 28, 2014. https://www.npr.org/2014/07/28/335288388/when-did-companies-become-people-excavating-the-legal-evolution.

[422] Wikipedia Contributors. 2019. "With Great Power Comes Great Responsibility." Wikimedia Foundation, June 18, 2019. https://en.wikipedia.org/wiki/With_great_power_comes_great_responsibility.

[423] Jones, Dustin. 2023. "Bank of America to Pay $250 Million for Illegal Fees, Fake Accounts." NPR, July 11, 2023. https://www.npr.org/2023/07/11/1187060652/bank-of-america-250-million-illegal-fees-fake-accounts-fines.

Chapter 15: Make Income Taxes Fully Progressive

[424] Duehren, Andrew. 2024. "Trump Flirts with the Ultimate Tax Cut: No Taxes at All." *The New York Times*, October 24, 2024. https://www.nytimes.com/2024/10/24/us/politics/donald-trump-tax-policy.html.

[425] USAFacts. 2023. "How Much Money Does the Government Collect per Person?" USAFacts, February 6, 2023. https://usafacts.org/articles/how-much-money-does-the-government-collect-per-person.

[426] Luhby, Tami and Sullivan, Kate. 2024. "Trump Floats Ending the Federal Income Tax. Here's What That Would Mean." CNN, October 26, 2024. https://www.cnn.com/2024/10/26/politics/trump-income-taxes-tariffs/index.html.

[427] Whitten, David O. 2024. "The Depression of 1893." Economic History Association, 2024. https://eh.net/encyclopedia/the-depression-of-1893.

[428] Corrigan, David. 2019. "Hard Times Tokens." Museum of Connecticut History, January 30, 2019. https://museumofcthistory.org/hard-times-tokens.

[429] Wikipedia. 2021. "Willie Sutton." Wikipedia, December 13, 2021. https://en.wikipedia.org/wiki/Willie_Sutton.

[430] Piketty, Thomas and Saez, Emmanuel. 2006. "How Progressive Is the U.S. Federal Tax System? A Historical and International Perspective." DOI Foundation, 2006. https://doi.org/10.3386/w12404.

[431] McClelland, Robert and Airi, Nikhita. "Effective Income Tax Rates Have Fallen for the Top One Percent since World War II." 2021. Tax Policy Center, September 15, 2021. https://taxpolicycenter.org/taxvox/effective-income-tax-rates-have-fallen-top-one-percent-world-war-ii-0.

432 Americans for Tax Fairness. 2024. "Income Inequality Reached Record High In 2021, Even As Richest Paid The Lowest Tax Rate In 8 Years." Americans for Tax Fairness, September 16, 2024. https://americansfortaxfairness.org/income-inequality-reaches-record-high-2021-even-richest-paid-lowest-tax-rate-8-years.

433 Bonitatibus, Steve. 2023. "The 'Fair Tax' Act Would Radically Restructure the Nation's Tax System in Favor of the Wealthy." Center for American Progress, February 8, 2023. https://www.americanprogress.org/article/the-fair-tax-act-would-radically-restructure-the-nations-tax-system-in-favor-of-the-wealthy.

434 Knutson, Jacob. 2023. "How a Proposed IRS Tool Could Disrupt the Billion-Dollar Tax Prep Industry." Axios, May 19, 2023. https://www.axios.com/2023/05/19/irs-direct-file-proposed-tool-tax-preparation-industry.

Chapter 16: Protect Political Expression

435 Equal Employment Opportunity Commission. "3. Who Is Protected from Employment Discrimination?" www.eeoc.gov, n.d. https://www.eeoc.gov/employers/small-business/3-who-protected-employment-discrimination.

436 The Editorial Board. 2022. "America Has a Free Speech Problem." *New York Times*, March 18, 2022. https://www.nytimes.com/2022/03/18/opinion/cancel-culture-free-speech-poll.html.

437 New York Times/Siena College Research Institute. 2022. "The New York Times/ Siena College Research Institute February 9-22, 2022." *The New York Times*, 2022. https://int.nyt.com/data/documenttools/free-speech-poll-nyt-and-siena-college/ef971d5e78e1d2f9/full.pdf.

438 Morabito, Greg. 2017. "Uno Pizzeria Fires Employee Who Marched in Charlottesville White Supremacist Rally." Eater, August 17, 2017. https://www.eater.com/2017/8/17/16161330/uno-pizzeria-charlottesville-marcher-fired.

439 Judkis, Maura. 2017. "Charlottesville White Nationalist Demonstrator Loses Job at Libertarian Hot Dog Shop." *Washington Post*, August 12, 2017. https://doi.org/10-2019/WashingtonPost/2017/08/12.

440 Reuters. 2021. "Some at US Capitol Riot Fired after Internet Detectives Identify Them." Voice of America, January 8, 2021. https://www.voanews.com/a/2020-usa-votes_some-us-capitol-riot-fired-after-internet-detectives-identify-them/6200469.html.

441 Noah, Timothy. 2004. "The Insubordinate Bumper Sticker." Slate Magazine, September 14, 2004. https://slate.com/news-and-politics/2004/09/the-insubordinate-bumper-sticker.html.

442 Moyer, Justin Wm. 2022. "Nonprofit Founder Says She Was Fired for Being Conservative Republican." *Washington Post*, December 12, 2022. https://www.washingtonpost.com/dc-md-va/2022/12/12/audrey-henson-interns-capitol-hill.

443 Palestine Legal. 2023. X (Formerly Twitter), October 24, 2023. https://twitter.com/pal_legal/status/1716931448643649964.

444 Velazquez, Eddie. 2023. "Workers Say Employers Are Retaliating against Them for Voicing Support for Palestine." Prism, November 13, 2023. https://prismreports.org/2023/11/13/workers-retaliation-supporting-palestine.

445 Elassar, Alaa. 2023. "A Palestinian Student Was Expelled from a Florida High School after His Mom Made Pro-Palestine Posts on Social Media." CNN, December 15, 2023. https://www.cnn.com/2023/12/15/us/palestinian-student-expelled-pine-crest-florida/index.html.

446 Dev, Krish, and Maisie Zipfel. 2023. "NYU Langone Physician Facing Termination after Reposting Pro-Palestinian Content." *Washington Square News*, November 6, 2023. https://nyunews.com/news/2023/11/06/physician-terminated-nyu.

447 Schwartz, Brian. 2024. "Top Republican Donors Fund Group Doxxing Pro-Palestinian College Students." CNBC, May 13, 2024. https://www.cnbc.com/2024/05/13/republican-donors-fund-far-right-doxxing-palestinians.html.

448 Bacallao, Marianna. "Talking with a Vanderbilt Senior Expelled for Role in Pro-Palestinian Protests." NPR, May 10, 2024. https://www.npr.org/2024/05/10/1250589763/talking-with-a-vanderbilt-senior-expelled-for-role-in-pro-palestinian-protests.

449 Miranda, Shauneen. 2023. "CEOs Seek to Blacklist Harvard Students after Signing Pro-Palestinian Letter." Axios, October 12, 2023. https://www.axios.com/2023/10/12/israel-palestine-letter-ceos-blacklist-harvard-students.

450 Snider, Mike. 2024. "Google Fires More Workers over Pro-Palestinian Protests Held at Offices, Cites Disruption." *USA Today*, April 23, 2024. https://www.usatoday.com/story/tech/2024/04/23/google-firings-pro-palestinian-protests-cloud-computing/73427928007.

451 Nietzel, Michael T. 2024. "13 Trump-Appointed Judges Vow Not to Hire Columbia University Grads." *Forbes*, May 8, 2024. https://www.forbes.com/sites/michaeltnietzel/2024/05/08/13-trump-appointed-judges-vow-not-to-hire-columbia-university-grads.

452 Gilliland, Donald. 2019. "Is Political Affiliation the New Discrimination? Our Research Suggests 'Yes.'" *The Hill*, November 27, 2019. https://thehill.com/opinion/technology/472200-political-affiliation-the-new-discrimination-our-research-suggests-yes.

453 Ekins, Emily. 2020. "Poll: 62% of Americans Say They Have Political Views They're Afraid to Share." Cato Institute, July 22, 2020. https://www.cato.org/survey-reports/poll-62-americans-say-they-have-political-views-theyre-afraid-share#.

454 Vavra, Shannon. 2017. "Where You Can't Get Fired for Political Speech." Axios, December 15, 2017. https://www.axios.com/2017/12/15/where-you-cant-get-fired-for-political-speech-1513304949.

455 Yglesias, Matthew. 2020. "The 'Shy Trump Voters' Debate, Explained." Vox, November 2020. https://www.vox.com/2020/11/1/21544644/shy-trump-voters-polling-error-explained.

Chapter 17: Guarantee the Right to Bodily Autonomy

456 Alonso, Paola. 2018. "Autonomy Revoked: The Forced Sterilization of Women of Color in 20th Century America." *Health Equity* 2, no. 1 (September): 249–59. https://doi.org/10.1089/heq.2017.0045.

457 Luthra, Shefali. 2023. "California Promised Reparations to Survivors of Forced Sterilization. Few People Have Gotten Them." The 19th, September 5, 2023. https://19thnews.org/2023/09/california-forced-sterilization-incarceration-reparations.

458 Ko, Lisa. 2016. "Unwanted Sterilization and Eugenics Programs in the United States." PBS Independent Lens, January 29, 2016. https://www.pbs.org/independentlens/blog/unwanted-sterilization-and-eugenics-programs-in-the-united-states.

459 Greene-Santos, Aniya. 2024. "Corporal Punishment in Schools Still Legal in Many States." www.nea.org, May 20, 2024. https://www.nea.org/nea-today/all-news-articles/corporal-punishment-schools-still-legal-many-states.

[460] Brian P. Elliott, Capt. and Col. Steven Chambers. 2022. "A Historical Analysis of Vaccine Mandates in the United States Military and Its Application to the COVID-19 Vaccine Mandate." *Vaccine* 40, no. 51 (August). https://doi.org/10.1016/j.vaccine.2022.08.017.

[461] Omer, Saad B., Salmon, Daniel A., Orenstein, Walter A., M deHart, Patricia and Neal Halsey. 2009. "Vaccine Refusal, Mandatory Immunization, and the Risks of Vaccine-Preventable Diseases." *New England Journal of Medicine* 360, no. 19 (May): 1981–88. https://doi.org/10.1056/nejmsa0806477.

Chapter 18: Prioritize the Environment

[462] Cockburn, Harry. 2019. "'High Likelihood of Human Civilisation Coming to End' by 2050, Report Finds." *The Independent*, June 5, 2019. https://www.independent.co.uk/climate-change/news/climate-change-global-warming-end-human-civilisation-research-a8943531.html.

[463] Wikipedia. 2020. "Ecocide." Wikipedia, December 25, 2020. https://en.wikipedia.org/wiki/Ecocide.

[464] Ong, Sandy. 2023. "The World's Soils Are Becoming Dangerously Degraded, but Rare Microbes Offer Hope." *Wired*, October 19, 2023. https://www.wired.com/story/la-puna-extremophiles-soil-degradation.

[465] Shagun. 2022. "Land the size of South America will be degraded if current trends continue: UN Report." Down To Earth, April 27, 2022. https://www.downtoearth.org.in/environment/land-the-size-of-south-america-will-be-degraded-if-current-trends-continue-un-report-82595

[466] U.N. Department of Public Information. "World population projected to reach 9.8 billion in 2050, and 11.2 billion in 2100 – says UN." www.un.org, n.d. https://www.un.org/en/development/desa/population/events/pdf/other/21/21June_final%20press%20release_wpp17.pdf.

[467] Gillam, Carey. 2022. "Guest Column: Overfishing Poses Threat to Our Oceans." The New Lede, September 7, 2022. https://www.thenewlede.org/2022/09/guest-column-overfishing-poses-threat-to-our-oceans.

[468] NOAA. 2022. "Quantifying the Ocean Carbon Sink." National Centers for Environmental Information, August 17, 2022. https://www.ncei.noaa.gov/news/quantifying-ocean-carbon-sink.

[469] Cousteau, Jacques. 1971. "Our Oceans Are Dying." *The New York Times*, November 14, 1971, sec. Archives. https://www.nytimes.com/1971/11/14/archives/our-oceans-are-dying.html.

[470] Global Seafood Alliance. 2022. "Experts: World's Coral Reefs Could Vanish by 2050 without Climate Action." Global Seafood Alliance, April 20, 2022. https://www.globalseafood.org/advocate/experts-worlds-coral-reefs-could-vanish-by-2050-without-climate-action.

[471] Merchant, Brian. 2015. "The Last Time Oceans Got This Acidic This Fast, 96% of Marine Life Went Extinct." *Vice*, April 9, 2015. https://www.vice.com/en/article/the-last-time-our-oceans-got-this-acidic-it-drove-earths-greatest-extinction.

[472] Gain, Isabelle. 2023. "Hot Tub Heat: Understanding the High Ocean Temperatures off Florida's Coast." Thompson Earth Systems Institute, September 27, 2023. https://www.floridamuseum.ufl.edu/earth-systems/blog/hot-tub-heat-understanding-the-high-ocean-temperatures-off-floridas-coast.

[473] Audley Travel US. 2022. "Best Time to Visit the Caribbean | Best Months for Travel." Audley Travel, March 21, 2022. https://www.audleytravel.com/us/the-caribbean/best-time-to-visit#jan.

[474] Ditlevsen, Peter and Susanne Ditlevsen. 2023. "Warning of a Forthcoming Collapse of the Atlantic Meridional Overturning Circulation." *Nature Communications* 14, no. 1 (July): 4254. https://doi.org/10.1038/s41467-023-39810-w.

[475] World Wildlife Fund. 2020. "68% Average Decline in Species Population Sizes Since 1970, Says New WWF Report." World Wildlife Fund, September 9, 2020. https://www.worldwildlife.org/press-releases/68-average-decline-in-species-population-sizes-since-1970-says-new-wwf-report

[476] Hance, Jeremy. 2011. "How Genghis Khan Cooled the Planet." Mongabay Environmental News, January 20, 2011. https://news.mongabay.com/2011/01/how-genghis-khan-cooled-the-planet.

[477] Baylor University Media and Public Relations. 2011. "Baylor Study Shows Native Americans Significantly Modified American Landscape Years prior to the Arrival of Europeans." News.web.baylor.edu, March 21, 2011. https://news.web.baylor.edu/news/story/2011/baylor-study-shows-native-americans-significantly-modified-american-landscape-years.

[478] World Economic Forum. 2024. "Sea Level Rise: Everything You Need to Know." World Economic Forum, September 20, 2024. https://www.weforum.org/stories/2024/09/rising-sea-levels-global-threat.

[479] Duff, Meg. 2023. "Which Islands Will Become Uninhabitable due to Climate Change First?" Livescience.com, November 12, 2023. https://www.livescience.com/planet-earth/climate-change/which-islands-will-become-uninhabitable-due-to-climate-change-first.

[480] Tabuchi, Hiroko. 2025. "Far from the Fires, the Deadly Risks of Smoke Are Intensifying." *The New York Times*, January 11, 2025. https://www.nytimes.com/2025/01/11/climate/wildfire-smoke-risks.html.

[481] Sustainability. 2024. "Assignment: Earth." Sustainability, September 9, 2024. https://sustainability.usc.edu/assignment-earth.

[482] O'Neill, Tegan. 2024. "Thawing Permafrost: What Does It Mean? And What Can Be Done?" The Salata Institute, June 11, 2024. https://salatainstitute.harvard.edu/thawing-permafrost-what-does-it-mean-and-what-can-be-done.

[483] Iberdrola. "Melting Permafrost: Why Is It a Serious Threat to the Planet?" Iberdrola, n.d. https://www.iberdrola.com/sustainability/what-is-permafrost.

[484] Mayorquin, Orlando. 2023. "Worms Revived after 46,000 Years Frozen in Siberian Permafrost." *The New York Times*, July 29, 2023, sec. Science. https://www.nytimes.com/2023/07/29/science/roundworm-nematodes-siberia-permafrost.html.

[485] Matthews, Dylan. 2023. "An Unusual Way to Figure out If Humanity Is Toast." Vox, July 10, 2023. https://www.vox.com/future-perfect/23785731/human-extinction-forecasting-superforecasters.

[486] Krol, Aaron. 2023. "Will Climate Change Drive Humans Extinct or Destroy Civilization?" MIT Climate Portal, October 20, 2023. https://climate.mit.edu/ask-mit/will-climate-change-drive-humans-extinct-or-destroy-civilization.

[487] Carrington, Damian. 2022. "Climate Endgame: Risk of Human Extinction 'Dangerously Underexplored.'" *The Guardian*, August 1, 2022. https://www.theguardian.com/environment/2022/aug/01/climate-endgame-risk-human-extinction-scientists-global-heating-catastrophe.

[488] Kemp, Luke, Xu, Chi, Depledge, Joanna, Ebi, Kristie L., Gibbins, Goodwin, Kohler, Timothy A. and Rockström, Johan et al. 2022. "Climate Endgame: Exploring Catastrophic Climate Change Scenarios." *Proceedings of the National Academy of Sciences* 119, no. 34 (August). https://doi.org/10.1073/pnas.2108146119.

ABOUT TED RALL

Ted Rall, born in Cambridge, Massachusetts, and raised in Kettering, Ohio, is a provocative voice in American political and cultural discourse. A syndicated political cartoonist, opinion columnist, author, and radio host, Rall has spent decades challenging power structures and amplifying leftist perspectives. His education began at Columbia University's School of Engineering and Applied Science, where he majored in Applied Physics and Nuclear Engineering for three years until a medical emergency led to his expulsion. Returning after six years working on Wall Street and in banking, he graduated with honors in 1991 as a History major, a journey that shaped his analytical approach to societal and economic issues.

Rall's political significance lies in his fearless critique of U.S. imperialism, capitalism, and bipartisan hypocrisy. His cartoons, published in outlets like *The New York Times, Rolling Stone, Los Angeles Times* and *The Wall Street Journal*, blend biting satire with radical insight, earning him two Robert F. Kennedy Journalism Awards and a Pulitzer Prize finalist nod. His work transcends commentary, serving as a cultural artifact of resistance against mainstream narratives. Books like *The Year of Loving Dangerously*, chronicling his 1984 homelessness in New York, and his critiques of post-9/11 America underscore his commitment to exposing systemic injustices.

Culturally, Rall bridges punk ethos and intellectual rigor, influencing a generation of activists and artists. His involvement in movements—from Columbia's apartheid divestment campaign to Occupy Wall Street, where he led study groups—marks him as a participant, not just an observer. Rall's radio presence and columns further amplify his reach, offering unfiltered takes on war, police brutality, and economic inequality. He remains a polarizing figure: a hero to the disenfranchised, a gadfly to the elite. His legacy is a testament to art's power to provoke, inform, and inspire revolutionary thought in a conformist age.

ALSO BY TED RALL

Waking Up In America, Cartoon Collection, 1992
All the Rules Have Changed, Cartoon Collection, 1995
My War With Brian, Graphic Novel, 1996
Real Americans Admit: The Worst Thing I've Ever Done!, Graphic Novel, 1996
Revenge of the Latchkey Kids, Nonfiction Current Events, 1998
2024, Graphic Novel, 2001 (Updated 2024)
To Afghanistan and Back: A Graphic Travelogue, Graphic Nonfiction Current Events, 2002
Attitude: The New Subversive Political Cartoonists, Anthology (Edited by Ted Rall), 2002
Search and Destroy, Cartoon Collection, 2004
Attitude 2: The New Subversive Alternative Cartoonists, Anthology (Edited by Ted Rall), 2004
Wake Up, You're Liberal!: How We Can Take America Back from the Right, Nonfiction Current Events, 2004
Generalissimo El Busho: Essays & Cartoons on the Bush Years, Nonfiction Current Events, 2004
America Gone Wild, Cartoon Collection, 2006
Attitude 3: The New Subversive Online Cartoonists, Anthology (Edited by Ted Rall), 2006
Silk Road to Ruin: Is Central Asia the Next Middle East?, Nonfiction Current Events, 2006
The Year of Loving Dangerously, Graphic Novel, 2009
The Anti-American Manifesto, Nonfiction Current Events, 2010
The Book of Obama: From Hope and Change to the Age of Revolt, Nonfiction Current Events, 2012
After We Kill You, We Will Welcome You Back as Honored Guests, Nonfiction Current Events, 2014
Snowden, Graphic Biography, 2015
Bernie, Graphic Biography, 2016
Trump, Graphic Biography, 2016
Francis: The People's Pope, Graphic Biography, 2018
Political Suicide: The Fight for the Soul of the Democratic Party, Nonfiction Current Events, 2020
The Stringer, Graphic Novel, 2021

www.ingramcontent.com/pod-product-compliance
Lightning Source LLC
Chambersburg PA
CBHW080549030426
42337CB00024B/4813